McSWEENEY'S BOOKS
SAN FRANCISCO
www.mcsweeneys.net

McSweeney's and colophon are registered trademarks of McSweeney's,
a privately held company with wildly fluctuating resources.

Printed in Dexter, Michigan, by Thomson-Shore.

PAGE
244

GRANTLAND

TABLE OF CONTENTS

The inside book jacket features the classic Nike poster of George "The Ice Man" Gervin, originally released in 1976.

EDITOR IN CHIEF
Bill Simmons

DEPUTY EDITOR
Dan Fierman

DIRECTOR,
BUSINESS DEVELOPMENT
David Cho

EDITORS
Jay Caspian Kang
David Jacoby
Sarah Larimer
Rafe Bartholomew
Mike Philbrick
Chris Ryan
Mark Lisanti
Robert Mays
Megan Creydt

CONSULTING
EDITORS
Dave Eggers
Malcolm Gladwell
Chuck Klosterman
Jane Leavy
John A. Walsh

GRANTLAND

QUARTERLY

Designed by McSweeney's
in San Francisco, CA

MANAGING EDITOR
Juliet Litman

ART DIRECTOR
Brian McMullen

DESIGNER
Walter Green

DISTRIBUTION & BUSINESS
Laura Howard
Adam Krefman
Sam Riley

ALSO HELPING
Jordan Bass, Chelsea Hogue, Rachel Khong, Sunra
Thompson, Andi Mudd, Ethan Nosowsky, Alyson Sinclair,
Matt Gillespie, Belle Bueti

BIGGER, FASTER, STRONGER, SAFER

*The end of the
NHL headhunter*

by KEN DRYDEN

MIKE HIRSHON

It was an extraordinary press conference. Four people were at the media table in a spare setting at Pittsburgh's CONSOL Energy Center—Penguins general manager Ray Shero, Dr. Michael Collins, Dr. Ted Carrick, and Sidney Crosby. They were serious and straightforward. Through nearly 45 intense minutes, they offered almost no smoke or spin.

The doctors, not the GM nor the player, spoke first. Dr. Collins, head of the University of Pittsburgh Medical Center's Sports Medicine Concussion Program, laid out the events surrounding the injury, Crosby's resulting symptoms, the diagnosis, the treatment, and the ups and downs of Crosby's recovery since January. He was patient and thorough. He spoke as if he knew his audience was intent to hear what he said and, despite his occasional medical jargon, would understand him in all the ways that mattered. With a few lapses, Dr. Carrick, a chiropractor and founder of the Carrick Institute for Graduate Studies in Florida, did the same. Beyond the details, the doctors needed to convey that they were competent, professional, and responsible—that Crosby was in good hands.

At times, the doctors talked about Crosby's brain as if Crosby wasn't there himself. Yet Crosby seemed undistracted. Respectful, he watched and listened as if the doctors were only his trusted advisors. He was still the captain of his own ship.

When it was his turn to speak, Crosby was composed and informative, seeming to not hold anything back. He spoke of how he felt at each stage after his injury. At first, he had felt himself in a fog, he said, as if he were living one step removed from his own life, a spectator to it. Objects around him weren't quite where he knew them to be; once, Dr. Collins related, Crosby, feeling he was falling, found his body reacting when he wasn't falling at all. Even the flickering images on a TV screen moved too fast for him, making him dizzy; this in someone who had always seen everything so acutely, who at only 24 years old had seemed somehow to figure out hockey and life. Now his board had been scrambled. Normal life, his doctors said, would return when, at full exertion, his headaches stayed away. Normal life as Sidney Crosby would return when everything went back into its proper orientation and, when confident of that, Crosby could resume his Crosby-like creating, scrambling the board for everyone else instead.

A Long History of Violence in the NHL

Violence has always been a part of hockey. At least three professional North American players have died as a direct result of on-ice head trauma since 1907, when Owen McCourt of Canada was injured, leading to murder charges being levied against members of the opposing team. 2011, though, may end up being remembered as the year in which a sea change began in the NHL. It was a year that saw three well-known enforcers—Rick Rypien, Wade Bleak, and Derek Boogaard—die at their own hands before their 40th birthdays, all three suffering from forms of mental or physical deterioration thought

The doctors and Crosby said no one could pre-
dict when that would occur. Given where he had
been and where he was now in his recovery, and
pushed by the media's questions and by their own
professional and human hopefulness, the doctors
and Crosby put science to one side and declared
that it *would* happen. Asked if he had played his
last game, Crosby replied without bravado, "I wouldn't bet on that."

Before the press conference, it was clear; after, it is even clearer. The
NHL season that began October 6, 2011—whether Crosby plays at all, or
how well—will be about Crosby.

Crosby...
watched and
listened as if the
doctors were
only his trusted
advisors.

This is a difficult time for the NHL, for its commissioner, Gary Bettman,
and for hockey. It's no less difficult for the NFL, for its commissioner,
Roger Goodell, for the NCAA, and for football. Head injuries have become
an overwhelming fact of life in sports. The immensity of the number, the
prominence of the names, the life-altering impact on their lives, and, more
disturbing, if that's possible, the now sheer routineness of their occurrence.
The Crosby hit didn't seem like much. If it hadn't been Crosby, the clip of the
incident would never have made the highlight reel. And if so much can happen out of so little, where is all this going? Who else? How many more? How
bad might this get? Careers and lives of players, we know now, have been

---

to be caused or exacerbated by years of violent play. After several of the league's brightest
stars—including its very brightest, Sidney Crosby—were sidelined for significant periods of time
due to head injuries, the NHL appointed former Detroit Red Wings star and future Hall-of-
Famer Brendan Shanahan to act as the league's Chief Disciplinarian. Changes have been swift:
Shanahan suspended eight players for head-hits during the preseason, and each time Shanahan
shared videos with the public in which he narrated precisely why a player received a certain
punishment. It seems to be the hopes of the league and an increasing number of its fans, tired
of the tragedies and career-ending injuries, that the Shanahan era will lead to a new kind of
hockey in North America.

Our players will
not get smaller,
they will not
skate slower, the
force of their
collisions will
not diminish.

shortened, diminished, snuffed out by head injuries. What once had seemed debatable, deniable, spin-able, now is not. What once had been ignored now is obvious. Not just contact or collision sports, hockey and football are dangerous sports.

Bettman, Goodell, and sports leaders who came before them have done only what the players, fans, and media have wanted them to do. They know we want our athletes to be better than they've ever been. We want them to be superhuman versions of ourselves—faster, bigger, stronger, more skilled, more committed. We want them, no matter the risk or pain, to prove beyond even unreasonable doubt that they're not in this for the money but for the love of their/our sport and their/our team, and to demonstrate that at every moment by being willing to do whatever it takes. The players, fans, and media want great plays and thunderous hits. They need "wows" to compete against every other challenge—in sports, entertainment, news, politics—for the public's attention. And the players and their commissioners, Bettman and Goodell among them, for the most part have delivered.

If the result has been collisions that are too dangerous, you "tweak" the rules, "tweak" the equipment, "tweak" the strategies of play, often in the face of great resistance—and the leagues have done this. But still, the careers and lives of their players are being compromised, and now everybody can see it.

As a hockey or football commissioner today, you can't not know that many of your players this year, next year, and every year will suffer head injuries. Some will have their careers ended; some, like Paul Kariya and Eric Lindros, before age gets them will begin their downward slide from superstar to journeyman; and some retired players will die long before their time, their final years for themselves and their families in the living death of dementia. This isn't being alarmist. This is alarming.

Bettman and Goodell can see this. So can the heads of the hockey and football players' associations. So, increasingly, can the players, their wives and families, and their lawyers. The commissioners and their leagues—mostly—are now beyond simple denial, defensiveness, and counterattack. The challenge is no longer awareness of the problem. It's awareness of the solution. If you are Gary Bettman or Roger Goodell, what do you do?

I come back to the Crosby press conference. I'm not sure how it could have been done better. The message was that we are in uncharted territory. We know some things, there is much more we don't know, and we're going to do what we know and respect what we don't until we know better. This is serious, and we are serious. And we want you—all those who are watching—to experience what we have experienced and learn what we have learned, because as people who love sports, we're in this together. It is this same tone, attitude, and approach on head injuries that Bettman and Goodell need to take.

For Bettman, it's time to say: This is a great game, but it has a big problem, one that will only get worse if we don't do what needs to be done now. Our players will not get smaller, they will not skate slower, the force of their collisions will not diminish. The equipment they wear will not improve fast enough to mitigate the greater risks they will face. "Tweaking" is not the answer.

Immediately, Bettman can say, we need to treat any hit to the head as what it is: an attempt to injure. A hit to the shoulder, torso, or hip—depending—is understood as good positioning and good defense; not so a hit to the head. The head has always been thought of differently, requiring special protection with its own peculiar penalties. High sticking is not for a blow to the shoulder, nor elbowing for a blow to the chest. In the future, if a play results in an incidental and minor hit to the head, or one that is the fault of the player's being hit, no penalty need be called. But now the presumption needs to be that every hit to the head is an attempt to injure, with the onus on the player doing the hitting, through his actions and in the eyes of the referee, to defeat that presumption. As Crosby said in his press conference, if the league requires players to be responsible for their sticks, why not their bodies? Further, if an opponent purposely puts his head in a position to draw contact to cause a penalty to be called, just as with "diving" now, it is that player as an "instigator" who will receive the penalty.

But what about the player who is carrying the puck with his head down, another oft-cited example intended to show how impossibly complicated it is to ban headshots? In years past, the best way to move the puck forward was believed to be for a player to do it himself, stickhandling up the ice. Having his head down with his eyes focused on the puck was considered an advantage to him. It was only fair, then, that a defender have his own advantage and, unseen by the puck-carrier, be able to blast him. Now the best way to advance the puck is seen to be by passing, so a player with his head down is at a disadvantage already and doesn't require further punishment. He can be easily stopped with no more than incidental contact. In such cases, a crushing hit to the head (e.g., Stevens on Lindros) is nothing less than an attempt to injure. The common explanations—"Because he deserved it" or "Because I can"—are not good enough in this age of concussions and dementia.

What then about fighting? If hits to the head are banned, why not punches to the head? This isn't the time to reengage the debate over fighting. Not directly. That will only distract from the more critical issue that must now be addressed. The problem of fighting, for most critics at least, isn't fighting itself. It's the consequences of fighting. To many, fighting seems out of place in sports, turning away prospective fans from a game that needs many more. To some, rather than acting as a "safety valve" to reduce further fighting, it creates increased ill-will and generates more fighting. So why allow it?

What is relevant here is whether fighting relates to head injuries. Is fighting dangerous or not? Once, hockey players did their own fighting. An elbow to the nose or a slash on the arm, and—big or small, good fighter or not—a player had to right his own wrong. Most players were bad fighters. On their skates, they wrestled, slipped, and flung themselves around. It was vaudeville. Now most fights are between designated fighters. Each such fighter knows what he's doing, and though usually well-matched enough to be able to protect themselves, these fighters are also skilled enough to hurt each other. And questions have now arisen: Why did postmortem studies on the brains of Reggie Fleming and Bob Probert, two brawlers of different eras, show brain damage? Why did three contemporary fighters—Derek Boogaard, Rick Rypien, and Wade Belak—who were young, rich, and seemed to have everything to live for, die in recent months? We don't know the answers, but we know enough to know we need to find them.

Fighting seems out of place in sports, turning away prospective fans from a game that needs many more.

The NHL rulebook is judicious in distinguishing a bodycheck to the head from other contact to the head, treating fighting as its own separate category. For an illegal check, it is necessary that "the head is targeted and the principal point of contact." But in a fight, is the head not "targeted?" Is the head not "the principal point of contact?" Is a fist not part of the body? And in fights today, with fighters who can truly fight, what's the difference between being hit in the head by Niklas Kronwall's shoulder or Zdeno Chara's fist? This is about head injuries, not fighting's place in hockey. This is about the outrageous damage that hits to the head are doing to lives and to a sport.

Every time big changes are discussed, the same flood of examples comes forward in support of the aggrieved hitter and the historical game—*but what about, butwhatabout*—and every time it steals focus from the gravity of head injuries and derails significant action. No more. The truly aggrieved is not the player or the team who receives the occasional unjust penalty. There's only one *but what about* that matters. It's the player or family who has to live with years of an unfull life."

For Gary Bettman, the challenge is not to be distracted by history, by the voices of those who grew up as "hockey people," or by the overwhelming power of the status quo. He is the central custodian of the game. If he takes on head injuries aggressively—and he must—some of his changes might be ineffective, others may be embarrassingly inept, and he may very well be mocked by fans and the media. But he and we will learn, and it is far worse to be mocked by damaged players for not doing what clearly needs to be done.

Many of these steps can be implemented this season, and with significant impact if their purpose—to prevent or otherwise minimize head injuries—is not forgotten and the rules to support that purpose are applied unfailingly. Other steps will take longer and be of greater effect, but they can be set in motion.

Most important, however, it's time to think about our sports a different way.

What would hockey look like if it were played in a "head smart" way? If the safety of the brain were central to the rules? What about football and other sports?

What would we have to do differently? When do hits to the head happen? In what circumstances? On what parts of the ice? Against the boards? Against the glass? By whom? With shoulders? With elbows or sticks? They don't happen often. During most of the game, with most of the players, they don't happen at all. Why then? Why them?

What about the big hits?

What would we need to do to minimize the risk? Because this isn't about no risk. It's about smart, informed risk. How would we make hockey safer?

What would need to change? How would this game feel different to play? To watch? What would be lost? Unable to do some of the things they did before, what would players do instead?

My guess is that a lot less would change and for many fewer players than we think. My guess is also that many of the changes would make our games better, and not only for reasons of safety. If some rules are changed, players and coaches will find ways to adapt and to gain a competitive advantage, because that's what players and coaches do. They're dreamers and imaginers. They're competitive. They need to win. Once, players and coaches came up with

> If some rules are changed, players and coaches will find ways to adapt... because that's what players and coaches do.

the forward pass in both hockey and football, and gave flight to sports that had become a static snarl of bodies. They'll do it again. The mediocre will dig in their heels—they fear they can't change—and usually that's enough to stop everything in its tracks. But this time we have no choice. Not everyone will be affected the same way. Some things will change more for young kids but not for adults, or for girls and not boys, or for boys and not girls. The crucial point is that at every age and every level "head smart" will become the way we play.

This "head smart" movement should be global, not North American. We all face the same problems. Efforts might begin by gathering the most thoughtful coaches and players of a sport—in an area or in a country—and the best head-injury experts to begin putting together a "head smart" model for their sport. These models, as well as those created by other individuals and groups, would be put forward to the public and tested and debated through websites and later through local and international workshops and conferences. "Head smart" models generated in one place and in one sport would challenge and inform models in others to make each model continually better.

The NHL, NFL, and other sports leagues would engage with these efforts, sometimes as partners (in studies, in testing out proposals), sometimes financially, always in promoting the importance of the work. The Crosby press conference suggests an opportunity. The future doesn't have to be one of pointed fingers and shouted denials. None of us knows the answer. All of us know the problem. We are all in this together. We love our sports. We love to play them and watch them. We love to argue over them. We love the inspiration and the excitement they bring. We want sports to be part of our lives forever. We know that sports will not go away, but we also know that the role they play in our lives is at risk. This is a fearful time, but it can be an exciting time.

The NHL and Gary Bettman and the NFL and Roger Goodell have an opportunity. This is the moment.

Originally published September 30, 2011.

Novak Djokovic hit a number of improbable shots against Roger Federer, eventually winning the match and the 2011 US Open.

A SERIES OF UNBELIEVABLE EVENTS

*What the hell happened
at the US Open semifinals?*

by BRIAN PHILLIPS

by BRIAN PHILLIPS

One way to think about losing a tennis match, and specifically to think about the pain and disappointment of losing a great, tense, five-set tennis match the way Roger Federer did on Saturday, is to imagine yourself walking in to talk to the media afterward. Imagine that you have just spent several hours doing a physically exhausting, phenomenally difficult thing; that many thousands of people, and several television cameras, were watching you do this thing; that you could not look up while doing it without seeing a giant image of yourself hovering overhead; that your entire life revolves around this thing to the point that most of your waking hours are consumed by your obsessive work toward the goal of doing it successfully; that this has been the case since you were very young, so that succeeding in moments such as the one you have just been through is effectively

When you've
won sixteen
Grand Slam
titles... dazedness
at a tennis
tournament is
the equivalent
of anyone else's
existential panic.

the only purpose you have ever known; that you have just done the aforementioned thing at such a high level that almost no one in the history of the world could claim to have done it better; that you failed anyway; and that you failed because of an outrageous bit of bad luck, which came out of nowhere and upended all your work at precisely the moment when you thought you had succeeded. There: Now ready to answer some questions?

There's a certain death-type imagery from movies and TV shows that the situation calls to mind: a tight shot of a man walking down a long corridor toward a set of double doors; other people's hands reach out on either side of him to open the doors; he steps through into a blinding white light. If you or I were to face this situation, having lost the way Federer did, there's a very good chance that our quotes in the next day's paper would be dominated by transliterated weeping and hysterical blasphemy:

> But the five-time champion, who hasn't won a major since last year's Australian Open, never recovered from the loss of those two match points, dropping the final four games of the fifth set and falling to a 7–6 (9–7), 6–4, 3–6, 2–6, 5–7 defeat. "Nyrrrrrrggggh!" he said after the loss. "Nyyyrrrrrrrgggh aaahh-ahh ahh-nrrrrrm! There is no God in the universe! Do you hear me, CBS??"

To his credit, Federer didn't do this. Having played astonishingly great tennis against the world's runaway no. 1 player, Novak Djokovic, whom no one else has even pushed to five sets this year, and having lost anyway, Federer mainly seemed dazed. That in itself was revealing; when you've won 16 Grand Slam titles, the way Federer has, dazedness at a tennis tournament is the equivalent of anyone else's existential panic. But what left Federer stunned was one moment in particular, and at this point we need to pause to discuss that moment, because without understanding it we can't understand either the match or, more generally, what can be so devastating and unfair about top-flight tennis.

For the sake of clarity, we can divide the moment into two parts, which I'm going to call The Shot and The Confrontation. The Shot came late in the fifth set. Federer had looked staggeringly good in winning the first two sets, almost like his old self, but then turned passive and sluggish in the third and fourth sets, both of which Djokovic won easily. In the final set, Federer surprised everyone, including the hugely pro-Federer crowd, by rallying, breaking Djokovic at love at 4-3, then giving himself two match points while serving at 5-3. On the first of the two, Djokovic flicked back Federer's serve with a slappy, haphazard forehand—The Shot—that looked doomed but happened to drop inside the line. The crowd cheered, thinking the match was over, then fell into a murmury silence when it became clear that Djokovic had just hit a bafflingly great shot. That was when Djokovic produced The Confrontation. Turning toward the stands with an incredulous look on his face, he raised his arms up over his head like a pro wrestler, then broke into a dufusy grin. The crowd, uncertainly, started cheering. Djokovic kind of rolled his eyes and went back into his return stance with a look like, *these people*. After that, he loosened up, reeled off four straight games against a staggered Federer, and took the match.

That was why Federer was stunned. Having spent his entire adult life consciously molding himself into one of the best high-stakes tennis players in history, he'd just been beaten by an almost random sequence of events. Djokovic's snapped return happened to land in bounds; the crowd happened to set something off in Djokovic's head; this happened to inspire him to play better tennis. "I had it," Federer said about the match. "There's no more I could do. He snaps one shot, and then the whole thing changes … To lose against someone like that, it's very disappointing, because you feel like he was mentally out of it already. Just gets the lucky shot at the end and off you go."

We want athletes to be able to explain sports. Sport, at its most basic, is about physically realizing intentions—calculating the angle, plotting the spin, executing the shot. So surely the people who have the intentions, the people whose inner lives sport is expressing in some complicated way, are in the best position to tell us what really happens on the court. And to a certain extent that's true. But one of the reasons it's so scary to imagine going into the postmatch press conference as a loser is that it's not entirely true. What happens during a match may concern you to an emotionally devastating degree, but what happens can also turn on tiny fluctuations of chance so complicated that they are astoundingly difficult to articulate—minute physical differences that fall within any conceivable margin of error, emotional swings that could have gone either way and went against you, who knows why. These sorts of breaks are often monstrously unfair. And as with The Shot and The Confrontation, they tend to take on outsize importance in matches that are otherwise very close. Meaning that the greatest contests, the ones whose outcomes are most exalting for the winners and most devastating for the losers, are the ones most likely to be decided by infinitesimal turns of luck.

I want to be precise about this, because it's not the case that Federer's loss was purely arbitrary—had he not double-faulted on break point at 5–3 in the fifth, or committed 59 unforced errors, he could have won regardless of that one match point. But because all the athletic-skill stuff was so evenly matched, because the mistakes and heroic deeds all worked out to a stalemate, that one lucky shot—and even Djokovic agreed that it was lucky, although it's possible that he was being modest—was able to change everything. If Djokovic wins against Nadal in the final, it won't be an exaggeration to say that it changed tennis history.

Think about it: Djokovic goes from being a very good player whose season was

> What happens can also turn on tiny fluctuations of chance so complicated that they are astoundingly difficult to articulate.

tarnished by his inability to beat Federer (in the French Open semis and here) to holding three Grand Slam titles at once while being well on his way to completing maybe the best season in tennis history. Federer goes from being a player who can still beat the best to a definitively past-his-prime ex-champion who's dropped two straight late-round matches in majors after winning the first two sets. Nadal goes from having yet another crack at his rivalry with Federer to losing to Djokovic for a legacy-unsettling sixth straight time in a final. All because of that one shot.

So it's not hard to understand why Federer seemed dazed. The game can be pretty unjust. Actually, you could even say that what made this match so intense was not the quality of play—really high at times, but with a lot of errors—so much as the way all the minor injustices converged on each other. For instance: It was unfair that the crowd was dead set against Djokovic, who has worked like crazy (dancing, mugging, clowning around with various McEnroes) to win New Yorkers over since he first alienated them during a 2008 spat with Andy Roddick. It was unfair that the draw pitted these two players against each other while the second-seeded Nadal got to feast on Andy Murray. It was unfair that The Shot dropped in. It's unfair, really unfair, that Federer is getting old. There was just an air in the stadium of quiet, objectless frustration, which hummed along under the tennis, raised the stakes, and helped the match feel semiclassic. But if you think about it too much, you wind up nearly as dazed as Federer.

Originally published September 12, 2011.

BUSINESS VS. PERSONAL

Owners, players, agents, lawyers, and the
interview that blew the NBA lockout wide open

by BILL SIMMONS

HAGEN: Your father wouldn't want to hear this, Sonny. This is business not personal.
SONNY: They shoot my father and it's business, my ass!
HAGEN: Even shooting your father was business not personal, Sonny!
SONNY: Well then, business is going to have to suffer.

That's one of the most famous scenes from one of the most famous movies ever made. You know how things end for Sonny Corleone—he ignores his *consigliere*, makes it personal, and ends up gorging on a bowl of bullets parmigiana. His brother Michael assumes command and remains all-business for his first few years, slowly losing perspective and becoming more and more paranoid. He stops trusting his inner circle, grows apart from his family, and murders his bumbling brother. Killing Fredo is strictly business for Michael, a warning that nobody should ever cross him. He can't see anything beyond making money and keeping power. He's dead inside. No different than Sonny, really.

What does this have to do with the NBA lockout? The owners wanted to blow up their current model; the players gave them gas and matches. But why? I think the answer lies in that Godfather scene. The owners treated these negotiations as a natural extension of their business, only caring about their bottom line and nothing else. The players took the proceedings much more personally. After things fell apart on Monday—when the NBPA rejected David Stern's "take it or leave it" ultimatum and decided to decertify, a confusing move (because of the timing) that almost certainly wrecked the 2011–12 season—agent Aaron Goodwin made a telling comment to the *Washington Post*'s Mike Wise.

"For years owners have treated players as if they are just their property," Goodwin said, "fining them over how they dress, act, everything. This is the first time the players have the opportunity to say no.

Whoa. For months and months, bubbling beneath the surface of the posturing and rhetoric, buried under anonymous leaks, veiled threats and everything else that makes any professional sports lockout or strike so insufferable, a dynamic had been swelling that was entirely, 100 percent personal. Let's look at Goodwin's take a second time.

For years owners have treated players as if they are just their property …

That's a recurring theme of this lockout, something Bryant Gumbel broached on *Real Sports* when he compared the NBA owners to plantation owners, then festered when nobody on the players' side distanced themselves from Gumbel's words (if anything, you could almost feel them silently nodding). A few days later, Wise's column "Negotiations could be hijacked by racial perceptions" publicly nailed many of the points that NBPA insiders had been whispering privately for weeks. Why isn't anyone pointing out that Peter Holt is one of Rick Perry's biggest donors? Why isn't anyone remembering that Donald Sterling battled those racial discrimination housing lawsuits, or that Dan Gilbert skewered LeBron James after The Decision and made him seem like, as Jesse Jackson said later, "a runaway slave"? Why hasn't anyone noticed that 28 of these 29 owners are white, or that everyone in David Stern's inner circle is white except for Stu Jackson? Race overshadowed these negotiations more than anyone wanted to admit. Gumbel recklessly ripped that scab open. The NBPA's lead negotiator, Jeffrey Kessler, reopened it last week by stupidly saying, "Instead of treating the players like partners, they're treating them like plantation workers."[1] Goodwin (an African-American) revisited the theme a little more diplomatically on Monday, but still … calling the players "property" is pretty telling.[2]

Is this what happens when twenty-eight wealthy white guys (plus Michael Jordan, who emerged to everyone's surprise as a leader of the "let's screw the players over as much as we possibly can" side) keep trying to impose their will on a collection of not-nearly-as-wealthy-and-mostly black guys? This was one of Stern's biggest mistakes—believing the league had squashed their race issues decades ago, that his record was impeccable on this front, that he could negotiate one last labor deal without worrying about things like, "The players won't care that nearly everyone on my side for this meeting is white, right?" Stern would disagree—vehemently—with Goodwin's assertion that owners treated players like "property." But Goodwin isn't some low-level flunkie. He has represented superstars like Jason Kidd, Paul Pierce, LeBron James and Dwight Howard over the years. He represents Kevin Durant right now. He has a better feel for these

1. This was such an idiotic statement by Kessler, and so counter-productive, that Hunter and his cronies quickly distanced themselves from it AND made Kessler apologize. Somehow, he's still in charge. Go figure.

2. Here's where it gets tough for me. I am white. Jackson's "runaway slave" remark never sat well with me for the simple reason that—in my mind—slavery should never be brought up with professional sports (no matter the topic). My friend Michael Wilbon disagreed. He thought Gilbert's remarks failed the racism "smell test" and mentioned that, independently of Jackson, he read Gilbert's

guys than Stern does. And if he truly believes the players feel like "property," that's pretty frightening.

Let's look at the second part of Goodwin's quote …

For years owners have treated players as if they are just their property—fining them over how they dress, act, everything.

That's not an outlandish claim. For the past twelve years (since our last labor shutdown), Stern capped contracts and rookie deals so players didn't get paid too much (or too much right away). He instituted a mandatory dress code so injured players looked more professional (translation: less "urban"). He cracked down on taunting during games, physical play, leaving the bench during altercations and anything else that might lead to another Artest Melee or Kermit/Rudy scenario. He pushed players to participate in "NBA Cares," fined them for not showing up on time to All-Star Weekend, fined them for avoiding the press during the playoffs and basically treated them like an overbearing high school principal. And, of course, he made every decision in his typically smug, sarcastic, endearing-or-bullying-depending-on-how-you-feel-about-him manner.[3]

He's clearly wearing out the players … and not in a good way. During one of Stern's typically biting lectures in a crucial labor meeting two months ago, Dwyane Wade snapped and yelled at him, "Don't you point your finger at me!" That was personal, not business. That was Wade telling Stern, "Fuck you, you're not my dad. We're tired of your condescending bullshit. It's not happening anymore." Same with Kobe Bryant, Kevin Garnett, and Paul Pierce staging their infamous (and totally ill-conceived) "We're not budging from 53 [BRI]" walkout a few weeks later. Even more interesting: Stern and

rant and wondered, "Wow, did one of (Gilbert's) cotton-pickers get away?" Wilbon is one of the smartest, most rational people I know, some-one who succeeded by positioning himself as an entertaining writer and TV personality who happens to be black. He never makes race an issue without a reason. Wilbon was bothered by something in Gilbert's letter that I couldn't see. His life experiences were different than mine.

3. For the record, I find it endearing. Then again, I've never been on the opposite side of a bargaining table with him.

24

his inner circle were (and are) genuinely dumbfounded by the players' growing enmity toward them.[4]

Quick tangent: My father served as the superintendent of schools in Easton, Massachusetts, for nearly twenty years. He retired in the summer of 2009, at the age of 62, for a variety of reasons … but mainly this one. He didn't want to stay too long. When you're a superintendent, it takes only one renegade school committee member, one unexpected budget cut, one scandal, or one tragedy to shift momentum against you. Once it happens, you can't get it back. Adversaries smell your weakening power the same way zombies smell blood. You start getting undermined or browbeaten into ideas you never wanted to do. By the time you finally resign or get replaced, those final years become part of your legacy, the last thing anyone remembers about you (whether you like it or not). My father never wanted that to happen. He left one year too early instead of one year too late. He has no regrets.

And as an NBA die-hard and 38-year season ticket holder for the Celtics, he watches what's happening with David Stern right now and has one reaction: "He stayed too long. That's exactly what I didn't want to happen to me."

I don't blame Stern—sometimes you're the last to know. I think that he thought his track record was impeccable. He can't see how his players see him in 2011—as the little/old/sarcastic/white/out-of-touch dictator who patronizes them, orders them around, genuinely feels like THEY should listen to HIM, and by the way, works for the owners (and not them). And it's not like fans are delighted with him, either. He stopped thinking outside the box years ago.[5] It's funny that the league obsesses over its big market/small market issue, revenue sharing, and international growth, and keeps trotting out the same laborious 82-game regular season with

4. Something that probably didn't help—unlike in 1999, every twist and turn during this lockout was dissected immediately on Twitter, sports blogs, and websites, and any player could become a character in the negotiations just by tweeting something either inflammatory or defensive. The coverage of this lockout, in general, was incredibly comprehensive and so pointed that I can't even imagine how casual fans followed it. Even if the players barely (if ever) heard from their player reps, they could have certainly educated themselves about the day-to-day proceedings of the lockout if they had wanted.

5. I'd list some examples but I've written about this 275 times.

the same jacked-up prices and the same annoying issues (like tanking for draft picks or exhausted teams playing their fourth road game in five nights). You know what was really telling these past few weeks? We were coming off of one of the top-five NBA seasons ever, now it's November, the league isn't playing … and nobody really cared. Imagine the outrage if pro football disappeared for an entire month. Where's the clamoring for regular season pro basketball?

If anything, it's swung the other way. Many season ticket holders don't care if they miss these first six weeks of games, feeling their tickets are overpriced, anyway. Casual fans only care during the playoffs; for them, it was always a nine-week sport and that's it.[6] Only the junkies are pissed off. And even then, you don't REALLY feel the NBA's loss until after the holidays, when college football is gone and the NFL playoffs are winding down. No wonder the league claims to be losing money even after a godsend of a two-year stretch (pre-Decision and post-Decision) in the midst of a historic talent boon. When you remember it happened on Stern's watch, then factor in his disconnect with the players, it's sure starting to seem like one of the greatest sports commissioners ever overstayed his welcome.

Which brings us to the last part of Goodwin's quote …

This is the first time the players have the opportunity to say no.

That's a pretty bold statement. And by the way … I don't disagree. When can you remember NBA players truly standing up to Stern before these last few months? See their quotes or tweets dating back to the summer and the same themes keep popping up. Why should we trust the owners' numbers? We already gave back; what are they giving up? Why are we the ones making all the concessions? How is this a partner-

6. That apathy vindicated the owners' position to some degree: in case you were wondering, nobody really gives a crap that we're not playing right now. By blowing up the NBA and trying to create a more logical model, we weren't exactly breaking up the '27 Yankees here.

ship when one side is telling the other side what to do? Why do they claim so many franchises are in trouble when people are still buying them? Who was putting a gun to the owners' heads when they were giving out all those contracts that they knew were dumb?

Some arguments make sense; others are too idealistic. But there is definitely an overriding theme. We don't trust them, we're tired of kowtowing to them, we're standing up for ourselves. The players would rather implode a season than accept an unfavorable deal—not as a business move, but for their own sanity, because they're over competitive, proud people who no longer want to be told what to do. They convinced themselves (perhaps foolishly) that there's a greater good here, that their collective dignity was worth sacrificing a paid season of their preciously short playing careers. They believe they conceded enough (a 10 percent drop of their revenue share, basically), they're worried about protecting future generations of players (or so they claim), and deep down, it pisses them off that the Old Haughty White Guy Who Bossed Us Around For Years basically told them last week, "Here's our offer, here's our deadline for you to take that offer, and if you don't like it, I am going to ram that offer up your asses and you won't play this year."

Really, they're just rebelling. And over everything else, that's why the 2011-12 season is about to get canceled.

O f course, these things don't just blow up by themselves. Everything described above was the "gas." We still needed matches, and we still needed people lighting those matches and tossing them toward the gas leak. Here were the offending parties in no particular order.

1. BILLY HUNTER AND DEREK FISHER

Imagine riding in a car with someone who doesn't care if he dies. He's driving 100 miles an hour on the highway and cackling like a maniac. You're asking him to slow down. He asks, "What's it worth to you?" You stammer. He says, "Unless you give me everything in your wallet right now, I'm driving into that highway divider up there." You have to make a decision: do you pay him, or do you think he's bluffing?

Well, you pay him. Quickly. You don't want to find out if he values his life less than you value yours.

Guess who had the leverage that whole time? That's right … the suicidal maniac driving the car. And really, that's how the latest NBA lockout played out. We have known for nearly three years that the NBA owners (a) wanted to change the financial structure of their business and (b) didn't care how they did it, just that it happened. If they lost 30 games of the 2011–12 season to get what they wanted, fine. If they lost the season, fine. If they lost three seasons, fine. They didn't care. Just don't ask them a question like, "If you're so unhappy owning your NBA franchise, why don't you just sell it?" See, heading into the summer of 2011, your average NBA franchise was more valuable for the investment itself than for the revenue it yielded. That's pretty liberating—if you don't care that your business stops, how can anyone possibly negotiate with you? You're basically driving them toward that highway divider and asking for their wallet.

You could see the owners' devious plan percolating as far back as All-Star Weekend in 2009, when I wrote my "No Benjamins Association" column[7] and predicted doom. You know who else could see it coming? Billy Hunter! You know, the guy who admitted last week to knowing this day was coming for two or three years. That begs the question, "Why didn't you start the decertification process on July 1 instead of November 14, Billy?" It's like losing your house to an earthquake and

7. One prediction from that column: "The owners will happily lock out players as soon as the current CBA expires, then play the same devious waiting game from the summer of 1998 … will the league

saying, "I knew we were going to have another earthquake, I've been saying this for years," only never buying earthquake insurance. Excuse me? Maybe Hunter doesn't realize it yet, but he's become a permanent punchline for playing the decertification card so late (and for how he handled the past six months in general). I wouldn't let Billy Hunter negotiate an eBay bid for me at this point.

As a friend who works in professional sports (not the NBA) pointed out by e-mail this week, "When one party has all of the leverage (like the NFL lockout once the Court of Appeals ruled the lockout could continue, or the NBA lockout until now), it does not necessarily mean the other party has to hit its head against the wall. What is wrong with figuring out, well in advance, that you have a weak position and cutting the best deal you can? This notion that a good negotiation lasts right up until a deadline (or past a deadline) is stupid. A good negotiation is understanding your position and getting a deal done before bad things happen. That is where the NBPA (Kessler, really) screwed this up. Sometimes you just have to understand that the best deal to be made (under any circumstances) CAN be made early. If you get criticized as a Gene Upshaw-type lackey, then so be it. By the way, when you are willing to do a deal early, you can sometimes get peripheral issues your way, because the other party does recognize the value of avoiding a fight and missed games."

And sure, if the league suddenly started making boatloads of money, that leverage would shift, and the players could say, "Everything stops unless we get more." But those weren't the stakes this time around. Hunter and Fisher failed to prepare the players, fed their anti-Stern neuroses, never unearthed a decent strategy, and misread every conceivable tea leaf. Their goal from Day One should have been, "We have no lever-

survive a year-long disappearance? What about two years? We're less than 29 months from starting to find out. If you think it's a good idea to disappear for even six months in shaky economic times, ask any Writers Guild member how that turns out. These wealthy or used-to-be-wealthy owners don't want to keep losing money just to feed their ego by continuing to own a basketball team. They will make other arrangements, the same way they would arrange to sell their favorite yacht because they didn't feel like splurging on gasoline anymore. These guys don't want to fix the system; they want to reinvent it."

age, we need to get the best deal we can without missing any paychecks." Even last week, they mistook Stern's ultimatum as "take it or leave it" when it was really an "S.O.S."—with his influence eroding, Stern barely had enough owner votes and knew small-market teams (along with Washington and Denver) wouldn't back any other offer unless it pillaged the players.[8] Hunter and Fisher thought he was bluffing. They were wrong. Dead wrong. That offer is gone. And it's not coming back.

You can't oversell how disorganized Hunter's side has been—especially last weekend and on Monday, when they never allowed the players to vote, failed to give them enough information, and couldn't even wrangle every player rep to Monday's meeting in New York. It took them five solid days to respond to Stern's offer; instead of countering with four or five system tweaks like Stern expected (he would never admit that publicly because it would belie his whole "take it or leave it" stance, but it's true), the players simply shredded it and launched the NBA's "nuclear winter" (Stern's words, and really, his only inspired moment of the past few months). Anyone who commends the players for standing up for themselves should mention that, during those five days—which doubled as the five most essential days in the recent history of the players association—many players couldn't even get in touch with their team reps (much less Hunter or Fisher). Those players were standing up for themselves, all right—they were standing up to make sure they had cell phone reception, because nobody was e-mailing them any updates. What a mess. If I wrote a book about the 2011 NBA Lockout, it would either be called Clusterfuck! or CLUSTERFUCK!

8. We learned these past few weeks that Stern barely has enough juice to mobilize his owners any more. There's too much new money in the league and too many owners who weren't around during Stern's prime. Goes back to my dad's whole "stayed too long" thing.

2. THE OWNERS

Either they never wanted a season (and lied this whole time), or they badly misread the players' resolve and their growing contempt for Stern. It's one or the other. Hmmmmmmmm. Let's lie and pretend they wanted a season. Who "negotiates" like that? Why were they going for Eff You touchdowns like the post-Spygate Patriots? Why weren't they more magnanimous? Why did they try to win every single issue? Whatever happened to the concept of "I want to win, but I also want to be fair, because these are my partners for the next 10 years?"

Players are competitors. They don't want to be "embarrassed" or "broken." It's easy for them to confuse "taking a stand" with "not making the best available deal given the limited leverage you had." Why didn't the owners find a few subtle ways to let the players save face? Didn't they learn anything from how Roger Goodell and his owners handled those few days after their NFL agreement, when they effusively praised the deal for both sides even after working the players like a speed bag? And if Team Stern expected the players to counter, why not say that? Hell, why not say, "We screwed that 'last offer' thing up; so we're revising our offer as a sign of good faith in one last attempt to save the season?"

One thing's for sure: if Stern believed they were that close (and I know for a fact he did), then he *totally* failed and *totally* underestimated how the players felt. Not their resolve, just how they felt. Maybe that's why he seemed visibly stunned afterward, blaming Hunter and Kessler when the reasons were so much more complex. The players know they have terrible leadership. Their agents have been telling them that for months and months and months. And at this point, they don't care. Even though Hunter was an unequivocal disaster these past few months—his lack of urgency was stupefying, his lack of a coherent strategy was almost criminal, his summer media strategy couldn't have been worse, and his inability to keep his 450 players in the loop from day to day was inexplicable—the players kept following him and Fisher if only because the other option (trusting Stern and the owners) was less palatable. How can someone run a sports league for 28 years and lose the trust of his players that completely? And how could he possibly expect to win that trust back? (The short answer: He won't. It's gone.)

3. THE PAMPERING ISSUE

Your typical NBA owner operates like a sugar daddy of sorts. He coddles his players, flies them on chartered planes, serves them gourmet meals on those planes, puts them up in five-star hotels, builds them state-of-the-art practice facilities, hires them the best possible training staffs, sneaks them extra tickets for every game, enables their entourages, builds ticket campaigns around them, kisses their asses and (in some cases) even allows their friends to hitch rides on team charters. That's the real reason Dan Gilbert was so pissed off two years ago—after giving LeBron everything he wanted for years and years, LeBron never had the courtesy to call before he picked Miami. Gilbert felt more like a spurned boyfriend than anything (and acted like it).

I thought we had something! What about all those times I let your buddies ride on our team charter! You used me! I'm throwing away everything you ever gave me!

Once Gilbert flipped that switch and went after LeBron so ferociously, the players took it personally ... just like they took it personally when the owners started playing hardball this summer. (You can only imagine how the players would have reacted had the owners pulled "chartered planes" and "suites in every five-star hotel" out of their last proposal. Then we REALLY would have had a problem.) There's a general disconnect here that almost feels like a bad marriage. Follow me here ...

- The owners bitch about the players being greedy, and yet all they've done is enable that greed.

- The players claim they're being disrespected, and yet no group of professional athletes has ever been more spoiled.[9]

- The owners claim they care about the quality of the game, and yet every player says the ideal number of regular season games—if your goal is to have healthy, rested players entertaining your fans to their best ability every night—is somewhere between 70 and 74 games. (The owners, of course, ignore this.)

- The players claim it's not their fault that owners keep handing out lavishly dumb deals to forgettable players, and yet they ignore that their fans—the people who pay their salaries and keep their league afloat— hate nothing more than seeing overpaid assholes jogging through games, faking injuries, showing up for camp 20 pounds overweight, clogging their team's salary cap, and making it harder to improve their team's roster. The fact that they don't realize this reflects on them is kind of alarming. Can you really be that self-absorbed?[10]

- The owners claim they need a better financial model, and yet they're the ones recycling the same incompetent executives—seriously, someone is hiring Ed Stefanski again????—and handing out cringe-worthy contracts year after year after year after year. I wrote the "Atrocious GM Summit" column in 2006—four years later, with a lockout looming, we watched more moronically dumb contracts handed out than EVER

9. No American professional sports league ever had a higher average salary.

10. The counter-argument to that point (as Stein & Bucher made in our podcast on November 15): Come on, you'd want yourself or any other writer to make as much money as they could! I would have rebutted this more effectively if Bucher's crappy cell phone didn't make it impossible to interrupt him. Here's the problem with that argument—a

before. These guys can't stay out of their own way, and even worse, the players want to keep it that way.

Aren't they "partners" here? Don't they care about the league as a whole? Don't they want fans to like their product? The players want it both ways—please, keep the chartered airplane seats, hotel suites, crab legs, and stupid contracts coming; just don't ask me to care about the quality of my league. In a perfect world, both sides would work together and create the best and most fan-friendly NBA model possible. But the world ain't perfect.

You know what the real irony is? The owners' last proposal actually made a ton of sense. Read Howard Beck's breakdown of what it would have looked like, potentially, and try to find ONE thing that isn't logical. Contracts should be shorter so fans aren't getting constantly turned off by that relentlessly overpaid mediocrity. The gap between big market teams and small market teams should be smaller. A team like Cleveland should have a more favorable chance to keep its best player. A star like Carmelo *shouldn't* be able to force a trade and get rewarded with a mammoth extension. The mid-level exception *should* be tempered—it spawned too many dumb contracts and made it harder for teams to improve. What's wrong with coming up with a smarter model in which the right money goes to the right people? That's a bad thing?

As my aforementioned pro sports friend says, "In every part of life there are systems that protect people from doing things that will ultimately hurt themselves—its why banks don't charge $30/month for debit card usage; it's not like they don't want to, and it's not like some people wouldn't pay for it. Once you have the BRI split, then EVERYONE should be working toward a better system. The NFL got to the dollars,

professional sports league only has a certain amount of money to give its players. Why do you want too much of that money going to the wrong players? Why not come up with a better model, something that addresses the issues of rookie contract guys outperforming their deals (like Derrick Rose or Russell Westbrook) or meal tickets like LeBron and Durant making less money than Vernon Wells or John Lackey? I'm fine with players making as much money as they can—can we just make sure those players are good and deserve the money? God forbid we figured out how to work performance-based incentives (like All-Star or All-NBA appearances, top-5 MVP votes, the Finals MVP, or someone who spends a certain number of years with the same team) into the labor negotiations these past few months.

got to the cap, then tried to make it so the rookie pool made more sense. This is a system issue that benefited everyone. It doesn't make sense for Sam Bradford to make more than Drew Brees, right? The key with any system issue is trust—you tell the NBPA that the money WILL be in the system no matter what—don't they want it to go to guys like Wade or Dirk or Monta Ellis (early in his career) instead of mediocre veterans like Darko or Cardinal? This is where the agents have too much power—some of the powerful ones benefit from certain system structures even if the overall cash doesn't change—they just need to be ignored, and the players need to really trust that the system change won't cost them dollars in the aggregate."

Which leads us to …

4. THE AGENTS

If the players don't trust the owners or Stern, and they're losing trust in Hunter and Fisher, who's left?

You guessed it … it's those shrewd and lovable legal minds who negotiate for players, call them every day, know their kids' names, won them over years ago, spent the last few months quietly undermining Hunter, know how to butter up media members and curry favor, and currently have their clients lathered into an anti-The-Man frenzy. The agents despised the owners' latest proposal—they don't want the middle class compromised in any way, or sign-and-trades, or the luxury tax, because that might curtail player movement (their bread and butter). They would rather lose a season to protect what they have, knowing they have much longer careers and they'll make those commissions back over time as long as they can prevent the NBA's model from changing against them too drastically right now.

Make no mistake: the agents are the single smartest group involved in this lockout. They make absurd commissions working over general managers (usually ex-players) who are almost always unequipped to negotiate with them. You know that saying "laughing all the way to the bank"? That's what the best sports agents do. Trust me, they have done the math. They figured out exactly where this lockout needs to end for them—repeat: for them—and advised the players accordingly. Meanwhile, these players can NEVER get that lost season back from three standpoints: how it affects them financially, how it affects their playing careers, and how it affects their fans (especially the casual ones who hopped on the bandwagon these past two years and will just as quickly hop off). The agents were supposed to be protecting these guys; instead, they protected themselves. Of course ...

5. JEFFREY KESSLER

The agents could never act more selfishly than Kessler, who waited his whole career for the right antitrust suit and finally found his patsy. It's his chance to become the focal point of an HBO documentary, bring the NBA to its knees, and maybe become the Marvin Miller of antitrust lawyers. (It's a longshot, and we might lose a couple of NBA seasons in the process, but who cares, right?) Those just-as-ruthless NFL owners sniffed him out early, chopped his balls off, and eventually shut him out of the final negotiating process, knowing he didn't totally care about getting a deal done. Now he's operating in a much bigger vacuum—thanks to a leadership void, Kessler kept amassing power even after his "plantation owners" comment backfired so spectacularly.[11]

Again, one of the world's leading experts in antitrust law is mobilizing NBA players toward a potentially historic antitrust suit that could wipe away multiple (repeat: multiple) seasons. You don't see anything shady there? Giving Kessler a significant say in these proceedings makes about as much

11. A cynic would say that Kessler deliberately tried to undermine negotiations with that comment in a last-ditch attempt to mess things up so he could get his antitrust suit.

sense as putting Kris Jenner in charge of a Parents Shouldn't Exploit Their Kids support group.

6. THE VETERAN SUPERSTARS

That would be Steve Nash, Grant Hill, Kobe Bryant, Tim Duncan, Dirk Nowitzki, Ray Allen and Paul Pierce … seven of our wealthiest, most-thoughtful and most-accomplished NBA players. Five of them have been missing in action— most disappointingly, Nash, one of the smartest athletes in any sport. Kobe can't decide whether he wants to cross Fisher and Hunter or not; he's done everything but call them out, he's allegedly leaked information to writers, he pushed hard behind the scenes for the 50/50 deal, he obviously wants to play … and yet there's an invisible line he won't cross.[12] Pierce has gone the other way—he's been the union's most vocal "veteran star" voice, and if there's been a revelation these past few months, it's that Pierce carries more weight with other players than anyone else.

All right, so let's look at Pierce for a second. He's one of my favorites. As a Celtics fan, I stuck with him through thick and thin. I remember when he was nearly stabbed to death, how that incident affected him, how his personal issues nearly led the Celtics to trade him in 2005, how that moment didn't happen only because Boston's new owner stuck up for him, how he reinvented himself over the next three years, how he graciously stuck around during a rebuilding process, because his GM promised him help, how he thrived during that championship season, how he soaked in that special moment during Game 6 (in the fourth quarter against the Lakers at home, when the crowd was going bonkers and Pierce turned toward the stands, nodded

12. I thought for sure that Kobe would be our saving grace here. Of everyone, he has the most to lose—a chance at a title, 2,000 more points toward Kareem's scoring record, maybe one last elite year from his knees, and oh yeah … $25 million. By the way, I hate this lockout for so many reasons, but the fact that it's making me root for Kobe ranks right up there.

happily and seemed to be saying to himself, "I've been waiting my whole life for this"), how he tried so valiantly to win a title these past three years as his body slowly betrayed him. He's one of the toughest (and most durable) Celtics ever. He could have played with Russell, Cowens, Bird, you name it.

I'm not surprised that Pierce emerged as a behind-the-scenes leader during this lockout. Every Celtics fan knows how he's wired. Here's what surprises me: knowing how competitive he is, knowing how much he cares about one more title, knowing how much he loves playing in Boston, knowing how much he appreciates how Wyc Grousbeck and Danny Ainge stood by him over the years, knowing how he thinks about his career in a big-picture sense, knowing that he's a pretty rational guy, it frightens me that Paul Pierce cares *this much* about standing up to the owners and potentially losing a season. It makes me think the owner/player relationship (and the Stern/player relationship) is significantly more damaged than we want to believe. I don't agree with many of the reasons why we arrived there, or with the motives of the people who either conspired to get us there (or pushed us there with their own ineptitude), but we're there … and really, that's all you can say.

For that reason and all the others, I keep saying "no" whenever anyone asks me if there will be a 2011–12 NBA season. Just know that there's no side to take—it's mutually assured destruction in its purest form. That's difficult to explain to anyone losing his or her job over these next few months. I work across the street from the Staples Center at L.A. Live, in a complex that houses something like 10 restaurants and three bars within a two-minute walk of Staples. They were expecting three or four NBA games every week from now until next spring. Now on those nights, it's quiet as hell. A little eerie, even. Bartenders, waiters, bus boys, and cooks will start getting axed soon. Same for many Clippers/Lakers employees across the street, and for every other team, and for everyone else who works near an NBA arena, and for every media entity that covers one of the 30 teams, it's a ripple effect that keeps going and going, and it's happening because this lockout went soooooooooooooo much deeper than just "we're taking a stand."

I can't see the players caving at this point. They're too entrenched and too rankled. Stern and Hunter are too stubborn to step aside; it's like they're trapped in the same neverending hockey faceoff, only the referee won't ship them off. Kessler and the agents only care about themselves. Same for the small market owners and even a few of the bigger market ones. If you're looking for a voice of reason[13], a veteran star[14] to throw his hands up and say, "Wait a second,[15] we're not really throwing this season away,[16] right?", you're going to be disappointed.[17] That renegade player[18] would have emerged by now.

For the owners, nothing has changed—it's strictly business. For the players, something has changed—it's almost entirely personal. You can't find a middle ground between those two worlds. You just can't. Maybe it's the opposite of how definitively *The Godfather: Part II* ended—with Michael Corleone sitting outside by himself, lost in thought, alone in every sense, a ruthless businessman with no personal connection to anything—but even so, that deafening silence sounds the same.

Originally published November 18, 2011.

13. Kobe?

14. Kobe!

15. "I'm Kobe Bryant"

16. "For Kobe Bryant"

17. KOBE!!!!!!!!!!!!!!!!!!!!!!

A NEW KIND OF CARRIE FOR CABLE TV

*Homeland's heroine is on the offensive against al-Qaeda, the
United States government, and the heroine archetype altogether*

by ANDY GREENWALD

On television, women are allowed to be good wives or new girls. They
can break hearts or fix them, be criminals or cops. But for the most part, the
one thing they can't be on television is a mess. And not a cutesy, unable-to-
decide-between-handsome-boyfriend-and-dream-job, panic-eating and klutz-
falling cue-the-Fray-on-the-soundtrack sort of mess, either. I'm talking an honest-to-goodness shitshow—a complicated, complex character who manages to
be both brutally effective and titanically troubled. Think Andy Sipowicz, Tony
Soprano, George Costanza: charismatic, memorable men allowed to be more
than one thing at any given time, and most of them terrible. After only two
hours of screen time, it might be time to add Carrie Mathison to the list.

To be clear, the protagonist of Showtime's new *Homeland*, as played by
Claire Danes, is extremely good at her job. Too good, perhaps. As a CIA

counterintelligence officer, Carrie is as comfortable behind the wheel of a jeep in Baghdad as she is behind a conference room table in Langley. She's brittle and single-minded, so driven to prevent another 9/11 she'll seemingly sacrifice any life, including her own, in the process. She defies authority and wears an engagement ring so her one-night stands won't get any long-term ideas. Her refrigerator is empty, save for a solitary pack of rancid yogurt. Her aspirin bottle, though, is full of antipsychotic pills—a no-no at her clearance level—that she gets on the sly from her soccer-mom sister. Carrie thinks nothing of whore's bathing before a top-secret debriefing or throwing herself at Saul (an excellent Mandy Patinkin), her bearded mentor, when he uncovers the extra-legal lengths she's willing to go to in order to prove herself right. She's a walking weapon of mass self-destruction.

What's exhilarating about *Homeland*—and Danes's performance in it— is that Carrie can be all of these things and still, indisputably, be the hero. Of course "hero" is a problematic word in any context, particularly so on this show, which spins on the homecoming of Nicholas Brody (Damien Lewis), a POW marine who went missing in Iraq eight years before. Carrie, though, is certain an Al Qaeda bombmaker whispered a warning about an American turned terrorist during the off-reservation op that got her pulled from the field ten months prior. Now, despite the wishes of the entire United States government, Carrie launches a one-woman stakeout of Brody: camping out on her couch in front of two giant monitors, spying on the most intimately twisted moments of Brody's rapprochement with his wife (who's been

---

A Select List of Other Honest-to-Goodness Shitshow Heroines

Jo March
Little Women by Louisa May Alcott. One of four sisters, Jo is the sassy tomboy writer who cannot fathom staying home from the Civil War battlefield. In her own words: "I detest affected niminy-piminy chits!"

Amelia Bedelia
Amelia Bedelia by Peggie Parrish. The heroine of several "I Can Read Books," Amelia Bedelia does everything so right, it's wrong. She squarely tells her boss, "The list said to put all the lights out. It didn't say to bring them back inside."

sleeping with his best friend), his attempts to reconnect with his confused children, and his kung-fu chopping of overly ambitious tabloid reporters.

A lot of this stuff is played with the paranoia set to 11 and bears the aggro thumbprints of the executive producer's previous gig at *24*. There's also a worrying whiff of the same sort of isolated ambition—an entire season to figure out if one guy is bad or not?—that sunk recent cable duds *Rubicon* and *The Killing*. But the first two episodes of *Homeland* are legitimately gripping, able to toggle gracefully between TV tropes (Lynn, Carrie's asset who may have information on Brody's militant puppetmaster, is a sexy, occasionally topless, kept woman) and HBO-ish depth (Carrie lies about the danger she's putting Lynn's excellent body in while trying to crack the case). Lewis is suitably haunted in a challenging role—anyone gone from the comforts (and pancake griddles) of home would be a total wreck regardless of whether he's a born-again Islamist or not. But this is Danes's show, her focused, relentless performance the true heir to Helen Mirren's original *Prime Suspect*, not the neutered, be-hatted version currently treading whiskey-and-water on NBC. It's been two weeks, meaning there's plenty of time to get on board with the fall's best new drama. Get to know Carrie Mathison before she has a chance to clean herself up.

Originally published October 11, 2011.

Irina Spalko
Indiana Jones and the Legend of the Crystal Skull. Her self-described credits: "Three times I have received order of Lenin. Also medal of Hero of Socialist Labor, and vhy? Because I know things. I know things before anyone else. And vhat I do not know, I find out."

Lisbeth Salander
The fearless heroine of the Millenium books, she survives getting shot by her father and being buried alive by her brother while still hacking computers and stealing billions of dollars.

Ree Dolly
Winter's Bone by Daniel Woodrell. A seventeen-year-old girl who takes care of her inept mother and younger siblings when her meth addict father disappears. She knows exactly what she is: "a Dolly, bred'n buttered."

 Member teams, geographic region, and all other defining characteristics subject to change.

THE ERA OF THE SUPER-CONFERENCE

Embracing NCAA realignment

by MARK TITUS

Now that Ohio State's national title hopes were dashed by those cheaters from Miami earlier this month, it seems like the hot topic at the college football water cooler has shifted from how dominant the Buckeyes are to all this conference realignment going on.

As far as I can tell, most fans seem to be against the changing of the conference landscape either because it has the potential to end some of college football's most historic rivalries, or because they fear that too many teams in each conference will make them nostalgic and long for the good old days when the "ten" in Big Ten represented how many teams were in the conference and wasn't just an arbitrary word. Well, luckily, I'm here to explain why you should embrace this change, because conference realignment has the potential to be the best thing to ever happen to college football. In fact, I support conference realignment so much that I think there should be mandated realignment every year in the form of promotion and relegation. Yeah, I said it—relegation. Before you grab your pitchfork and start yelling, "Keep your pansy soccer concepts out of my college football!" hear me out.

Here's how it would work: Most people agree that super-conferences are the only logical ending point for all the realignment. Some think there will eventually be four 16-team conferences, and others believe that the remaining teams in the Big 12, after all the shifting is done, will merge with the remaining teams in the Big East. For our purposes, let's assume the latter will happen. This will leave us with five power conferences in college football—Pac-12, Big Ten, ACC, SEC, and the Big East/12. Coincidentally, there are five other conferences in FBS that are considered to be a step down from these power conferences—WAC, MAC, C-USA, Sun Belt, and Mountain West.

The way I see it, the powers that be should pair up each power conference with one of these lesser conferences and create a relegation system like foreign soccer leagues use. Geographically, it would make the most sense for the Pac-12 to pair up with the WAC, the Big Ten to pair up with the MAC, the ACC to pair up with C-USA, the SEC to pair up with the Sun Belt, and the Big East/12 to pair up with the Mountain West. Even though the NCAA has proven time and time again that doing whatever makes the most sense is typically not an option, let's give them the benefit of the doubt here and assume that they'd get these pairings right. From there, it's simple—the last place team from the power conference would play the conference champion from the lesser conference in a bowl game at the end of the season to determine who gets to be in the power conference the following year.

This system would be awesome. For one thing, it would put an end to the perpetual outcry to give the little schools like Boise State a shot at the national championship, because the elite small schools would be able to play their way into a power conference and then rightfully earn their spot at a national championship the next season. Instead of guessing how well Boise State would do if they had to play schools from a power conference week in and week out, we'd get a definitive answer. I fail to see how this could possibly be a bad thing.

Secondly, relegation could be used as a way of punishing schools that cheat, much like how Juventus was relegated to the Italian league's Serie B in 2006 for fixing matches. Instead of getting a slap on the wrist in the form of scholarships taken away or restrictions on recruiting, schools like USC, Miami, North Carolina, and of course Michigan (which have all recently been found to have committed or been accused of NCAA violations) could get sent down to a lesser conference for a year or two as punishment. Sure, being put on probation by the NCAA kinda sucks, but nothing would deter a team from cheating more than the threat of having to spend a season in the WAC and play in places like Moscow, Idaho, or Ruston, La.

Perhaps the best thing about a relegation system, though, is that it would make the throwaway bowls (like the GoDaddy.com Bowl) suddenly relevant. Instead of virtually nobody watching a 9–4 MAC team play a 6–6 Sun Belt team, a legitimate audience would actually tune in to see if Florida International could take Ole Miss's spot in the SEC or if Toledo could knock Indiana out of the Big Ten. (Spoiler alert: they absolutely could.) Casual fans would no doubt be much more intrigued if the stakes were raised and fans of the terrible teams from the power conferences would have a reason to keep actively rooting for their team at the end of the year, when they would've otherwise lost hope and given up on their team's season.

Just think about all the legitimate questions to consider concerning a relegation system: How would it affect recruiting? Could Boise State win the Big 12/East? What about if Oklahoma and Texas were in the Big 12/East too? Would Indiana ever play in the Big Ten again? If Florida International played in the SEC and had back-to-back games against LSU and Alabama, would they still have enough healthy players to field a team the following week? Is this the best idea that has a 0 percent chance of actually happening?

Since we're on the topic of college football reform, I don't see any reason why conference realignment can't also serve as the first step toward implementing a playoff. Every conference will end up playing a conference championship game, so there's no reason why we can't just take the 10 teams that make it to the conference championship from the five power conferences, throw in two at-large bids (for the independent teams to still have a shot and for any really good one-loss teams that didn't make their conference championship because their loss came to a team in their division), and play a 12-team tournament. The four best teams per BCS rankings would get a bye, and the next four best teams would all host a home game on their campus against one of the last four teams in the first round. The four second-round games would then be played as the BCS bowls (Rose, Sugar, Orange, Fiesta), with the winners of those games advancing to the BCS Final Four, which would take place over the course of two weeks and rotate its location between the BCS bowls like the national championship does now. Meanwhile, the non-BCS bowls that we've all come to love (Cotton Bowl Classic, Capital One Bowl, Outback Bowl, etc.) could still take place as usual with the teams from the power conferences that don't qualify for the playoff and the teams from the lesser conferences that don't win their conference.

It sucks how much sense all of this makes because that guarantees that none of it will ever happen.

Originally published September 26, 2011.

JALEN ROSE
in conversation with
DAVID JACOBY

Every Friday, Jalen Rose chats with
Grantland *editor David Jacoby. Their*
discussions cover an astounding amount of
ground, usually using Rose's experience as
an NBA player as their point of entry.

DAVID JACOBY: An ex-athlete just told
me something interesting, which I
think is contrary to the public perception. I always thought that Performance Enhancing Drugs (PEDs) were
used by athletes to get bigger, stronger,
faster, but an ex-athlete told me they're
a recovery drug.

JALEN ROSE: It's all about recovery

JACOBY: Now tell me about that.

ROSE: You have back-to-back games.
Four games in five nights. You have a
Monday night football game, and then
you have a game Sunday. It helps your
body recover, heal itself, get you to the
position where you can still train, you
can still condition, and get ready for
the next practice or the next game.

JACOBY: Has anyone ever offered you
PEDs?

ROSE: Yes.

JACOBY: How did that happen?

ROSE: In the mid-'90s, at the gym,

trying to do different things to keep
myself in shape—cross-training, kick
boxing, throwing some punches, trying
to do whatever I could to get an edge.
So you get exposed to all types of
things and supplements. I was aware
of them and was exposed to them.
But as you saw me over thirteen years,
obviously
I didn't use them. If I were to use
them I—

JACOBY: You're pretty skinny!

ROSE: I probably could've been Magic
Johnson if I used them. [He laughs.]
Oh well.

JACOBY: And you've never used PEDs?

ROSE: No, not at all.

JACOBY: Good, now—

ROSE: I don't do anything knowingly that
influences my heart rate. So when I'm
watching infomercials about Viagra, and
they say, "Oh man, if you have any heart
issues or blood issues, don't take this!"
I'm the person that's not taking that.

JACOBY: When I said PEDs, I wasn't
thinking about Viagra.

ROSE: That's a PED! [Laughter.] You
know, our country makes billions off
pharmaceuticals. They sell us anything, sun up to sun down. Everything
has a prescription for it.

Continued on page 89.

INNOCENCE LOST

*The end of all fantasies
in State College*

by MICHAEL WEINREB

THOMAS JAMES

Something terrible happened on my street when I was kid, something that I had screened from my consciousness for many years until last weekend. My neighbor Scott Holderman and I were futzing about near the side of his house, setting up one of those epic *Star Wars* tête-à-têtes or digging for earthworms or doing whatever children do on nice days in quiet neighborhoods, and then there came a horrible screeching, the braking of an automobile that could not stop in time. The car had crested the steep hill of our street and slammed into a child who wandered into it. I can still see the child lying there, and I can still hear the mother's tortured shriek when she realized it was one of hers. An ambulance arrived, and then a medevac helicopter touched down 30 feet from our house, and they took the child away. He survived, but he wasn't the same.

A few years earlier, back when I was five, my parents moved from suburban New York City to State College, Pennsylvania. They did this because my father took a job as a professor at Penn State, but I assume they also did this because State College was considered a good place to raise children, a placid college town set in the geographic center of Pennsylvania. Those of us who grew up there like to say we lived three hours from everywhere. We resided in a development called Park Forest, on a street named after a British county.

The kids from the neighborhood would gather to play basketball in my driveway, not because I was particularly popular, but because we had a good hoop. In high school, we engaged in epic pick-up football games in Sunset Park, a little patch of grass right next to a house owned by Joe and Sue Paterno. In the second grade, my Little League coach was an enormous neighbor of ours named Mr. McQueary, and his son Mike was the best player on our team.[1] We went to school at Park Forest Junior High, and then we went to State College High School, where we learned how to drive and how to date and how to do quadratic equations. We were the sons of farmers and college professors and football coaches. One of my brother's classmates was named Sandusky; one of my classmates was named Sandusky, too.[2] I goofed off in the back of Latin class with a kid named Scott Paterno.[3] We knew who their fathers were; their fathers were royalty to us, even if we acted like it was no big deal. Our football team's nickname was the Little Lions. There was no way to extricate the happenings at our school from the happenings at the university, and the happenings at the university always centered around football. Everything in State College—even the name of our town—was one all-encompassing, synergistic monolith, and Joe Paterno was

1. Mike McQueary, now an assistant coach at Penn State, was allegedly the graduate assistant in the horrifying grand jury report who witnessed Sandusky in the showers of the Penn State football building with a young boy in 2002. The graduate assistant allegedly reported it to Paterno, who passed some form of this information on to his superiors, but no one in the chain of command ever called the police. The outrage at both Paterno and the graduate assistant appears to be moral

our benevolent dictator, and nothing truly bad ever happened, and even when it did, it was easier just to blot it from our lives and move on.

I can't add a lot to what's been written about the facts of the burgeoning scandal at Penn State, except to tell you how strange it feels to type the phrase "burgeoning scandal at Penn State." I know that I'm in denial. I know that I'm working through multiple layers of anger and disgust and neurosis and angst. I know that I'm too emotionally attached to the situation to offer any kind of objective take, though I don't think I realized how emotionally attached I was until this occurred. I never understood how much of an effect both football and a sense of place had on my persona. I apologize if what follows seems disjointed, because I am still coming to terms with the fact that this is real. "What can I say?" my mom wrote me from State College on Monday afternoon. "We're sort of going around in a daze."

I do not mean to make excuses for anyone involved, nor have any of the alums or townspeople I've spoken to or corresponded with, including my friend Brad, who is the most rigidly optimistic Penn State booster I've ever met. There's a group, about 15 or 20 of us, who have kept in touch since college, and I haven't seen some of them in years, and I've never met some of the others, but I still consider them close friends because we share a bond that was forged through football. And I know that, if you attended a secondary institution where football was not a priority, that sounds like an absurd basis for a relationship. But this is why college football evokes such extreme emotion, and this is why schools work so damn hard and often take ethical shortcuts to forge

rather than legal, none of which makes it any less of an emotional bombshell.

2. While the Sanduskys could not have children of their own, they adopted six, which is one of those facts that feels telling only in retrospect.

3. Joe Paterno's youngest child. One of Scott's older brothers, Jay, was also a quarterback at State College High and is now the quarterbacks coach at Penn State. He often serves as a ready scapegoat for the Penn State fan base when things go wrong.

There will always be those of us for whom college football is … the purest emotional attachment of our adulthood.

themselves into football powers: if they are successful, then the game serves as the life-long bond between alums and townspeople and the university, thereby guaranteeing the institution's self-preservation through dona-tions and season-ticket sales and infusions into the local economy. It is a crass calculus, when you put it that way, which is why there will always be skeptics and there will always be those of us for whom college football is (other than our own families) the purest emotional attachment of our adulthood, and there will always be some of us who bound between those two poles.

Every year, Brad sends out an eight-page e-mail, a meticulous scouting report on a team that is inevitably destined for an Outback Bowl berth but that Brad believes really has a shot at 12–0 this time around. This is what Brad wrote on September 6, a few days before Alabama pounded Penn State in a game none of us believed we could win: "We're gonna hang on Saturday. I think we're gonna give 'em a run."

And this is what Brad wrote on Monday: "The nature of this crime is the worst that has ever happened anywhere."

We moved to State College in 1978, the season Penn State lost to Alabama on a goal-line stand in the Sugar Bowl. I was in first grade, and I didn't have much in the way of social skills, and Penn State football was the language by which I could relate to the world and through which I could speak to the adults around me. I drew pictures of Curt Warner and Todd Blackledge; I memorized the rosters so that when people in our sec-tion at Beaver Stadium would ask who made that play, I could tell them. To this day, when I try to recall the combination of my gym locker or a friend's birthday or the license plate of my rental car, I think in terms of uniform numbers. It is not 31–17–03; it is Shane Conlan-Harry Hamilton-Chip LaBarca. Those were great years, and Penn State was in its heyday and Joe Paterno was the Sportsman of the Year and State College was a community that never gave in to the ethical lapses of the '80s and early '90s, because our coaching staff would not stand for it. One former player called it Camelot, and that sounds apt enough.

Jerry Sandusky had been promoted to defensive coordinator the year before we arrived in town. For decades, Penn State defined itself through its ability to stop people when it mattered, and, speaking from a strict football perspective, Sandusky was as responsible for the school's glory years as Paterno was. Linebacker U. thrived under Sandusky, and Penn State won its first national championship in 1982, and then won another in 1986, defeating Miami 14–10 in the Fiesta Bowl in a game predicated entirely on defense. It is widely acknowledged that Sandusky's game plan was the difference, that he rattled Vinny Testaverde and Miami's impetuous wide receivers by devising confusing coverage schemes and instructing his defensive backs to hit Michael Irvin until he cried. The day after it happened, they played that game on a continuous loop in our high school cafeteria. It is still my favorite football game of all time, a metaphoric triumph of the unadorned hero over the flamboyant villain. I wrote a long piece about it for ESPN, and a portion of a book, that now rings completely hollow. I have the original video recording of it in my living room, and I have thought several times over the past couple of days about taking a hammer to it.

I remember one Saturday morning in the autumn of my adolescence, the coach shambling along in his parka, brow furrowed, glasses shadowed in the sharp glare of the sun, black sneakers kicking at the leaves as they eddied and then parted on the asphalt path before him. I did not intend to follow him; it just happened that way, so that one moment I was headed to a football tailgate and the next moment I was trailing along behind Joe Paterno.

I walked behind him for several miles that day. Back then, in the late 1980s, it was still a routine of his to walk from his house to the stadium where he coached, slipping across the Penn State campus, past science labs and classroom buildings and parking lots occupied by stunned tailgaters who could never quite get over the fact that it was really him. Sometimes we were guilty of regarding him as more deity than man,[4] as if he presided over us in mythological stand-up form. He was as much our own conscience as he was a football coach, and we made that pact and imbued him with that sort of power because we believed he would wield it more responsibly than any of us ever could. Maybe that was naïve, but we came of age in a place known as Happy Valley, and naïveté was part of the package, and now that word isn't in our dictionaries anymore.

4. The irony to this, of course, is that Paterno tried so hard, at least in the media, not to present himself as anything more than a common man. And yet this only elevated his public stature.

As a journalist, of course, you're taught to be skeptical of everything, and in college, we tried our damndest at the college newspaper to cover Penn State football like professional journalists did. At one point, a talented young reporter thought she'd caught Paterno in a loophole regarding the housing policy at the school, but nothing much ever came of it. Most of the time, Joe got what he wanted. We grew older, and we came to understand one of the central truths of human nature, which is that when you brush up against a truly powerful force, it is never quite as benevolent as you imagined it to be. In order to acquire power, you have to be at least a little ruthless.[5] All you can hope for is that those who do acquire power operate by some sort of rough ethical standard, and even if I no longer deified Paterno, I continued to believe that the monolith I'd grown up inside was essentially a force for good. They did things I found untoward, but I always presumed they did them for the right reasons.

A few years ago, I drove down to the University of Maryland to research a story on Len Bias. I'd gone to see his mother speak at a high school, and now I sat in her office, and I asked her what went wrong at Maryland, whether the administration and the people in power deserved to share any of the responsibility for her son's death, and I remember precisely what she told me. "There was no covering," she said.

We came of age in a place known as Happy Valley, and naïveté was part of the package.

I don't know if there are any apt analogies to anything when it comes to this case, but this seems a little bit like our Len Bias moment at Penn State. Our leaders failed to cover, and while they deserve the benefit of due process, they deserve to be held accountable for whatever mistakes they made. If it means that this is how Joe Paterno goes out, then so be it; if it means that 30 years of my own memories of Penn State football are forever tarnished, then I will accept it in the name of finding some measure of justice. Every sane person I know agrees on this. It took Maryland the better part of two decades to regain its soul, and it will take us many years, as well, and in some way it will never be the same. We've come to terms with the corruptibility of the human soul in State College, and we've swept away the naïve notion that this place where we lived so quietly was different from the rest of America.

I have two close friends, a husband and wife, both alums, who moved to State College from New York City a few years ago. They did this because they couldn't afford to raise children in Manhattan, but they also did it because he couldn't imagine a safer place to raise their kids than a little town in a valley situated three hours from everywhere. I don't know what it feels like to grow up there now. I want these things to disappear from my consciousness, but they won't. The place where I grew up is gone, and it's not coming back.

Originally published November 8, 2011.

THE BRUTAL
TRUTH ABOUT
PENN STATE

*The problem can't be solved by prayer or piety—
and it's far more widespread than we think*

by CHARLES P. PIERCE

*"But you, when you pray, go into your inner chamber and, locking the door,
pray there in hiding to your Father ... "*—Matthew, Chapter 6

It was midway through the pregame prayer session that the gorge hit high tide. There is always something a little nauseating in large spectacles of conspicuous public piety, but watching everyone on the field take a knee before the Penn State-Nebraska game, and listening to the commentary about how devoutly everybody was praying for the victims at Penn State, was enough to get me reaching for a bucket and a Bible all at once. It was as though the players and coaches had devised some sort of new training regimen to get past the awful reality of what had happened. Prayer as a new form of two-a-days. Jesus is my strength coach. Contrition in the context of a football game seemed almost obscene in its obvious vanity.

God help us, let us not hear a single mumbling word about how football can help the university "heal."

So, when the feeling had subsided somewhat, I dropped by the sixth chapter of Matthew, and then I went on to the Teacher in Ecclesiastes, who warned his people: "For God will bring every deed into judgment, including every hidden thing, whether it is good or evil."

And I felt better, but not much. There is solace in Scripture, but there are also too many places where the guilty and the morally obtuse can hide.

The crimes at Penn State are about the raping of children. That is all they are about. The crimes at Penn State are about the raping of children by Jerry Sandusky, and the possibility that people lied to a grand jury about the raping of children by Jerry Sandusky, and the likelihood that most of the people who had the authority at Penn State to stop the raping of children by Jerry Sandusky proved themselves to have the moral backbone of ribbon worms.

It no longer matters if there continues to be a football program at Penn State. It no longer even matters if there continues to be a university there at all. All of these considerations are trivial by comparison to what went on in and around the Penn State football program.

(Those people who will pass this off as an overreaction would do well to remember that the Roman Catholic Church is reckoned to be a far more durable institution than even Penn State University is, and the Church has spent the past decade or so selling off its various franchise properties all over the world to pay off the tsunami of civil judgments resulting from the raping of children, a cascade that shows no signs of abating anytime soon.)

There will now be a decade or more of criminal trials, and perhaps a quarter-century or more of civil actions, as a result of what went on at Penn State. These things cannot be prayed away. Let us hear nothing about "closure" or about "moving on." And God help us, let us not hear a single mumbling word about how football can help the university "heal." (Lord, let the Alamo Bowl be an instrument of your peace.) This wound should be left open and gaping and raw until the very last of the children that Jerry Sandusky is accused of raping somehow gets whatever modicum of peace and retribution can possibly be granted to him. This wound should be left open and gaping and raw in the bright sunlight where everybody can see it, for years and years and years, until the raped children themselves decide that justice has been done. When they're done healing—if they're ever done healing—then they and their families can give Penn State permission to start.

If that blights Joe Paterno's declining years, that's too bad. If that takes a chunk out of the endowment, hold a damn bake sale. If that means that Penn State spends some time being known as the university where a child got raped, that's what happens when you're a university where a child got raped. Any sympathy for this institution went down the drain in the shower room in the Lasch Building. There's nothing that can happen to the university, or to the people sunk up to their eyeballs in this incredible moral quagmire, that's worse than what happened to the children who got raped at Penn State. Good Lord, people, get up off your knees and get over yourselves.

There is something to be said, however, for looking at how it happened. Which is not the same thing as trying to figure out how it "could" have happened. The wonder is that it doesn't happen more often.

(How many football coaches out there work with "at-risk" kids? How many shoes are there still to drop? Unfair? Ask one Bernard Law, once cardinal archbishop of Boston, if you can pry him out of his current position at the Basilica of Our Lady of the Clean Getaway in Rome.)

It happens because institutions lie. And today, our major institutions lie because of a culture in which loyalty to "the company," and protection of "the brand"—that noxious business-school shibboleth that turns employees into brainlocked elements of sales and marketing campaigns—trumps conventional morality, traditional ethics, civil liberties, and even adherence to the rule of law. It is better to protect "the brand" than it is to protect free speech, the right to privacy, or even to protect children.

If Mike McQueary had seen a child being raped in a boardroom or a storeroom, he wouldn't have been any more likely to have stopped it, or to have called the cops, than he was as a graduate assistant football coach at Penn State. With unemployment edging toward double digits, and only about 10 percent of the workforce unionized, every American who works for a major company knows the penalty for exercising his personal freedom, or his personal morality, at the expense of "the company." Independent thought is discouraged. Independent action is usually crushed. Nobody wants to damage the brand. Your supervisor might find out, and his primary loyalty is to the company. Which is why he got promoted to be your supervisor in the first place.

Further, the institutions of college athletics exist primarily as unreality fueled by deceit. The unreality is that universities should be in the business of providing large spectacles of mass entertainment. The fundamental absurdity of that notion requires the promulgation of the various deceits necessary to carry it out. The "student-athlete," just to name one. "Amateurism," just to name another. Of course, people involved in Penn State football allegedly deceived people when it became plain that children had been raped within the program's facilities by one of the program's employees. It was simply one more lie to maintain the preposterously lucrative unreality of college athletics. And to think, the players at Ohio State became pariahs because of tattoos and memorabilia sales.

By an order of magnitude, the Penn State child-raping scandal is miles beyond anything that ever happened with the Ohio State football team over the past five years, miles beyond anything that happened with the SMU football team in the 1980s, and miles beyond anything that happened with the point-shaving scandals in college basketball. It is not a failure of our institutions so much as it is a window into what they have become—soulless, profit-driven monsters, Darwinian predators with precious little humanity left in them. Penn State is only the most recent example. Too much of this country is too big to fail.

On July 20, Enda Kenny, Taoiseach of the Republic of Ireland, Rose before the Dail Eireann and excoriated the Vatican and the institutional Roman Catholic Church for the horrors inflicted on generations of Irish children, horrors that they both committed and condoned. This was an act of considerable political courage for Kenny. The influence of the Church had been a deadweight on Irish politics and the secular government since the country first gained its freedom in the 1920s. Nevertheless, Kenny said:

> *Thankfully ... this is not Rome. Nor is it industrial school or Magdalene Ireland, where the swish of a soutane smothered conscience and humanity and the swing of a thurible ruled the Irish-Catholic world. This is the Republic of Ireland, 2011. A Republic of laws ... of rights and responsibilities ... of proper civic order ... where the delinquency and arrogance of a particular kind of 'morality' will no longer be tolerated or ignored ... as taoiseach, I am making it absolutely clear that, when it comes to the protection of the children of this state, the standards of conduct which the Church deems appropriate to itself cannot, and will not, be applied to the workings of democracy and civil society in this Republic.*

He did not drop to his knees. He did not ask for a moment of silence. He did not seek "closure" but, rather, he demanded the hard and bitter truth of it, and he demanded it from men steeped in deceit from their purple carpet slippers to their red beanies. Enda Kenny did not look to bind up wounds before they could be cleansed. And that is the only way to talk about what happens after the raping of children.

Originally published November 14, 2011.

The institutions of college athletics exist primarily as unreality fueled by deceit.

NOTES TOWARD A RENEGADE LEAGUE

So the NBA is broken.
Why not start over?

by JAY CASPIAN KANG & BILL SIMMONS

Back in early October, we seemed poised to lose the entire 2011–2012 NBA season to a lockout. Die-hard basketball fans Jay Caspian Kang and Bill Simmons were frustrated—so much so that they decided to exchange e-mails all day about a hypothetical renegade pro hoops league that will never happen. Here's what transpired.

Jay Caspian Kang: This NBA lockout has me thinking about Marx and Engels and a bunch of stuff I should have learned in college about labor power and alienation and how the worker should have control over his own economic fate. Specifically, I'm remembering a part of Ken Burns' *Baseball* documentary, in which George Will says that baseball is the one instance where a worker-driven system makes sense. To paraphrase, he says that in the history of the game not one person has bought a ticket or turned on a television to watch an owner. As such, because the products are the players, the players should control the majority of the wealth.

And so, with no really positive news coming out of the labor meetings in New York, I was thinking about alternatives that would save our NBA stars from the indignity of playing in Europe.

Here's the basic idea for a player-owned league, which I would call "The Oracle."

Bill Simmons: "The Oracle?" Nice name! It sounds like either a renegade professional basketball league, a new cable movie channel, an AMC drama or Dr. Dre's next comeback album. I'm in on The Oracle no matter what it ends up being.

Kang: Glad to see we're in agreement about the name! It also allows fans to make O's with their hands like they do for Oregon football.

First, we need a commissioner/bankroller. Larry Ellison has to be the man to spearhead this league. He's pissed because he got shut out in the Warriors sale (by the way, if you're looking for another reason to get angry at the owners, how about the fact that they wouldn't allow the third-richest man in America to be a part of their little club?). Oh, and he also spent $200 million to win an effing yachting competition. He wouldn't need too much more than that to start The Oracle, and if he somehow replaced the NBA with some weird proto-Communist version of professional basketball, it would be the greatest double-barreled middle finger to anything, ever.

Simmons: I like the way you're thinking here. To be fair, Ellison choked on the Warriors purchase—he lowballed them with his initial offer, then increased it at the last minute only when Joe Lacob and Peter Guber were closing with their $450 million bid. And the NBA blocked Ellison's Hornets play only because they knew he planned on breaking the team's New Orleans lease and moving it to San Jose. But this works for your commissioner/bankroller purposes: At this point, Ellison has probably convinced himself that the NBA is cockblocking him, even if that's not necessarily true. Who better to launch a spiteful renegade league? If not him, we'll find another billionaire with deep pockets, thin skin and a big ego. The bigger questions: Where would you put the teams? And how many?

Kang: I'm thinking eight teams in New York, Chicago, Miami, Atlanta, Los Angeles, Boston, Las Vegas, and Seattle.

There are no basketball antitrust laws in place. NBA arenas can rent their spaces out to all sorts of things right now: concerts, monster truck rallies, gymnastics competitions, Globetrotters exhibitions, etc. Unless there's language in a contract that specifies, "In case of a lockout, you CANNOT host another basketball team," there shouldn't be a problem. And if there is, then screw it, they can just play in a college gym.

The team names would be sponsored. Like the Atlanta Waffle Houses or the Subaru Dealerships of Greater Seattle.

Simmons: The Atlanta Waffle Houses would have the greatest uniforms ever. Also, they would make me hungry. Constantly. You're smart to go with sponsored names, even if that ruins my idea to have teams called the Seattle Nirvana and the Baltimore Wire. But it's too risky to mess around with existing NBA cities/stadiums; because television/Internet revenue will be driving this league anyway, they should pick medium-size cities that don't have teams but could easily accommodate them. You're right about Las Vegas and Seattle. Two killer choices. I'm already welling up at the thought of pro hoops returning to Seattle. Seriously, get me some Kleenex. The first "Fuck you, Stern!" chant during the first quarter of their first home game will be one of the best sports moments of the year. Instead of Los Angeles, I would grab Anaheim as the token SoCal team—it's only 50 minutes from L.A., it has a solid stadium in place, and it wants pro hoops so desperately that it did everything short of building an avoid-bankruptcy-and-keep-your-team parachute for the Maloofs last spring (before the NBA blocked the move). The fourth West Coast team should be Vancouver since it's pushing so hard for an NBA team, although you could also talk me into San Jose for the Silicon Valley money.

And Kansas City is a no-brainer as the fifth team: It has a state-of-the-art NBA arena, and it's also on suicide watch right now with the Chiefs and Royals. Nobody needs this league more than Kansas City. You're right, Seattle needs it more. My bad.

From there, you need two East Coast teams: I'd go with Baltimore OR Pittsburgh (can't have both), then Hartford (midway point between New York and Boston, plus it still has its renovated 16k-seat arena from its Whalers days). And for the eighth team, do we need to go South or could we add another Western team? Let's see, Austin, Jacksonville, Tampa or Nashville … (Thinking.) Screw it, let's go with the 'Burgh. My final picks: Seattle, Las Vegas, Vancouver, Anaheim (West); Baltimore, Hartford, Kansas City and Pittsburgh (East). And yes, I know Kansas City isn't technically "East." I'm well aware. Thanks for pointing this out. I got it. By the way, don't put it past Ellison to stick one of the eight teams in Malibu—he already owns half of Carbon Beach. Maybe the SoCal team could play at Pepperdine right down the street. If Pepperdine could handle a couple dozen Battle of the Network Stars shows once upon a time, I'm pretty sure it could handle "The Oracle."

"Instead of seeing Penny Marshall at Clipper games, you could see Mark Zuckerberg, Peter Thiel, and Meg Whitman whenever the San Jose Cisco Wireless Routers were in action."

—Jay Caspian Kang

Kang: Kansas City does have that arena and might draw some of the Jayhawk crowd, especially if you stocked the team with KU alums. I'm in on that. Vancouver's interesting because of Steve Nash's potential involvement, but I don't know if you want to put two of eight teams in the Pacific Northwest. San Jose works—it'll make commissioner Ellison happy, draw in the hoops-crazy population of the Bay Area, and bring forth an entire new type of celebrity. Instead of seeing Penny

Marshall at Clipper games, you could see Mark Zuckerberg, Peter Thiel, and Meg Whitman whenever the San Jose Cisco Wireless Routers were in action.

Simmons: Good call. I'm excited to see those San Jose courtside seats go for $375,000 per game. That could pay for the league right there. How would the "Player Draft" go? This is crucial—we need a format that would produce at least seven different mock drafts by Chad Ford.

Kang: Here's my vision: Eight entrepreneurial stars would "buy" franchises from Ellison and serve as captains. And then, in a huge pay-per-view event, those eight captains would pick their teams.

Simmons: Whoa!!!!!! Snake fashion?

Kang: Snake fashion.

Simmons: And pay-per-view?

Kang: Pay-per-view.

Simmons: I'm giddy.

Kang: Every player who wants to play in The Oracle would be required to be in attendance for the draft. The captains would take home the largest portion of any money the team made, obviously, but they'd also be taking on risk. The other players would be paid at the player/owner's discretion. But can you imagine how many awesome stories would come out of contract negotiations alone?

Simmons: I like the thought of Kobe Bryant negotiating with really anybody. That alone is reason to do this league. The only potential stumbling block: How would they decide the eight captains? On paper, the captains SHOULD be Kobe Bryant, Dwight Howard, Chris Paul, LeBron James, Dwyane Wade, Kevin Durant, Derrick Rose and Dirk Nowitzki, since those are the eight best players in the league. But how do we trust that Wade wouldn't make all of LeBron's decisions for him like he did in the summer of 2010? And do you really think stars like Deron Williams, Carmelo Anthony and Amar'e Stoudemire are signing off on NOT being captains? No way. Too many egos.

Here's the move: What if we went with co-captains for the eight teams, with the rule that current NBA teammates cannot be Oracle co-captains. (Sorry, Wade and LeBron.) I like these pairings: Nowitzki and Nash (cue up Peaches & Herb!); Carmelo and Deron Williams (a possible 2012–13 Knicks preview); Russell Westbrook and Kevin Love (an emotional reunion of their eight months at UCLA pretending to be students); Blake Griffin and Chris Paul (let the alley-oops begin!); Rose and Amar'e Stoudemire (high screens galore); Durant and Zach Randolph (the new "Odd Couple"); Wade and Dwight Howard (your favorites—we need a "front-runner" team that will convince everyone to pick them, then eventually let everyone down, a la the 2011 Red Sox, Heat and Eagles); and Kobe and LeBron (how fascinating would that be?). Kang, find a flaw with this plan. You can't.

Kang: This is why there needs to be a commissioner who also happens to have $33 billion. We'll have the captains pair up, as you suggested, and then everyone can submit their applications to a committee headed up by me, you, Ellison, Bill Walton, and Barack Obama.

Simmons: I'd like to include Justin Bieber as well.

Kang: Fine. The Oracle Committee decides which captain duos get to participate in the live pay-per-view draft. Shit, we could even pay-per-view the selection process, right? One wrinkle: Every player in the draft pool has one veto, meaning they can refuse to play for a certain team. What would be the best possible veto outcomes?

Simmons: For me, the remaining Lakers all using their "Veto" on Kobe's team would be the funniest veto, narrowly edging Baron Davis using his veto on gluten-free food. Wait, I have two more tweaks: First, we should only have 10 players per team. That's it. Second, since 10-player rosters means 80 players total (counting the 16 co-captains), shouldn't we invite 64 players total to the draft, if only to see who'd be the 64th and last guy selected? I'd be more fascinated in that 63rd selection than anything. What an ego slam for the last guy standing. Sorry, John Salmons, you were No. 64. We could bet on this and everything. That reminds me, what happens to undrafted guys?

Kang: Couldn't we just have 65 players at the draft, so that one of them gets left out? And if we did, I'm going with Brandon Roy. The entire city of Portland would call for a boycott of The Oracle. Three games into the season, Portland would return to combing its beard and crashing its fixed-gear bike into "_____ly responsible" latte stands/record stores. A collective sense of relief (and self-satisfaction) would wash over the city's residents, who finally realize that they don't really like basketball. They just really, really like regionalism and pronouncing "O-reh-GONE," and yelling at other people about how "great" Portland is, when it's really just—

Simmons: Tread carefully, Kang. I felt the wrath of the Portland soccer moms once. It's like swimming in a pool and suddenly being attacked by piranha. You don't even know what's happening, just that you're surrounded by your own blood and flesh.

Kang: Anyway. For guys like Roy, I'd set up a second division, a la the Premiership, where undrafted players could set up their own teams and play their way into the first division. This league would be set on a barnstorming schedule, with a league-wide cap of 20 franchises. Going off something you wrote in a mailbag last month about teams based on alma maters, my personal fantasy here would be if every old Carolina player got together and formed a team to play in the old Carmichael Gym in Chapel Hill. Of course, Duke would also have a team of old guys who didn't make the Oracle League.

A sample Carolina starting five: PG: Ed Cota; SG: Rashad McCants; SF: Tyler Hansbrough; PF: Rasheed Wallace; C: Brendan Haywood.

A sample Duke starting five: PG: Steve Wojciechowski; SG: Chris Collins; SF: Chris Burgess; PF: Christian Laettner; C: Cherokee Parks.

Simmons: Love how you started five white guys for Duke. Your Carolina bias didn't show at all there. Anyway, I love relegation in all forms, so you don't need to twist my arm. They should have done this for the fall TV schedule—"Sorry, Playboy Club, you've been relegated to the USA Network." Plus, you could stick a pro hoops team filled with alums in any college hotbed; those fans are so rabid, they'd come out regardless of the talent level, how fat or drunk the alumni players were … it just wouldn't matter. Duke, Carolina, Kansas, Arizona, UCLA, Georgetown, Gonzaga (yes, Gonzaga), Syracuse, Florida, UConn, Ohio State and Maryland should all have their own alumni-heavy teams. Total no-brainer. That's 12 for the relegation league right there. You're telling me UConn fans wouldn't fork money over to see Travis Knight and Khalid El-Amin running a high screen down memory lane? Come on.

Kang: UConn would have to happen. Georgetown would also be awesome. Iverson and Vic Page reunited in the backcourt, Hibbert in the post. Actually, maybe this is the way Big East fans could deal with the decimation of their league. Every Big East fan I know just wants to go back to the days of John Wallace and Donyell Marshall. The Oracle could make that dream happen. I'd also pay to see Georgia Tech, with Will Bynum, Jarrett Jack, Derrick Favors, BJ Elder, Kenny Anderson, and Anthony Morrow a.k.a. @blackboipachino.

Also, can you imagine what would happen in San Jose? Once Zuckerberg, Meg Whitman, and Sergey Brin start showing up at games, they are going to immediately go out and back their own franchises. Zuckerberg would pay $80 million for Yi Jianlian in an effort to bring Facebook to China. Sergey Brin would counter with Wang Zhizhi. And how long would it take for the Palo Alto eBays to buy everyone from Kobe's team, make the jump to the A League, and contend for a championship?

> "You're telling me UConn fans wouldn't fork money over to see Travis Knight and Khalid El-Amin running a high screen down memory lane?"
> —Bill Simmons

Simmons: I'm fine with up to eight Silicon

Valley teams. In the words of the immortal philosopher Rasheed Wallace, "CTC." CTC, rich billionaire software nerds. CTC. Here's another idea for two more relegation teams: Hey, Austin Rivers and every other McDonald's All-American from last summer … feel like ending the college charade, leaving the corrupt NCAA and making cash right away? Feel free to join The Oracle. We'd love to have you. And it's not like the season would be longer, right? How many games were you thinking?

Kang: In the A-League, I'd go with a 29-game regular season, with room for All-Star Weekend (including a $2 million dunk contest open to anyone in the world), then a playoffs with four teams making it, best of seven each round, and the entire postseason gate going to the winning team. The team that wins the championship wins some portion of the league's total TV revenue. With Ellison's money, his maverick personality, and his team of lawyers, can you tell me one reason why this wouldn't just be a better version of the NBA?

Simmons: And we haven't even split up the TV money yet. NBC Sports would jump at the chance to shed its WEN (White Entertainment Network) image and turn Versus into a network that, you know, occasionally might have black people on it. Plus, they'd get a TON of programming out of it. And better ratings than you'd think. Did you see 1.1 million people supposedly watched Chris Paul's pay-per-view pickup game last weekend? Jeez, even I wouldn't have watched that—who wants to see NBA players jog around, hog the ball, jack up threes and play matador defense? Well, other than James Dolan? And why should I be impressed that Kevin Durant dropped 60 against a bunch of scrubs? Isn't that exactly what he should be doing to a bunch of scrubs? We need to organize this stuff, Kang—we need coaching, practices, hastily done uniforms and obnoxiously integrated sponsor names, we need co-captains, we need billionaire owners, and we need to start drafting this stupid league that will never happen because it makes too much sense right now. Come up with a draft order already.

Kang: By random number generation, we've come up with the following Draft Order: Westbrook/Love; Carmelo/Deron; Rose/Amar'e; Wade/Howard; Kobe/LeBron; Dirk/Nash; Griffin/CP3; Durant/Z-Bo. Let's do three mock rounds so each team has a starting lineup. Quick question: Do we include KG and Duncan?

Simmons: I say no. Just cross 'em off. Those guys are too old, too rich, too banged-up and too pissed off that we didn't make them co-captains. I like my ridiculously hypothetical drafts that would never actually happen to be as realistic as possible. Let's switch off picks. I'll make the first pick of Round 1 …

Westbrook/Love take … Pau Gasol, and only because it's too early for them to take a third UCLA guy. Gasol should have been a co-captain, but we had to penalize him for turning into a chalk outline in the 2011 playoffs.

Kang: Carmelo/Deron take … Andrew Bynum. They need a defensive center and fall into the Bynum trap.

Simmons: Rose/Amar'e take … Al Horford. The run on big guys is officially on! Also, this allows Amar'e to never worry about guarding anybody. I mean, ever.

Kang: Wade/Howard take … LaMarcus Aldridge. Unselfish guy who spaces the floor, feeds off Wade's energy, can overplay on defense because he knows Howard is protecting the rim, and knows how to play third fiddle after years of being the overlooked star in Portland.

Simmons: Wow, you just turned into Jay Bilas. You forgot to mention Aldridge's length. Kobe/LeBron take … Nene, and only because they know they can get a point guard coming back in Round 2. Meanwhile, the big-guy run has turned into a big-guy panic! I just looked up DeMarcus Cousins' 2011 stats to make sure you won't laugh when I pick him next round.

Kang: Dirk/Nash take ... Josh Smith! Nash throws three alley-oops to Josh per game. Dirk doesn't have to work as hard (or at all) on the boards and Josh Smith finally finds his true basketball calling: playing with two white guys who make his life easier. He goes for 15–14 with 3 blocks and 2.5 steals every game. This team, by the way, sells millions of jerseys.

Simmons: Griffin/CP3 take ... Manu Ginobili. That's a really interesting top-three. If this were a 10-year draft, I'd take Eric Gordon here. For 29 games? MA-NEWWWWWWWWW!

Kang: Durant/Z-Bo take ... Rajon Rondo. I don't think there are three people with less in common.

Simmons: All right, I'll plow through Round 2 and you take Round 3. We're going in snake fashion, so ...

- Durant/Z-Bo/Rondo take ... Marc Gasol (that's suddenly a ridiculous team, and yes, we kept the "nothing in common" theme alive).

- Griffin/CP3/Ginobili take ... Chris Bosh (good value and he's already used to being a spare part).

- Dirk/Nash/Josh take ... Eric Gordon (it's a smallball fest a la the 2006 Suns!).

- Kobe/LeBron/Nene take ... Stephen Curry (giving them a potentially devastating offensive team).

- Wade/Howard/Aldridge take ... Rudy Gay (best swing guy on the board).

- Rose/Amar'e/Horford take ... Paul Pierce (pissed that nobody took him yet, by the way).

- Carmelo/Deron/Bynum take ... Joe Johnson (remember, his monstrosity of an NBA salary doesn't count in The Oracle, although

Ellison could always decide to give him $50 million per year to keep the balance askew).

- Westbrook/Love/Gasol take … Andre Iguodala (defensive stopper, glue guy). Take us home, Kang.

Kang: OK, here's Round 3 … Westbrook/Love/Gasol/Igoudala take … John Wall. We're not picking benches yet, but consider what would happen if you took out Love and put in, say, Tony Allen. Westbrook, Wall, Gasol, Igoudala, and Grime-N-Grit would tire out every team in the Oracle. And once the opponent's legs started to go, it would be a dunk competition for Westbrook, Wall, and Iggy.

Carmelo/Deron/Bynum/Joe Johnson … take Khloe and Lamar. The team needs a versatile three, sure, but more than that, they need someone to spice up the roster. I think this team has massive attendance problems. Might want to place them in one of the cities that will just be happy to have basketball around. Seattle, get ready to get Kardashian-ed.

Rose/Amar'e/Horford/Pierce take … Ray Allen. Again, it's a 29-game season. Whenever Rose and Amar'e can't quite generate the pick-and-roll dunk, Rose just tosses it out to Ray, who should be wide open from long-range. At first, I thought this team was going to finish in the bottom half. Now, I'm convinced they can make the finals.

Wade/Howard/Aldridge/Gay take … Serge Ibaka. Bringing back Bilas, this would be the lengthiest, girthiest team in the history of the league.

Kobe/LeBron/Nene/Curry take … Tyson Chandler. This is where Boogie Cousins could have gone, but contract negotiations broke down with Kobe.

Dirk/Nash/Josh Smith/Eric Gordon … take Boogie Cousins! Sets up a wonderful locker room, with Boogie and Josh Smith on one side, Dirk and Nash on the other, and poor Eric Gordon stuck in the middle. If this team gets the right coach, they'll make the playoffs. If they get, say, Mike Brown or Eric Musselman, they might not win a game.

"This team has massive attendance problems... Seattle, get ready to get Kardashian-ed."
—Jay Caspian Kang

Blake/CP3/Ginobili/Bosh take ... Paul Millsap. Gives them everything they need and provides CP3 with a second alley-oop partner.

Durant/Z-Bo/Rondo/Mark Gasol take ... Monta Ellis. Might not be the best fit, because Monta needs the ball in his hands, but this team can't pass on the talent/scoring. They'll average 120+ points per game.

Simmons: Wow. Danny Granger is walking around aimlessly, sobbing and wondering what he did to you. He didn't make out with your girlfriend once, right? Just checking. All right, I'm ranking the teams and assigning cities to them ...

Anaheim Activision Call of Duty: Modern Warfare (no. 1 seed): Kobe, LeBron, Steph Curry, Nene, Tyson Chandler. That's a borderline juggernaut. Especially when Kobe flies everyone to Italy right before the season to rejuvenate their knee joints by genetically screening them, treating their blood, then culturing that blood with chemicals and re-injecting it back into their knees, because this sounds totally legal and not like blood doping at all.

Hartford Lux Bond & Green (no. 2 seed): Wade, Howard, Aldridge, Gay, Ibaka. They're too big upfront, but we could address that pretty easily in Rounds 6 and 7 by grabbing a point guard (Tony Parker?) and second swing guy (James Harden?). Unrelated: I love that Parker didn't get picked. It's like the entire renegade league did a silent protest in Brent Barry's honor. Also, how great would an Anaheim-Hartford Finals be? Wade and Howard vs. Kobe and LeBron? And wouldn't NBC Sports go nuts for a (90 Minutes From) New York vs. (50 Minutes From) Los Angeles Finals? That could be (not really that) HUGE ratings!

Kansas City Klondike Bars (no. 3 seed): Rose, Amar'e, Horford, Pierce, Ray Allen. Our most complete team from a position-by-position standpoint. Couldn't you see Pierce thriving for the Klondike Bars with all the Jayhawks fans screaming for him? And Kang, can you believe how seamlessly I'm working Grantland's sponsors into this column? This doesn't feel forced at all!

Seattle's Best (no. 4 seed): Durant, Z-Bo, Rondo, Marc Gasol, Ellis. You screwed them over with your last pick. Should have taken Danny Granger. Chad Ford is giving you an "F" in his report card tomorrow, Kang. Anyway, I am excited to (a) watch this team, (b) reunite Gasol and Z-Bo, (c) call a professional sports team "Seattle's Best," and (d) reunite Durant with Seattle. You hear that, David Stern? We're reuniting Durant with Seattle! Don't you point your finger at me! I'm not your child!!!

Kang: Monta was the right pick there! They'd just have to draft some stiff to shoot 3s, put Monta on the bench (if things got too clogged at the start of the season) and you'd have Durant, Z-Bo, Rondo and the greatest bench scorer (irrational confidence guy) maybe in history???

Simmons: Don't complain to me, complain to Chad Ford. He just called you David Kahn 2.0 in his draft report card and wrote "KANNNNNNNN NNNNNNNNNNNNNNNNNNNNNNG!" As for our non-playoff teams ...

Pittsburgh Five-Dollar Footlongs (no. 5 seed): Dirk, Nash, Josh Smith, Gordon, Cousins. Weird team. I don't love the pieces as a whole, although I like them separately and the Dirk/Nash reunion makes me so happy that I don't know what to do with myself. To be honest, I'm afraid to put these guys in Pittsburgh because that sneaky Canuck Nash might undermine the team's Pittsburgh relationship (a la Sienna Miller a few years ago) in a nefarious attempt to move them to Vancouver after four games. Always be careful of Nash. I wouldn't be surprised if Jared Dudley filed for dual Canadian citizenship soon—Nash is to Canada what Tom Cruise is to Scientology.

San Jose Intel Core i7's (no. 6 seed): Carmelo, Deron, Bynum, Joe Johnson, Lamar Odom. This group leaves me cold for some reason. They need a little more personality. Kind of like Silicon Valley. I'm excited for these uniforms, though. And for the $375,000-per-game courtside seats. It doesn't ultimately matter if this team wins or loses, their attendance money will be funding most of the league.

Baltimore Barbasol (no. 7 seed): Blake, CP3, Ginobili, Chris Bosh, Millsap. Too small for my liking, although that's not stopping me from being excited for their alley-oops and their marketing campaign. Blake Griffin, you're looking good. Handsome, free and tall. Close shave, America. The Baltimore Barbasol. By the way, I thought about naming this team "The Baltimore Netflix Qwiksters," but Netflix will be bankrupt by the time this league starts.

Las Vegas Lexus (no. 8 seed): Westbrook, Love, Pau Gasol, Igoudala, John Wall. For comedy purposes, and for the sake of the sports-blog industry, it's crucial that we put our youngest team in the city with the most distractions. I see them swinging a big "Gasol for Cousins and cash" trade midway through the season, then things really falling apart, somebody eventually going missing and everything ending with a humiliating relegation and possibly someone losing a thumb.

My finals pick: Hartford over Kansas City in the finals. That's right, Hartford and Kansas City ... bathe in those big-market ratings, Kang! What about you?

Kang: I've got Seattle's Best over Hartford in six. I think you're underestimating what would happen if Rondo, Durant, M. Gasol, Monta, and Z-Bo ever stepped on a court together. That team might shoot 60 percent for the season. And Seattle would have the biggest home-court advantage in the league. (Actually, that might be Vegas. Not because of the crowd, but more because of the 90 percent chance that Lamar flips out and is last seen entering Cheetah's at three in the afternoon.) Hartford Lux Bond & Green gets to the finals on size, but they don't have anyone who can guard Seattle's quick point guards. After he's eliminated, Wade sits up on the podium with Dwight Howard and answers all his questions for him. Dwight only speaks to tell everyone who is not a star in The Oracle to "go back to their miserable lives." Hilarity and joy ensue.

Simmons: So why wouldn't this work? I can only come up with seven reasons ...

1. The league is geared toward the top 80 guys ... which is only 20 percent of the players union. If I'm Delonte West, or Josh Powell, I'm

definitely not excited about The Oracle.

2. The insurance premiums would be massive. How do you insure dozens of guys who already have contracts guaranteeing them eight figures a year?

3. We need Worldwide Wes to sign off. He could squash the league singlehandedly. Maybe we could throw him the Fab Five Alumni relegation team as a bribe and let him coach it.

4. How much time does it take to organize things like ticket-sales staffs, coaching staffs, medical staffs, schedule-makers, travel schedules, a governing body (someone who decides on rules, penalties and so on), drug testing (half The Oracle guys just shuddered), PED testing (20 percent of The Oracle guys just shuddered), a television infrastructure (remember, you have to televise every game, whether it's on TV or the Internet), Internet streaming, merchandise sales and everything else that makes a professional sports league work? Fine, you're right—we'll just unofficially legalize drugs and PEDs in a wink-wink way like the NBA does to make things easier. But everything else? I don't know how long that takes to figure out. If it's four weeks, we can pull the league off. If it's four months? That's too long.

5. Two words: Gus Johnson. If we don't get him, we're just making our lives more difficult. I want our no. 1 announcing team to be Gus Johnson and Tommy Heinsohn, with Kate Upton and Sloane from Entourage as the sideline reporters. Anything less is a failure.

6. I'm worried about finding enough groupies for these mid-market cities. Do we have to import some from the bigger cities? I don't want these guys to get into a series of Twitter/DM scandals on the road because they're horny and need some immediate affection, only they don't have their old standbys available. Let's make this a Level 1 priority.

7. Ellison turns us down. Larry, if you're reading, here's my plea: You

have 33 billion dollars. There's nothing—repeat: nothing—that one could do that would be cooler than funding a renegade professional basketball league that eventually broke David Stern and the greedy NBA owners. You could build the first-ever yacht/spaceship and it wouldn't be this cool. Just think about it. Kang, you're a genius.

Kang: Me and Kaaaaaaaaaahn.

If we don't get Ellison, we could always make a run at Zuckerberg. He's clearly in some weird over-tinkering mode with Facebook. Anyone over the age of 26 can't figure out how to use it anymore. And once the company goes public next year, his life is going to be filled with board meetings, shareholder conferences, etc. He might be looking for a new project.

Zuck, you know what's cooler than hanging out with Sean Parker? Playing craps in Vegas with Charles Oakley. Just please don't take the idea of "The Oracle League," rebrand it as "The Zucker" (later changed to just "Zucker") and yell at me at a deposition about whether or not you used any of my code. I don't even know how to make em-dashes in html. If you do, I'm coming for your league, and when I get it, I'm going to call it the "Winklevoss Google+ Finals Club Basketball League." (WGFBL.)

Cut me in 20 percent, Mark, and we're good.

Originally published October 4, 2011.

In the space of one half inning, Game 6 of the World Series turned from barely memorable to unforgettable

by JONAH KERI

Imagine living your life with no clock.

No more dragging yourself out of bed when it's still dark out. No more fighting through miles of traffic, everyone around you bound to the same schedule, stuffing muffins in their faces, spilling coffee on their laps, texting with one hand, driving with no hands. No risk of getting dumped or fired or scorned for being late. There are no deadlines. Only moments. Only possibilities.

You might go the rest of your life and never see a more perfect example of that existence than what happened in Game 6 of the World Series. Only baseball could have made that happen.

For the record, the Cardinals' 10–9, 11-inning win over the Rangers in Game 6 of the World Series on October 28, 2011 took four hours and 33 minutes to play. But this game, like every other baseball game ever played, wasn't bound by timed quarters, halves, or periods. Baseball games are marked only by outs. Never has getting those outs seemed more difficult.

After six innings, Game 6 looked poised to go down as one of the worst World Series battles of all-time. Hell, we even ran a data query for it. Mark Simon, the excellent researcher at ESPN Stats & Info, framed the question this way: "How many World Series games have featured a combined five errors, a pickoff at third base, and at least two wild pitches/passed balls combined?" Answer: none.

These were, admittedly, arbitrary parameters. Leaving aside the rarity of a third-base pickoff, there's no perfect way to measure the worst World

After six innings, Game 6 looked poised to go down as one of the worst World Series battles of all-time. Series game in history, just as there's no perfect way to measure the best one. But it certainly felt like something historic was going on. With all the miscues happening on the field, and all the preposterous decisions being made by the managers (mostly one manager), Game 6 was shaping up as quite possibly the most excruciating World Series game of our lifetime.

The carnage started in the fourth inning, with the score tied 2–2. Fernando Salas relieved Jaime Garcia, who looked nothing like the dominant pitcher he was in Game 2, and escaped with only two runs allowed thanks to some guile on his part and a whole lot of blown chances by Rangers hitters. Nelson Cruz, the first batter facing Salas, lofted a popup to shallow left. Rafael Furcal drifted back, onto the outfield grass, further and still further, well into Matt Holliday territory. The outfielder going forward must always call off the backpedaling infielder in that situation. Holliday did not. Replays would later show Holliday's furtive cry to Furcal: "Take it!" Furcal could not, nor could Holliday, and disaster ensued. When Mike Napoli cashed Cruz with an RBI single to right, you couldn't help but think the Rangers would win it all, and Napoli, with 10 World Series runs driven in and a long list of big moments, would be MVP.

Two batters later, more ugliness. Colby Lewis hit a tapper back to the mound. Salas wheeled and fired to second … air mailing everybody. Two on, one out, a chance for the Rangers to tack on more runs. Didn't happen. Texas put 14 men on base through the first five innings, but scored only four runs. Those early failures kept St. Louis in the game, as did the Rangers' own defensive breakdowns. Lance Berkman reached first to start the bottom of the fourth on an error by Michael Young, who booted the grounder wide of first, then made a poor throw to pull Lewis away from the bag. Holliday redeemed himself a bit with a walk and a takeout slide at second, forcing an errant throw by Andrus that helped set up the tying run. The Cardinals returned the favor, with David Freese bonking a routine popup by Josh Hamilton to start the fifth, and looking ridiculous doing it.

Then Ron Washington decided not to pinch-hit with a one-run lead, Salas on the ropes, the bases loaded, a deep, fully rested bullpen and several on-call starters standing by, and Colby Freaking Lewis the guy deemed irreplaceable.

Then, an inning later, Young made yet another error, this time doing nothing more than taking the ball out of his glove, only to drop it.

Then Washington decided he needed to go even further with Lewis.

Then Lewis, by now running on fumes, walked Freese to load the bases.

Then Washington looked down at the bullpen, considered an entire army of choices, and tapped the one guy who'd been a complete disaster throughout the World Series, Alexi Ogando.

Then Ogando walked in the tying run by very nearly hitting Yadier Molina in the face.

Then Holliday, failing spectacularly at bat and in the field throughout the World Series, completed the trifecta with brutal baserunning, getting picked off third by Napoli ... with the bases loaded ... on a throw from Napoli's knees.

Had the game kept going in that vein and ended in some generic way, this would have been a stinker for the ages. If you hadn't made a Tom Emanski joke by this point, you didn't have a pulse. But that's the thing about a sport with no clock. You don't have a finite amount of time to take a lead or mount a comeback. Anything is possible, so long as you have outs still left to burn. From this moment on, finding outs was something neither team could manage.

Leading off the seventh, Adrian Beltre launched a shot over the wall in right-center to reclaim the lead for the Rangers. Then Cruz bashed a ball into the stratosphere to make it 6–4 Texas. As Lance Lynn stood dejectedly on the mound, Tony La Russa no doubt had the same thought that he did during BullpenPhoneGate: What the hell is he doing out there? Four batters later, Ian Kinsler knocked home Derek Holland with the Rangers' seventh run, and the game seemed well in hand.

That's the thing about a sport with no clock. You don't have a finite amount of time to take a lead or mount a comeback.

But there were tactical errors, more heroics by the unkillable Cardinals, and more amazing moments still to come. Holland led off the bottom of the eighth by retiring the fifth straight batter he'd faced. He'd more than done his job, especially after throwing 116 pitches in Game 4, and with a cavalcade of right-handed hitters now coming up. The Rangers had spent two good prospects to get Mike Adams at the trade deadline. He was their clear eighth-inning guy, so much so that Washington wouldn't think to use him two innings earlier, when Lewis stayed in way too long and Ogando threw gas on the fire. Surely Adams was coming in now, right? Nope. First, Allen Craig blasted a homer to cut the lead to 7–5. Two batters later, Molina singled. Finally, only after La Russa sent punchless backup catcher Gerald Laird up as the potential tying run did Washington go to his setup man. The Cardinals followed with two straight singles, the first one a play that was a clear error by Andrus, which allowed pinch-hitter Daniel Descalso to reach. But Furcal, the only Cardinal rivaling Holliday for World Series futility, spoiled a bases-loaded rally by hitting the ball 40 feet. On the first pitch. Inning over.

When Texas went down quietly in the top of the ninth, the Cardinals were down to their final three outs of the season. But no matter what the Rangers tried from that point on, they couldn't seize that last out.

In what was supposed to be the final at-bat of his Cardinals career (again), Pujols lashed a first-pitch double. Neftali Feliz, a fire-breather of a closer with a 100-mph fastball but also some scary command issues, walked Berkman on four pitches. Still, the Rangers seemed ready to celebrate. Feliz struck out Craig on an unexpected slider, then got two strikes on Freese. One more strike and the Rangers would have their first World Series in their 50-year franchise history. Feliz threw a fastball. Freese drilled it. Cruz, playing all the way back near the warning track, needed just a few steps to get to the wall. Somehow, he still missed the ball by a mile, the carom whizzing by him, and Freese buzzing into third with a triple. A two-run, game-tying, down-to-their-last-strike, outfield-can't-possibly-allow-a-triple, triple.

From then on, you couldn't breathe. We'd crossed the plane of reality to some screenwriter's fantasy, a script so implausible that no one would ever greenlight it.

Josh Hamilton, he of the groin so wrecked that one jackass baseball writer told his manager he should be benched, walloped a two-run homer to give the Rangers a 9–7, 10th-inning lead.

Then Darren Oliver, a pitcher who's been around so long he was once Nolan Ryan's teammate, came in to face two Cardinals lefties ... and both of them scratched out singles.

Then La Russa used a pitcher, Edwin Jackson, to pinch-hit for another pitcher, Jason Motte. Then, before Jackson could get to home plate, he pinch-hit with another pitcher, Kyle Lohse, for Jackson.

Then after a Lohse sacrifice, Scott Feldman came in, looking for his first career save.

Then after Feldman notched the second out of the inning, Washington ordered the fourth intentional walk of Pujols in two games.

Then, down to their final strike once more, Berkman lined a single to center to tie the game, saving the season yet again.

Then with two outs in the top of the 11th and a runner on first, Washington sent up light-hitting, seldom-used utilityman Esteban German to die a quick pinch-hit death against Jake Westbrook, yanking Feldman out of the game in the process and leaving the Rangers bullpen exposed.

Then Washington went to his worst, and least-used reliever, Mark Lowe, with the game on the line.

And then, in a final masterstroke of temporal chaos, David Freese, the kid who grew up a Cardinals fan on the edges of St. Louis, the unlikely hero who hoisted his teammates on his back to get to the World Series, the man of destiny who waited until one strike remained in his season before granting his team deliverance, hit a cannon to straightaway center that sailed over the wall and into baseball history.

As the Cardinals piled onto the field and their fans reached a state of delirium, Joe Buck delivered an homage to his father, aping Jack's Game 6-ending call to the 1991 World Series, "We will see you tomorrow night."

And we will. Cruz and Holliday are both questionable with injuries, Napoli's hobbled after a badly turned ankle, the bullpens will get another full night, the Rangers will try to recover from the worst playoff loss since that other Game 6 a quarter-century ago, and Chris Carpenter will go for the win in a park where he's been nearly perfect all year.

But the Game 7 prognostication could wait. As Freese's teammates shredded his jersey at the bottom of a dog pile, the words of Buck's broadcast partner Tim McCarver kept resonating. Amid a din that engulfed half the state of Missouri, he could only rightfully ask, "How did this happen?"

It happened because only a game with no clock could give us a play-by-play graph that mimicked the roller coaster ride we all felt while watching. It happened because only a game with no clock could render one of the worst World Series games into one of the best, thanks to the wildest finish we've ever seen.

It happened because it's baseball, a game where time stands still, and the impossible becomes possible.

Originally published October 28, 2011.

"THE FABLED MEETING WHERE THE CHARLES BARKLEY AND CHARLES OAKLEY ALTERCATION TOOK PLACE."

(Jalen Rose and David Jacoby, continued from 49)

JACOBY: During the 1999 NBA lockout, were you focused on the way the negotiations were going? Were you involved with it, were you in touch with the people in the negotiations or were you kind of outside of it?

ROSE: I was in touch. I was trying to be a player that was knowledgeable about the facts, and the situations, and if we were putting ourselves in a position to lose money because of a lockout, or how time and the deal could shift, and then we started playing. I vividly remember going to a negotiation in New York. We were going to have a big meeting. It's the fabled meeting where the Charles Oakley and the Charles Barkley altercation took place.

JACOBY: Can you explain this altercation to me?

ROSE: Well it was really one person,

JACOBY: Take me through it, because I have heard bits and pieces and rumors.

ROSE: Well one person, Charles Oakley, was the aggressor. And Charles Barkley was the recipient.

JACOBY: Explain to me what you are talking about.

ROSE: Well, meetings in New York got a little contentious, and people have their personal dislikes for one another. Basically Charles Oakley took it upon himself to smack Charles Barkley.

JACOBY: Open-hand smack? [They laugh.]

ROSE: Pretty much. I don't want to be his agent, or bring up a bad memory so that people are going to be calling up Charles Oakley or Charles Barkley to talk about the story. But I'll just say it's an urban legend that that supposedly went down.

Paul Pierce had just gotten drafted— we're friends—and we're working out at UCLA with a lot of different pros. We fly to New York to be part of the negotiations. I just remember us, waking up in the morning: 'We're going to meet downstairs, we're going to make sure we that we go over there and that we get all of the facts, and we're all going to vote together.' We look at the TV, before we even left the hotel: they agreed to a deal.

(Continued on page 117.)

The Bad Old Days
are back again

by MICHAEL SCHUR

If the Red Sox had won two more games last year—one in early April, say, and one in September—would any of this be happening? What if they'd gotten hot (or, really, just lukewarm) and won the ALDS? The ALCS even? What if—and this was absolutely possible—they'd won the World Series?

We know the answer, actually. Bob Hohler's *Boston Globe* article probably isn't written, or if it is, it's one-fifth as long and entirely ignored, because: Who cares? Reports of fried chicken and beer in the clubhouse are seen as evidence of Texas Forever-flavored camaraderie. Carl Crawford and John Lackey get a pass because they hung in there under tough circumstances. Francona might still leave, and Theo might still leave, but the headline is "Nothing Left to Prove, New Challenges Await" instead of "Oh Holy God Make the Pain Stop." If the Sox even just barely make the playoffs, this script unfolds very differently; two games—one in April and one in September, maybe—form the thin line between "we'll get 'em next year" and an entire institution collapsing in on itself like a dying star.

The details are ultimately unimportant. I personally don't care whether the troublemaker was John Lackey or Josh Beckett or Nomar or Wil Cordero. Players can be traded. Contracts can be eaten. Leaders can emerge. Bad luck can turn to good luck. What worries me, and what should be worrying all Red Sox fans, is the return of the narrative that colored every moment of the franchise for 86 years. Specifically, to boil it down: "It Just Can't Work Here."

This narrative was never supposed to arise again in Boston after 2002. This is the old narrative—the one in which the team with (1) a license to print money, and (2) the most loyal fans in the world routinely screws those fans over with mismanagement, terrible decision-making, and dysfunction at every level. The one in which the team squabbles and fights and collapses under pressure and just can't get its shit together no matter what. This narrative, need I remind you, included a clause that the team might be cursed—like, by a mean ghost—and it was such a powerful narrative that some people believed it.

Obviously, the great irony at work is that this was all supposed to have been put to bed forever by the arrival of the very same guys who are now leaving. Because those guys were smart and good at their jobs and they won. The new narrative they brought with them was: "We have tons of money and we're not racist idiots, so we can win baseball games." In 2005, the last time Everything Was Falling Apart, Epstein somehow held it together, with nothing more than a gorilla suit and several rational conversations with the owners. This was the best evidence yet—yes, even better than actually winning the World Series a year earlier—that the old ways were banished forever.

But those smart and talented guys are gone now, and, worse, the old narrative is sneaky-peteing back into our lives and indeed has now expanded to include those smart and talented guys, even implicating them as part of the problem. That's right, people—this old, crappy, ugly, horrible narrative is now threatening to retroactively ruin the legacies of the best manager and the best GM this team has ever had.

This is why the details are unimportant.[1] The fact that Josh Beckett ate hot wings and played *Call of Duty 4* in the club-

1. I'd like to briefly address the complete moron in the Red Sox organization who insinuated to a reporter that Terry Francona had a problem with prescription pills.

Dear Moron,
Congratulations! You have just (a) attacked the best and most popular manager your team has ever had while (b)

house couldn't matter less to me, especially when juxtaposed with the fact that someone high up in the Red Sox organization told a reporter that maybe Terry Francona had a fucking drug problem. That's some old-school Boston Narrative bullshit. An anonymous team source just going to town on the ideas of loyalty, decency, and propriety, and (perhaps more immediately harmful) the idea of organizational cohesion.[2] This old narrative is stubborn, tenacious, and destructive. It ruins careers, forces bad trades, and drives free agents to other cities. This narrative has already, I would guess, driven David Ortiz away. It's made Jacoby Ellsbury dream about his press conference in San Francisco in 2013. It's causing people on Red Sox message boards to demand the trade of Jon Lester—the best pitcher on the team, who has a shockingly reasonable contract through 2014. It ruins everything it touches.

Boston, as cliché mongers are fond of pointing out, is a fishbowl. The narrative is like a hot pot underneath the fishbowl that cooks the fish alive.

In media offices all over the Boston metro area, long-dormant knives are being sharpened. Ancient attack angles are being mapped out. There's a frisson of negatively charged energy that hasn't been felt since 2002, when a smart, talented, and competent group of people took over the team (again, it's worth noting, marking the very first moment in the franchise's entire history that its team was, in any way, competent). Blame the players, if you'd like, but players come and go. The last time this narrative ran the joint, it took an executive as talented as Theo Epstein and a manager as patient and stalwart as Terry Francona to turn things around. And guys like that don't grow on trees.

Originally published October 13, 2011.

displaying a complete lack of institutional loyalty, which (c) pretty much guarantees that no one in his right mind will want to manage your team now, and (d) turned everyone against each other causing (e) massive paranoia which will undoubtedly lead to (f) a thousand more stories about how dysfunctional your organization is, which will only intensify the ill effects of (b,c,d,e). You are the worst person in the world. Quit.

2. For future reference, you fucking moron, when the greatest manager in the history of your team leaves, under any circumstances, you say the following: "He did a wonderful job for us, for many years, and we wish him only the best." You do not insinuate to a reporter that he had a drug problem or that he was distracted by a failing marriage. This is true whether or not he actually did have a drug problem, by the way. It's 100 percent irrelevant. You take the high road. Do I really need to explain this to you, you fucking moron?

THE VERTICAL PASS LIVES ON

*Al Davis's obsession with speed
revolutionized football*

by CHRIS BROWN

JOEL KIMMEL

In recent years, it became easy (and sometimes even appropriate) to mock Al Davis and his beloved Oakland Raiders. From the poor on-field results and questionable personnel moves to Davis' infatuation with speed and his seemingly never-ending quest to find a modern version of the "Mad Bomber," Daryle Lamonica, the past few years have been ugly. And nothing, perhaps, was uglier than the Raiders' ill-fated selection of quarterback JaMarcus Russell with the first overall pick of the 2007 NFL draft. Russell had a strong arm, but he ate and robo-sipped sizzurp until he became persona non grata in the NFL. But none of this should overshadow what Davis built and also what he left behind, even if at the end he seemed to be grasping at the shadows of the Raiders' past success. Among his greatest contributions is the least well understood: the vaunted Raiders "vertical passing game."

Davis picked up the aerial bug from passing-game guru Sid Gillman when he was one of Gillman's assistants with the San Diego Chargers in the 1960s. Gillman, the "Father of the Modern Passing Game," introduced several innovations to the air attack, the first of which was timing. Gillman preached meticulous practice to sync the precise timing between quarterback and receiver, or, more precisely, between the quarterback's dropback and the receiver's route. If the quarterback took a five-step drop, the primary receiver had to run his route based on a precise number of steps, such that quarterback would throw the ball before the receiver had turned to look for it. The secondary receiver in the quarterback's progression ran his route a split second after the first receiver, so that the quarterback could look for the first receiver, reset his feet, then look for the second and still throw before that receiver turned to look for the pass. Nowadays, this emphasis on timing is so universal—in theory if not entirely in practice—that it's difficult to believe how influential Gillman was in establishing it. His second insight was to understand pass defenses and how to defeat them at a level far beyond the old command to "get open." Defeating a man-to-man defense, then as now, is about identifying a receiver who can get open versus a particular defender. Zones, on the other hand, require more thought. Gillman realized that the key to defeating zones was spacing between receivers; specifically, if a defense had only four underneath defenders, then five stationary targets—even five trash cans spaced evenly horizontally across the field— are uncoverable. The defenders are outnumbered. Thus, the idea of the zone "stretch" was born.

When Davis left Gillman's staff he took Sid's playbook— and, more important, his ideas—with him.[1] But Davis wasn't

1. Taking Gillman's plays with him was no great crime. Indeed, the basic concepts and plays that Gillman developed remain the core of almost all modern college or NFL pass attacks.

content to stretch the field horizontally; he wanted to get vertical. If Gillman could get a trash can open against a zone, Davis tested how good he'd do if he added his favorite ingredient: speed. Gillman, of course, used "vertical stretches"—passing concepts that spaced receivers not left to right, butdeep to short—but for Davis they became the centerpiece of his offense. Indeed, this is what Davis meant when he brought the "vertical game" to Oakland. It was not a matter of throwing deep bombs (though it was sometimes), but was instead the science of stretching defenses to their breaking point. With receivers at varying depths, a small defensive error often meant a 15-yard pass play for Davis' offense, and a serious mistake meant a touchdown.

Davis continued to tweak the Gillman offense by adding more formations, adding options for running backs in the passing game, and generally expanding the possibilities of what an offense could do with the football. This was innovative stuff, so much so that it had an outsize effect on a young Raiders assistant coach by the name of Bill Walsh, who went on to craft his own multi-Super Bowl-winning offense with the 49ers that looked a lot like what Davis had created in Oakland. As Walsh explained in his book *Building a Champion*:

> [Al Davis'] pass offense included an almost unlimited variety of pass patterns as well as a system of calling them, and utilized the backs and tight ends much more extensively than other offenses … To develop ·an understanding of it took time, but once learned, it was invaluable.

This is not the description of the Al Davis offense you usually see—as some kind of simplistic, backyard, "heave it up" strategy. Sure, Al wanted to hit the long ball, but it was all part of his system. Al Davis' "vertical game" was, in short, built on stretching the defense vertically while using all available receivers—deep, intermediate, and short—to take what the defense gave up anywhere on the field. It's not Al's fault that defenses often yielded big plays to the Raiders.

In Davis' offense, as is the case today, the ultimate vertical stretch passes are true "flood" or three-level vertical stretches, with one receiver deep, another at an intermediate depth, and a third short. Pass defenses generally have

only two layers of defenders—deep safeties and underneath coverage players—so
when there are receivers at three depths
it is extremely difficult to cover them all.
For example, Davis' early Raiders teams
often used the "strongside flood" route, a
pass concept still popular today. On the
play, an outside receiver runs a "go" route straight upfield, trying to beat
his defender deep and otherwise taking the coverage with him. An inside
receiver—here the tight end—runs a corner route at 15 yards, breaking to
the sideline while an underneath receiver—here the running back—runs to
the flat. On the backside, the outside receiver runs a post route as an "alert"
for the quarterback. He's not the primary read, but if the deep defenders
overreact to the three receivers to the right, the home run shot is always
available. Because the defense has only two defenders (the corner and the
safety) to cover three receivers, it shouldn't be able to defend the play. Al's
secret—and it is the same secret Gillman discovered and Walsh extended—
is that the surest way to hit those deep passes is to consistently hit the
underneath ones.

Davis also pioneered the use of "slot" formations, in which the tight
end lines up to one side by himself, and two split receivers position themselves to the opposite side. From this they could run all manner of vertical
stretches, but one the Raiders used quite well (and which many teams also
use today) began with the slot receiver running vertically downfield and
the outside receiver on a deep square-in or "dig" route. This pattern more
directly attacked the deep safeties and linebackers, defenders Davis knew
would be vulnerable to his fleet-footed receivers.

These vertical stretch passes help explain why Davis became obsessed
with speed. Obviously, speed gives a vertical receiver a chance to get behind
the defense, but, even if he does not actually get open, he stillstretches the
defense, thus opening up the entire field. Speed distorts defenses, forc-

ing them to cover wider swaths of the field, and thus exposing the weak defenders and the voids around them. If Davis could have a receiver like Warren Wells, who in 1969 totaled 1,260 yards on only 47 catches for the Raiders—a staggering 26.8 yards per completion—then his other receivers would have plenty of room to roam.

And yet, while Davis may have been hooked on speed and the vertical game, those addictions weren't responsible for the Raiders' struggles in recent years. Instead, the Raiders have been derailed by weaknesses at the two most important positions for implementing Davis' vision as owner: head coach and quarterback. Throughout the 1970s, Davis had John Madden, a coach who could make Raiders football a reality. And for more than a decade Oakland had two quarterbacks, the "Mad Bomber" Lamonica and Ken Stabler, who could execute the sophisticated vertical passing game the way Davis wanted.

But long after Madden, Lamonica, and Stabler left the Raiders, Davis remained. As the years went on, Davis couldn't expect his coaches to run the offense exactly as he'd taught it to Bill Walsh—nor did he want them to, at least not exactly. But he always knew how he wanted it to look, and at times the Raiders achieved something close to the brilliance that had once been the norm. In football, great teams and great organizations exist only in the moments before the next signing season or injury or retirement, or even the next death. It's simply not reasonable to expect what Davis accomplished early in his Raiders career to continue into perpetuity. But, despite whatever bitterness or decay emanated from the Raiders in recent years, the fact remains that Davis gave all of us more than we gave him. He didn't just mold his football team and his coaches and his players in his image—he molded the game itself.

Originally published October 11, 2011.

JESUS CHRIST,
REALLY?

*God and country manifest
in a single quarterback*

by BRIAN PHILLIPS

Here's how I think it works, this Tim Tebow madness.

- Somewhere within all our reptilian hearts lurks an instinct for trial-by-combat. This instinct tells us that when a person is strongly associated with an idea, we can use that person's success or failure within the sphere of competitive athletics as a legitimate indication of the quality of the idea. Did the green knight kill the blue knight? Then the queen must be innocent![1]

- Tim Tebow has, for various reasons and despite the presence of many other religious athletes in the NFL, become the avatar or champion of evangelical Christianity in football.

- In doing so, he has managed to take on outsize significance in the league despite largely failing to excel on the field and despite the fact that the NFL already reads culturally like the result of a right-wing blogger shotgunning a wine cooler and deciding to "make things fabulous."[2]

1. Did Duke win a national championship? Abolish the capital gains tax!

• We all know that this is ludicrous, but we all kind of feel it anyway.

• As a result, it's basically impossible not to see Tebow's ability or inability to complete a 15-yard out pattern to Matt Willis as a referendum on the Book of Deuteronomy.

I'm not a churchgoer, personally. But even for me, Sunday's Miami-Denver game was a harrowing existential ride. For about three quarters, Tebow floundered, and it looked like the Living Water Bible Church out on Route 17 was wrong about pretty much everything. (Just as I suspected!) Then he rallied the Broncos for a heroic comeback and, d'oh, it seemed like there might be a god in the universe after all. And people called the win "overhyped"!

It's not as though, pre-Tebow, the NFL was lacking religiosity. I'm pretty sure Reggie White was actually a character in the Bible.[3] And every sideline reporter has lived through this scenario—

Sideline reporter: What defensive adjustments did you make after the half that let you stop the run so effectively in the third quarter?

Middle linebacker: I thank Jesus Christ my personal Lord and Savior thine be the glory baby [kisses finger twice, points up at sky]

—so many times that they must all be terrified it'll start to happen in their regular, non-football lives:

Sideline Reporter [at the UPS Store]: Does the 12-box jumbo pack come with bubble wrap?

2. The F-15 flyovers, the martial fanfares, the crisp green lawns, the body armor, the commercials in which giant whooshing branding irons burn the low APR of a Chevy Silverado directly onto the screen, etc. It's as if the guy who invented Branson, Mo., looked at his work and said, "Screw this, I can do better."

3. "And lo, by his totally just sweeping 300-pound offensive tackles aside with one arm shall ye recognize him. By his just absolutely body-slamming Doug Flutie shall the mark of his coming be known."

UPS Store Clerk: Hey, I just wanna give a shout-out to the Prince of Peace, Jehovah, my shepherd, everything I am is how He made me and all I do is for His name.

But Tebow's religiosity is different. For one thing, the public narrative of the Christian athlete normally involves a grown-up conversion experience: Deion Sanders on the Damascene Road. Tebow, by contrast, has been coming at the world with his own personal Good News since college, when he was still dewy from youth group. The son of missionaries, he always seemed religious in a way that, say, Kurt Warner didn't.[4]

The evangelical movement spends a lot of money and time coaching its kids on how to confront secular culture, but the kids don't usually reach a position at which they can confront it on a national-media scale—not as kids, anyway. But then here was Tebow, the quarterback at Florida, this articulate, successful young guy who was prepared to test all those techniques before a mass audience. He was calm. He was patient. He was totally committed, with the Bible verses on his eyeblack and his self-confessed virginity, but you never got the feeling he was judging you.

Instead, he was just respectfully taking in your mistakes and waiting to help you make a better call. At twenty, he was America's camp counselor at a camp half the country never meant to attend.

T ebow self-consciously presented himself as a defender of the faith, filming anti-abortion commercials, flying around the world to help with his parents' missions. A lot of athletes have been religious advocates or preachers over the years, but they've generally acknowledged some token separation between their private faith and their public lives, even

4. Even though Warner seemed weirder than Tebow in numerous other ways. Actually, it's Tebow's manifest nonweirdness that sets the rest of this up.

if the line often blurs. Reggie White appeared in ads opposing homosexuality, but not until after he retired. Tebow, on the other hand, gets press for circumcising Filipino babies. A trillion words have been written about this already, but suffice it to say that if you see him as the avatar of muscular Christianity in football, you know that in his bland, smiling, placidly self-confident way, he sees himself that way, too.

I'm sure there are people who manage to escape the demographic rooting pattern this creates. But in broad strokes, it's fair to say that how you feel about Tebow depends on how you feel about youth groups and Elisabeth Hasselbeck and, I don't know, WWJD bracelets and raft retreats with a lot of bonfires and swaying. Other religious players are religious individuals; Tebow is a whole culture. It helps that, as an NFL player, he's both nontraditional and kind of bad, which makes it easy to see his success as guided by a higher power—if a dude with that background and that throwing motion completes a touchdown pass, it almost has to be a miracle.

Whenever I catch one of Tebow's games, I tend to lose sight of the scoreboard and just focus on the metacompetition, the weird Joan of Arc drama that seems to go along with everything he does. I imagine a bar under a train station somewhere where the relevant ideas men gather to learn their fates. Did a receiver drop a pass? James Dobson just choked on a nacho. Did Tim throw an interception? Daniel Dennett just chest-bumped Richard Dawkins. Again, I realize that this is stupid, that it's beyond stupid, but compared to actually watching the Broncos? It'll do.

I find myself half-consciously rooting for Tebow to fail, even though I have nothing against him, have lots of religious friends, am not especially tribal by nature, and wouldn't want to be responsible for the nacho-related deaths of any prominent evangelical leaders, even if I detest their politics. Doesn't matter. The part of me that wants to eat pork and not stone people just switches on and cheers for the blitzing linebacker.

There's a problem with this, though, a problem that I'm convinced lies at the heart of the minor cultural puzzle that Tebow represents. The problem is that if you're rooting against Tebow because he's religious, you're giving way to the trial-by-combat impulse. And the whole idea of the trial by combat is that there's a higher power adjudicating the combat. It means something for the blue knight to kill the green knight only if God is moving the swords. So what I, many secular football fans, and Imaginary Daniel Dennett are really rooting for is for God to make Tim Tebow fail as a means of discrediting Himself, God, in accordance with our wishes, and against His, God's, own interests.

This—arguably—doesn't make a whole lot of sense.

For the sake of argument, let's say that the universe is radically meaningless. If that's the case, then when Tebow wins, it's a fluke that doesn't prove anything. When he loses, it's also a fluke that doesn't prove anything. For his losing to mean anything, it has to tie into some larger cosmic order, and if it does, then it can't prove that there isn't one. Since no one really knows whether the universe is meaningless or not, things rapidly grow confusing. Tebow scoring a two-point conversion on an off-tackle power play couldprove that Jesus Rose from the dead on the third day, or it could, well, not. Tebow's getting picked off after telegraphing a pass could doom us to a state of terrifying metaphysical uncertainty, especially if we are the Broncos' quarterbacks coach. (On the other hand, if we're a free safety on the opposing team, Tebow's throwing motion might make us suspect that there is a God after all.) But if you're against Tebow, you can't read too much into Tebow's failures, or else Tebow has already won.

From a theological standpoint, it's so hard to say what you're actually rooting for and how it aligns with specific on-field outcomes that it almost seems to make more sense not to bring religion or politics or philosophy into the NFL, or maybe any sport, at all. But then what the hell have we been watching?

Originally published October 25, 2011.

Olympic gold medalist Lindsay Vonn got into the Tebow pose at the Audi FIS World Cup on December 7, 2011 in Beaver Creek, Colorado.

Detroit Lions linebacker Stephen Tulloch Tebowed following his sack of the Broncos' quarterback.

TIM TEBOW AND THE MIRACLES

The quarterback gets a little help from his defense

by CHRIS RYAN

Let's start at the end, at the bottom of a pile-up of football players, with Mile High rocking and John Elway standing and applauding, Rex Ryan throwing up his hands in dismay and the NFL Network's Mike Mayock, who had spent the whole night excellently articulating the problems and promise inherent in the Broncos read-option offense, simply laughing.[1] He, like most of the people at home, was probably thinking the same thing, invoking that one place Tim Tebow is trying to avoid more than anything: "What the hell?"

Yeah, the circumstances demanded such a reaction. If, by some tilting of the Earth's axis, that had been Brady Quinn leading the Broncos on a 95-yard game-winning

TOP: ASSOCIATED PRESS
BOTTOM: GETTY IMAGES

1. The New York Jets played the Denver Broncos at Mile High Stadium in Denver on November 17, 2011.

drive, I'm sure he would have gotten a couple of man-hugs out of the bargain as well. But this was different. This was a team that had just received one of the greatest rewards you can get in life; the one where putting your faith in someone else pays off.

After every underthrown ball and every broken play, the Denver Broncos came back to the huddle with their heads held high, never showing up their quarterback, no matter how off target or out of his depth he was. And when Tebow couldn't get anything going, which, let's be clear, was the majority of the game, the defense came out and played like highly irritated Mongol raiders.

For most of the night, I was looking for a reason why. Why Mark Sanchez (who, for all his problems, *has* led the Jets to consecutive AFC Championship games) was getting nothing but shade from Plaxico Burress and hot, angry breath from offensive coordinator Brian Schottenheimer

This Broncos supporter avidly believes in the power of Tebow and Tebowing: "If you Tebow, good things happen."

while Tebow, who was playing quarterback with the grace of an ice-skating Bambi, was getting the undying support of his teammates.

For the answer, go back to 3:55 remaining in the fourth quarter. Tebow, barely bothering to look upfield, cradles the ball and takes off like a Greyhound bus driven by a meth head. There on the horizon, he sees the usually unwelcoming vista that is Revis Island. And what does he do? Does he trot out of bounds and save some clock and spare himself the contact? Nope. He barrels over Revis like a hurricane, stays in bounds, and gets that much closer to the end zone.

That's why you block for a guy like that. That's why you run route after useless route and try to save play after broken play. That's why, if you're on defense, you are just trying to keep it close, just trying to ding Sanchez up enough to make him jumpy, just trying to frustrate the Jets receiver corps enough to make them give up on their game plan.

Because at the end of the game, it might just be 13–10 and you might just have a shot. You might just be 20 yards out and your quarterback might just be able to run like Mike Alstott. And with the home crowd losing their minds in the thin air, and the terrifying Jets defense on their back foot and everyone in America watching because your very average AFC West team has become the center of the football universe, your quarterback might just do the one thing he was put on Earth to do: make a perfect read on a safety who is overcommitted to the inside and take off with only one destination in mind. He might do what he said he would, what he asked you to believe he could do. He might just win the damn thing for you.

That's when you say, "What the hell." And that's when you block.

Originally published November 18, 2011.

THE ART OF
SEAT POACHING

*A poor man's guide
to a better view*

by SHANE RYAN

There was a time, when I was very young, when simply attending a live sport-ing event was something incredible. I grew up in upstate New York, about an hour south of Montreal, and each summer my dad would take me up across the border to see the Expos play. We'd arrive at the grotesque Stade Olympique, with its phallic tower looming over the clam shell roof, and my young heart would be thumping. It didn't matter that we were about to be treated to a miserable brand of baseball on an ugly turf field in front of his-tory's worst fan base; we were going to see the pros! And it definitely didn't matter where we sat.

Today, that's no longer true. I don't think I'm the most ungrateful sports fan in the world, but I have to be in the top tier. It's gotten to the point where if I'm sitting in the nosebleed section of a stadium, under almost any circumstance, I will not enjoy the game. Sure, I'll guilt myself into focusing for a few minutes, but soon I'll be back to obsessing on how I can get closer.

I've become spoiled. For better or worse, I need good seats. Unfortunately, at the same time, I'm not even close to having the kind of money required to get there legitimately.

As such, I've had to become a seat-poacher. Say what you will about my integrity or basic decency, but it's a title I embrace. I've even devised a comprehensive system, guaranteed to get you into the best seats at no cost, and today I'd like to share it with you. The tips and tricks that follow have been tested for five years against the stern ushers of two Yankee Stadiums, and I'm happy to report a success rate near 100 percent.

Fair warning: You'll be far more successful at applying these tips if you lose all sense of shame and pride. Also, you'll be required to do a lot of things that look sneaky, cheap, and downright pathetic, so be careful before you attempt them on a date.

1. GETTING THE TICKET

1. Don't buy the ticket in advance. With all the fees and taxes and nonsense, you'll be gouged even for the cheap seats. Buying tickets at face value is for suckers and cowards.

2. Forget the professional scalpers. Unless you want to wait until the game is under way, which is terrible, and even then they'll never come down to a reasonable price. It's too easy for them to find the bloated family of four from the sticks strapped with new hats, at least one fanny pack, and $500 cash. This is the only game they'll attend all year, by golly, and what's a few bucks for an afternoon of fun? Ignorance drives the market.

3. Find the man with the extra ticket. Maybe his buddy had to stay late for work, or his kid got sick, or he caught his wife having cyber-sex with his boss (awkward!) and is withholding her ticket as a small act of revenge.

Play to this man's sympathy; his memory, even, of being in your shoes. Personally, I used to stand on the subway platform at Yankee Stadium as people filed off the 4 train. "I'm just looking for one extra ticket!" I'd shout in an aggressively sheepish manner. "I'm not a scalper! Just a big fan trying to get into the game."

The downside is that hundreds of people will stare at you and feel embarrassed both for and with you. Attractive young women will give you a look that says, "If my boyfriend ever behaved like that in public, I would drink a gallon of paint."

The upside is that you will absolutely find the man with the extra ticket. When he approaches, get real sincere and say, "Hey, just so you know, I don't have a ton of money, so I might not be able to buy the ticket if it's too good. I hope I don't waste your time."

Make sure he doesn't feel like you're playing the class card on him; you should convey that you understandhis situation. He dropped real money for the tickets in the first place, and that's not to be taken lightly. But reality is reality—you're the kind of dude who can only dole out 15 bucks on a given night. He'll probably feel pity for you without feeling like he's being made to feel pity, which is crucial. Sometimes, you'll get superlucky and either get a free ticket or a really nice one for peanuts (note: not literal peanuts, peanuts are not a form of currency or legal tender).

2. GETTING INTO THE GOOD SECTION

The good sections always have ushers. Teams don't waste manpower on the crappy grandstand seats where the likes of you should be sitting. But field level or mezzanine? It's watertight. Still, there are ways to beat the system.

1. Get there early. In most stadiums, the ushers don't care who goes where in the early hours. Sometimes they'll flush you out as the game gets closer, but that usually only happens in the Goldman Sachs-type sections. This can be the easiest solution of all.

2. Find the section with the young, male usher. If he's wearing his hat slightly cocked to the side, even better—it speaks of a flippant nature. He's going to be the most casual and feel the most reluctant to call you out on your low-down tactics. It makes him feel like "The Man," and you can use this against him. Avoid sections with older ushers; they absolutely live to catch you red-handed. They're like sadistic soldiers given free rein in battle; they'll pounce with the slightest excuse, flashing their cruel grins. Mess with them, and they'll be boring their grandchildren for years with the story of how they ruined your day.

3. Try to sneak in behind a family. If there's a group streaming in, full of family chaos and confusion, fall in place in the back of their line. When you approach the usher, laugh really loudly at one of their jokes or start bickering with one of the younger ones. "Oh my god, Jessica," you should say, "I HATE YOU." The usher will group you in with all the legitimate tickets he's just seen from the rest of the family, and you're golden. (Note: This may lead to some awkwardness with the family afterward.)

4. If the usher turns his body in one direction to help someone or have a conversation, sneak in behind. This is a very risky maneuver, though; if he turns and catches you, you'll have no excuse since it's clear you were trying to pull a fast one. Your only defense at that point is to change the dominant narrative of the situation by immediately falling down the stairs.

5. Thank the usher as you approach the section for the first time. These guys see a ton of people at every game, and there's no way they can remember each face. If you say something like, "Thanks for the directions, I thought I'd never find the bathroom!" he'll assume you were in his section before and he helped you out. He'll also assume you're an idiot, since bathrooms are clearly marked in every single American stadium, but having him think you're stupid is a good thing.

6. Have a girlfriend lead the way, staring at her ticket and saying something like "is row G close to the bottom?" Unfortunately, my girlfriend gets absolutely terrified at even this simple maneuver. She'll actually start pan-

icking as we approach, and at the last moment she'll lose heart and back away. It's one of the real difficulties of our relationship. (One time, when we were about to sneak in, an usher turned around and his hand accidentally touched my girlfriend's butt. He was so apologetic that he didn't even bother to check our tickets, and we got excellent seats. I don't know how this could be incorporated into a consistent strategy, but it's something to think about.)

7. For any of these options, remember to always move fast without hurrying. Act like you know where you're going and have been there before. If you make eye contact with the usher, he has a much higher chance of noticing you, and that's always a bad thing. Also, try not to be too discouraged or humiliated if you get caught. It's all in the game. Believe me, they won't throw you out of the stadium for trying to get a good seat. If you let one failure stop you, for shame or for fear, you'll never be one of the great seat-snagging cretins like me. Live to fight another day, my brother.

3. STAYING IN THE GOOD SECTION

1. Often you'll find a nice seat, enjoy the first part of the game, and then some rich bastard will waddle up, look all flustered as though he's trying to solve a Chinese crossword, and say, "I, uh … I think this is myseat." He'll probably have a trophy wife who gives you a look like you just threw her poodle into the side of an old refrigerator. You'll absolutely detest these latecomers, who have no love in their hearts for the game, but the fact remains that they paid real money for the seats and have the law on their side. You're nothing but a wretched squatter.

So: ALWAYS HAVE YOUR NEXT SEAT IN MIND. More than one, preferably. Even if it's the fifth inning and you think nobody could possibly ruin your night now, emulate a great defensive back and keep your head on a swivel. The quicker you move when the fat cats finally come, the less likely they'll be to rat you out, and the more likely you'll be to avoid doddering around and attracting an usher's attention. The best seat-poachers are always thinking several seats ahead. (Note: You can also turn this situation to your benefit. One of the great satisfactions in life is actually sitting next to one of the richies and telling them how much you paid for the ticket. "Yeah," you'll say, smiling like you've known nothing but good fortune all your life, "15 bucks! Can you believe it? What'd yours cost?" Later, when he goes to the bathroom, ask his wife if she'd like a beer.)

2. The dreaded bathroom problem. At some point, you may have to leave your section to use the restroom, and you obviously don't have the ticket to get back in. The best strategy here relates to no. 5 above. Ask the usher something on your way out. It's crucial that they remember you, though, so try some sort of odd phrasing. Instead of asking for the bathroom or where you can get a beer, say, "Where would a gentleman find a working urinal?" or "Could you direct me to the safest saloon?" On your way back, say thank you, and they won't ask to see your ticket.

3. If you have two people in the section, you're golden. This is one trick my girlfriend can manage. On my way back, I'll start shuffling around and staring at the seats. She'll be waiting near the top of the section, cued by a text message, and when I come shambling along, she'll say, "Honey! Over here!" I'll turn, my jaw still slack with confusion, and be overcome by a look of total relief. The usher, having witnessed this drama, will let me pass without incident.

And that's all there is to it. I'm not saying it's easy—you'll face some real hardship and doubt along the way. But when those demons come, just remember: You, my friend, are a seat-poacher. You are a warrior, striving to leave behind the complacent and apathetic and take your rightful spot beside the fortunate sons who would see you starve. You are an honest-to-god, old-school American, and hell if a soul that hale will ever abide a bleeding nose.

Originally published August 16, 2011.

"ALL GREAT DEFENDERS KNOW WHERE THE HELP IS GOING TO BE."

(Jalen Rose and David Jacoby, continued from 89)

JACOBY: I want to talk about the 1997 NBA Eastern Conference Finals a little bit. You did a very good defensive job against Mr. Jordan.

ROSE: Yeah, when I was a young player, one of my roles was to play defense. [Laughter.] That was the way I was going it get minutes! And I got to play for Larry Bird? Are you kidding me? I played for Larry Bird!

JACOBY: What was Larry Bird like as a coach?

ROSE: He was terrific because he's such a straight-shooter. You hear about the player egos all the time, and he just cool as a cucumber. He's like, "I'm going it tell you what I expect of you and when you're not doing what I ask of you, come sit over here next to me." So there's no gray area. He would bring you to the sidelines and say "Jalen, what did I ask you to do? A, B, C and D. What were you doing? E, F, and G. Go sit down." And I loved that! I embraced that! I needed that!

JACOBY: Yeah, he didn't move, he was like a statue!

ROSE: Right! Rick Carlisle (who was our associate head coach and now the coach of the Dallas Mavericks) was like our offensive coordinator; and Dick Harter (long time successful coach in the NBA) was like the defensive coordinator, and Larry Bird was like the CEO. That worked for our veteran team, and it got us to the point where we were playing against Michael and the Bulls in the play-offs in a Game 7, which was something that was big for the fans of Indiana and big for that team because that doesn't happen every year.

JACOBY: You still haven't answered my question about that series. What was your approach to defending Michael Jordan, because you had a lot of success in that series.

ROSE: My approach was: Where's my help going to be? All great defenders know where the help is going to be, and they try not to contest shots, and they try not to back off an inch. Michael Jordan is arguably the greatest player of all time, so you give him an inch, he's going to take a mile; you give him a rope, he's going to turn into a cowboy. You got to find a way to know where your help is, stay up in his chest at all times, contest a shot, and hope he misses.

(Continued on page 167.)

(ALMOST) WINNING IN MILWAUKEE

The Brewers fall short, and fall in line with
the history of baseball in the upper Midwest

by CHAD HARBACH

On October 16, my father and I drove north from my parents' home in Racine to attend Game 6 of the NLCS—Brewers versus Cardinals. It was my first-ever playoff game, and I felt like an ancient wrong was being redeemed. In 1982, the Brewers appeared in their only World Series, against these same Cards. I was 6, and it was my first season of serious fandom. Someone gave my dad two tickets to Game 5, a Sunday-afternoon game, and my dad, with whom I'd attended many games that season ... took my mother. I was baffled. Did she even like baseball? It was unclear. My dad and I had been going all season long, she'd stayed home, and I saw no reason why I'd get demoted now. I consoled myself with the idea that, since it was a rare day game, I'd get to watch the whole thing on television.

Twenty-nine years later, minus one day, my time had finally come, and against the same despised Cards. Brewer fans still bear a grudge against St. Louis for ruining our lone shot at glory—our only World Series appearance in 42 years—and since the teams became divisional rivals in 1994 (through the machinations of Allan Huber Selig, on whom more later) there's often been a corresponding bitterness on the field. It's a rivalry born of intense identification: two medium-sized Midwestern industrial towns, one on a great lake, the other a wide river, impassioned and wise about baseball, with stadiums named after the lager empires that have partly sheltered their towns from the worst ravages of manufacturing's collapse. The only thing missing was a few more Milwaukee victories—the Cards have won 11 World Series, the Brewers none—and this seemed to be the year. But when it's never your year, it's never your year.

Miller Park rises from one of the cheerier expanses of sun-bleached concrete you'll find, amid a network of spur roads, stringy trees, and pedestrian overpass bridges three miles west of downtown Milwaukee. Around the parking lots' fringes lie various low-slung businesses—Badger Railing, Taylor Dynamometer, Wisconsin Highway Business Signs—whose names, like the old Brewers ball-and-glove logo, might have been designed especially for hipster T-shirts.

The stadium itself has a gigantic aspect—both familiar and alien, bigger than a ballpark, siphoning cars toward it. The pale-brick facades make it look like a shopping mall, or a train station in a gentrified downtown, but what stands out is the green retractable roof, swelling skyward, its raised iron beams running like spines over the mammoth length of the place. Presumably those beams serve some structural purpose, but they also make a nice piece of urban architecture, suited to Milwaukee but imaginable atop a cutting-edge art museum in a labor-minded European city.

We arrived at four o'clock as the parking lots opened, and by 4:15 the smell of charcoal filled the air. Wisconsin tailgaters, whatever the sport, move with a military efficiency, at least until they're drunk. Tables and camp chairs bloomed across the lot; the tables filled with meats, buns, condiments, Jell-Os, desserts, and a surprising number (at least to me) of full-on wet bars. Everyone played cornhole—so many bean bags flew toward so many wedge-shaped wooden goals (some with Brewers or Packers or Badgers logos, others marbled black and white like Holsteins) that it was hard to walk around.

A flag-stiffening wind blew from the west, calling to mind the windy day in 1999 when the Big Blue Crane, as it's known, collapsed against the side of the nearly finished stadium, killing three ironworkers. Today, the sun fell swiftly, casting parts of the parking lot in chilly shadow. All radios were tuned to WTMJ, which recounted highlights from the just-booked Packers win. The crowd, too, content and subdued, seemed yet to have turned its thoughts to baseball. No one was warmly dressed, because the stadium roof was closed, and so even when the night turned frigid it would be plenty warm inside. It has always struck me as odd and incongruous, a roof like this in Wisconsin for a summer sport, and no matter how many games I attend I still tend to forget it exists. Baseball, after all, is a summer sport, and we cherish our summers here.

At 5, the stadium gates opened, and my dad headed in to watch batting practice. I walked around, looking for old friends. I passed a pair of old women in crocheted Brewers sweaters, white with patterned versions of the ball-and-glove logo where the pumpkins or snowflakes would otherwise be. A guy walking ahead of me wore a Brewers jersey with NIXON between the shoulder blades. I was surprised to see two attractive women in proximity to one another (it's not that kind of crowd), until I realized one was a TV reporter—she held a microphone to the other's lips and nodded absorbedly for long stretches, relieved to have found someone almost as telegenic to talk to.

As I strolled through the tailgate, I saw virtually no black or Latino people, but I did soon run across the latter group's representative sausage: The Chorizo. The Chorizo is 10 feet tall and wears a sombrero and a green

T-shirt with his name and the number 5 emblazoned on the back. He was added to Milwaukee's sixth-inning Sausage Race in 2007 to honor the city's Latino population—which, though sizable, appears not to attend Brewer games, at least not playoff ones. The Chorizo, unfazed by this, was out shaking hands and posing for photos, no doubt striving, as the newbie, to build a following commensurate to those of the original four sausages: The Brat, The Italian, The Polish, and The Hot Dog.

I could tell the crowd was serious by how little Packers garb I saw despite the autumn Sunday—even in the height of summer there's usually more green and gold. Fans in red had to be vetted for Badger or Cardinal alliance—if they were wandering instead of tailgating, they were probably from St. Louis. The Cards fans' beefiness looked different from Wisconsin beefiness—healthier, heartier, as if they'd been eating organic meat. Everyone else wore the dark blue of the current Brewers or, almost as often, the paler blue of the 1982 team.

The mustachioed, beer-bellied shadow of 1982 hangs over everything to do with Milwaukee baseball—not just this season, but especially this season. Those Brewers are fondly remembered by fans in many places, and might be the most famous post-expansion team not to win a title. This year, on the night of Game 5, I found myself committed to a dinner in Nashville, unable to watch the game. When I asked my Tennessean

---

Notable Members of the 1982 Brewers and Their Notable Nicknames (Plus a Few Notable Mustaches, Too)

Paul "The Igniter" Mollitor
Position: third base
Series batting average: .355
Of note: Molitor holds the World Series record for most hits in a game with the five he hit in Game 1.

tablemates if anyone had a smartphone on which to check the score, they instantly, and for no other reason than the joy of reciting the names, rattled off the lineup of the '82 Brewers—Yount, Molitor, Cooper, Thomas, Oglivie, Gantner, Simmons, Vuckovich, Fingers. Throw in the handful of guys they forgot, like Moose Haas and Charlie Moore, and you have one of baseball's iconic teams, a supremely charismatic group that won back-to-back MVPs, back-to-back Cy Youngs, a home run title, and a pennant, but no World Series, and which faded to oblivion by the end of the following year.

There are reasons for their popularity. Those Brewers were, or at least resembled, a perfect manifestation of their place and time—beer-drinking, bike-riding guys in the city of Miller and Harley-Davidson. At the dawn of Reaganomics, amid the rise of the bond trader and a new corporate ethos, they found themselves already, accidentally, a crazily coiffed throwback to the supposedly freewheeling '70s.

The moustaches, and the heartening lack of guile when talking to the press, might have counted little if their style of play didn't exude the same careless excess. They were average in the field and on the mound (despite those back-to-back Cys for Fingers and Vuckovich), as though to deny the other team its share of runs would be stingy and wrong. To compensate they raked and raked and raked. They were a slow-pitch softball team in a big-park, dead-ball era. They led all of baseball by 30 home runs, while finishing second-to-last in strikeouts. They scored .45 runs per game more

"Stormin'" Gorman Thomas
Position: center field
Series batting average: .179
Of note: For the season Thomas had an AL-high 39 home runs, but in the World Series he was the final out, striking out.

Ted "Simba" Simmons
Position: Catcher
Series batting average: .174
Of note: Simmons, who played for the Cardinals before joining the Brewers, hit home runs in Games 1 and 2.

than anyone else—a gigantic margin.

Their manager was Harvey Kuenn, who suited them perfectly: a hometown boy, UW-Wisconsin star (before the Badgers canceled baseball), and AL batting champ who married a former Miss Wisconsin, and—no joke—bowled in the winter to stay in shape. In case that wasn't enough, he'd also, like Ahab, that coach of another unruly gang, had one leg amputated just below the knee.

Kuenn became manager only on June 2, after the team sputtered to a 23–24 start and Buck Rodgers was fired. Harvey's Wallbangers, as they were called, finished a formidable 72–43 to win the AL East, defeated the California Angels in a dramatic ALCS, then battered the Cardinals 10–0 in the opening game of the World Series. They parlayed that win into a 3–2 Series lead, then went to St. Louis and let it slip away. The team finished fifth the next year, and Kuenn was fired. Since then, Milwaukee fans have been frozen in time—forever celebrating, lamenting the loss of, and wearing the caps of, the only pennant-winning team we've ever had.

These 2011 Brewers, the city's most talented team since '82, seemed both buoyed and burdened by their old-school counterparts. Like their predecessors, they started poorly, beginning the season 14–20, then racked up the majors' best record thereafter. They, too, were charismatic sluggers who played suspect defense and relied on a well-coiffed closer—

Donald "Black & Decker" Sutton
Position: pitcher
Series record: 0-1
Of note: Sutton was the starting pitcher who clinched the AL East title for the Brewers in 1982.

Robin "The Kid" Yount
Position: short stop
Series batting average: .414
Of note: Yount is the only player in MLB history to have two four-hit games in the World Series (Game 1 and Game 5).

John Axford, winner of the Robert Goulet Memorial Mustached American of the Year Award, even though he's Canadian. Most important, they looked like they could win it all—on the last day of the season, still playing hard for home-field advantage, they won their 96th game, finally eclipsing the '82 team's record.

As always, the Cardinals loomed large. The teams went 9–9 against each other, and the games were exceedingly tense. In August, Jason Motte retaliated for a pitch that hit Albert Pujols by plunking Ryan Braun; later in the game, Cards catcher Yadier Molina went berserk on the plate umpire. In September, Brewers center fielder Nyjer Morgan, who'd been feuding for a while with Chris Carpenter, flung his tobacco in Carpenter's direction, enraging Pujols, whom Morgan then inelegantly slagged on Twitter, and inducing Tony La Russa to tell Morgan to get a clue. (La Russa, sometimes easily induced, also described Brewers fans as "idiots," and complained that Miller Park employees were altering the lighting depending on who was at bat.)

Morgan's erratic behavior had pretty much made him a pariah before he joined the Brewers this year, but his new teammates rallied around him in a fierce, palpable way. He became the team's focal personality, which reduced the pressure on Fielder and Braun and seemed to give the whole team confidence. Brewers fans loved him as much as opposing fans despised him—the jersey of his alter ego, Tony Plush (who was, weirdly, invented as a kind of Neil Strauss The Game-style avatar for picking up

---

Benjamin "Gentle Ben" Oglivie
Position: Left field
Series batting average: .222
Of note: Oglivie hit one solo home run in Game 7. It was the Brewers' only home run, and Oglivie's only home run of the Series.

Roland "Rollie" Fingers
Position: pitcher
Series record: 0-0
Of note: Fingers did not pitch in the world series, but it's impossible not to include him in the context of notable mustaches.

women in clubs), became the team's best-seller. An SI cover story about the Brewers' season morphed into a sympathetic profile of Morgan, perhaps the only black kid from San Jose ever to drop out of high school to move to Canada to play minor league hockey.

Even Brewers fans occasionally get annoyed with the garrulous Morgan and his proliferating alter egos—Tony Tombstone, Tony Gumble, Tony Hush, et alia—and when they do, they contrast his mania to the calm dignity of Yount and Cooper. But mostly fans can't get enough of Morgan, because he feels like a throwback to that premodern era when an athlete, unable to become a corporation, might decide to become a character. What we want from our ballplayers, apart from the beauty of their performance, is a little insight into the thoughts that make that performance possible. But they can't really talk about what they do —what they do is too delicate, too fragile, too elusive. And, in the age of endorsements and corporate sponsorship, they can't talk about much else, either. The athlete interview—and we watch and hear and read so many—is a deadening monotone. But Morgan talks and talks, wears his feelings on the outside, and so makes us feel like we're inside. It's a brave move, if an uncalculated one, especially for a black man; and it makes Morgan, more than any other Brewer, feel like a link to the league of 30 years ago.

Now as then, the Crew won their first playoff series in a deciding Game 5—this time in the bottom of the 10th, when Morgan bounced a single up the middle, scoring his platoon mate Carlos Gomez. Later that night, the Cards beat the Phillies, and it was on. Perhaps the exorcism could finally be performed, the heads snapped off all those endless throwback bobbleheads.

T he crowd streamed through the main entrance near home plate, slowed only by a perfunctory security check. Opposite that entrance stands an idyllic Little League field, built on the infield of old County Stadium, and in between stand four life-size bronze statues: Hank Aaron; the three ironworkers who died in the Big Blue Crane accident; and owner-turned-commissioner Bud Selig. The Selig statue was installed most recently, in August 2010, and I had somehow remained ignorant of its existence until I found myself standing before it.

Born in Milwaukee, Selig attended the University of Wisconsin, where he roomed with Wisconsin senator and Bucks owner Herb Kohl, and then entered the family auto-leasing business. He became a minority owner of the Milwaukee Braves, tried to keep the Braves in town, failed. Immediately he formed the Milwaukee Brewers Baseball Club, whose sole purpose was to bring baseball back to the city. He tried to spirit the White Sox away from Chicago, but that purchase was blocked, and then turned his attention to the Pilots, a bankrupt expansion club that had lasted a single season in Seattle—just long enough to have their awfulness immortalized by Jim Bouton in Ball Four. The cost was around $10.8 million, of which Selig himself put up a small fraction.

You could and probably should call Selig a local hero—a hometown boy who's devoted his life to keeping baseball in Milwaukee, and now occupies the game's highest office—and yet he's never played the part quite convincingly. His lifelong nickname stems directly from his role as a little brother; when his mom returned from the hospital with baby Allan in tow, she told her first-born, Jerry, "We brought you a little buddy." And indeed Buddy's relationship to Milwaukee, over the past five decades, has always had a big/little brother dynamic, with Buddy, no matter how powerful he becomes (and by certain measures he's one of the more powerful men in America), forever in the role of noogie recipient. He's remained perpetually loyal and eager to impress, which gives Brewers fans perpetual license to remain unimpressed. As fiercely as we'll defend Selig against outside attacks, among ourselves we'll say little that's forgiving about the guy. He wants our affection—has always openly wanted it—and that gives us the option to withhold it.[1]

He's also been willing to stir up trouble outside the family to protect what's within.

Much of what other fans chide Selig for are his pro-Milwaukee moves: First, his shrewd orchestration of the Brewers' switch from the AL to the NL, which saved us the cost of a DH; gave us endless cracks at the Cards; and replaced free-swinging White Sox fans with free-spending Cubs fans. Second, his willingness to raise the vexed question of contraction (to shrink, in the American imagination, is worse than death) while refusing to consider the then-struggling Brewers as a candidate.

Within Wisconsin, Selig's major shortcoming has always been not winning enough—which has meant, in large part, not being wealthy enough. He self-identified with his Brewers in a way Kohl, for instance, never has with the Bucks, and his team lost and lost and lost, confirming in fans' minds what they always sort of thought: Selig couldn't win. The Brewers won 65 games in their first season, one more than the hapless Pilots had, and things were rarely much better thereafter. Hence the enduring love for that '82 team; in the Selig family's 35 years at the helm, that was the only team that had a shot.

As the '80s wore on and professional sports became huge business, it became harder and harder for cities like Milwaukee to keep pace. They weren't cities, it turned out, so much as "markets"; economically and rhetorically, the distinction between small- and large-market clubs became the critical one. This language took some of the heat off Selig, even while it made it seem less likely that he'd ever redeem himself.

Then as now, the conventional wisdom was clear: A small-market club survived by building a big-market facility. This wasn't going to be easy for Selig, who didn't have any money, and so constructing a stadium in Milwaukee would

1. Bud's Jewishness is—has to be—some kind of factor in this equation. Until recently, Wisconsin had two Jewish senators, including Selig's ex-roommate Kohl, and yet all of the state's Jewish residents together couldn't come close to filling Miller Park. There are so few Jews in the state that the category barely exists, whether as a cultural entity, a stereotype, or anything else—like "US Senator" (a category with which it's oddly contiguous), "Jewish" is, in Wisconsin, a remote and rarified, if slightly suspect, title.

require, even more so than in most cases, a pure application of public funds: $310 million, which was raised through a controversial .1 percent sales tax on Milwaukee and four surrounding counties.[2] The bulk of the Brewers' contribution, meanwhile, came from a government loan and from leasing the naming rights to Miller—hardly much of a contribution at all.

In his two decades as commissioner, meanwhile, Selig has presided over a steady, massive expansion of the business of baseball. Although the sport's cultural primacy has been in slow decline for decades now, Major League Baseball has become, on Selig's watch, a gargantuan, healthy, and labor-strife-free $6.6 billion business. Smooth David Stern gets most of the press and the props, but you could easily argue that Selig has been the more successful CEO. He's been compensated in contemporary CEO fashion, i.e., absurdly: $18.4 million in 2010. To Milwaukee fans, such numbers beside our former owner's name seem unaccountably strange.

The statue, which stands in a spot of honor near Aaron and Yount, is a good one. It captures a midlife Selig in mid-step, besuited, tie aswing. He holds a baseball in his right palm, and his head is thrust forward, ahead of his body, in a way that's quintessentially Selig—brave, dogged, not to be denied, but also hunched and vulnerable, exposing a slice too much neck to ambushing enemies. ("Given that the guy didn't have much to work with," Selig has said, "I think he did a masterful job.") As I lingered by the statue, several people paused to photograph, or be photographed with, Bud's likeness. All of them did so with a wry irony, sometimes affectionate, sometimes snickering, but always meant to keep the commissioner in his place: Once a little brother, always a little brother.

2. Nowhere was it more controversial than in Racine, my hometown, and the last place to be added to the tax. Racine, an industrial town separated from Milwaukee not only by suburbia but by large tracts of farmland, possesses an identity and a tax base largely independent of Milwaukee. If the argument that a new stadium would contribute positively to "economic activity" seemed dubious in other places, it seemed downright silly in Racine. our state senator at the time, George Petak, cast the deciding vote on the tax, changing his vote from a promised No to a Yes at the last moment. This enabled the stadium to be built, and also got Petak recalled and defeated—the first successful recall election in Wisconsin state history, and thus a bizarre dress rehearsal for this year's even fiercer political battles.

I nside, Miller Park resembles a many-balconied combination of Grand Central Station and an overly flashy NBA arena. Before the game, the Diamond Dancers performed in brief, blue sequined dresses and nude slippers than made them look barefoot, finishing in splits on the warning-track dirt, and this was in keeping with the zonked, casino-like, noon-at-midnight feel of the place. Recently, the original scoreboard was replaced with a gargantuan 1080-pixel display, and a long ribbon of high-def video screen wraps, like a stock ticker, around the face of the third level from pole to pole. Several panels of the left-field wall, weirdly, are also big digital screens.

My dad, as he sipped the dark homebrew he'd smuggled in in plastic Coke bottles, beer—the better to circumvent the rules against glass and alcohol—kept complaining about the screens: Forget the fans—how could the players concentrate amid all that flashing? In this, it seemed, he had an ally in La Russa.

For days Milwaukee talk radio had been consumed by an awful certainty that starter Shaun Marcum wouldn't last into the second inning, and so it happened. By the time the game was 10 minutes old, the Brewers trailed 4–0, and the antsy crowd was booing. A buzzed-blond guy in a green Brewers jersey with shamrocks on the sleeves, loops of Mardi Gras beads around his neck, passed slowly down the aisle, touching elbows like an alderman. "Stay positive," he counseled. "Let's bring plenty of positive energy."

The Brewers kept it close with three home runs in the first two innings, but in the third Allen Craig snuck a painfully slow, bouncy single through the infield, making the score 9–4. The rest was anticlimax: a series of empty rituals. The sausage race used to provide a reliable minute of relief, but within the pixelated swirl of the newly souped-up park it seemed distant and lost. In the top of the seventh, the organ player embarked on a hopeful rendition of Sweet Caroline —then abandoned it after a few bars, as if realizing how gruesome it was to evoke the Red Sox just then.

The crowd clambered gamely back to its feet to begin the eighth—first to will Prince Fielder to start a rally as big as himself; and then, when Fielder tapped weakly to short, to commemorate his 230 home runs; his All-Star MVP; his one missed game in the past three seasons; and the fact that baseball's most electric slugger is a chubby, book-reading 5-foot-11 vegan. They gave a second ovation to gawky 41-year-old utilityman Craig Counsell, who'd subsisted of late on a series of increasingly unlikely one-year contracts, and is unlikely to return.

Late in the game, I took my dad's camouflage binoculars and peered down the first-base stands toward home, trying to catch a glimpse of Brewers owner Mark Attanasio, who always—when he's in town—sits in Row 1, Seat 1. Attanasio presents in Milwaukee as the anti-Selig: an East Coast Ivy Leaguer (Brown, Columbia Law) who made a clockwise progress around the country (born in the Bronx; founded an investment firm in Dallas, which was bought by a firm in L.A.) before purchasing the Brewers in 2004 for $200 million. If Selig seems the quintessential younger brother, Attanasio seems like Mark Cuban's older brother. The two men are oddly alike in their looks and builds and haircuts, and Attanasio is indeed 10 months older and as placid as Cuban is pugnacious. Where Cuban, like Superman, puffs his chest, strains against his tight shirts, and seems always to be exerting himself, Attanasio wears glasses and basic suits and hangs in the background like Clark Kent.

Like Cuban, Attanasio sits front row and brings a boy's bare passion to the game. He's a regular guy with a regular-guy image and several hundred million dollars—he sponsors exhibits at the Milwaukee Art Museum, says only good things, and has presided over as many playoff appearances in seven years as Selig did in 35. And so fans have embraced Attanasio in a way they never did his predecessor, even though—or precisely because—he's a super-wealthy financier who lives and works in L.A. and attends perhaps half of the Brewers' home games. (Selig, on the other hand, still basically lives in Milwaukee, though for two decades he's been running a giant corporation based in New York.)

The transition from Selig to Attanasio—from hometown striver to swooped-in savior, from land-grant scholar to Ivy Leaguer, business to finance, schlumpy to smooth, rich to superrich, and, ultimately, from losing to winning—seemed like a kind of lesson in modern life. If you live in a place like Milwaukee and you're looking to win, you'd better hope for intervention from far-off places. Money and power flow through the coasts, and around the world, but they favor the interior of the country only by happy accident. Brewer fans understood this and welcomed the replacement of Selig, whose chief shortcoming, in the end, was to be too much a part of the place, and so partake of its limitations. Selig, meanwhile, had to move in the other direction—had to leave and go to New York, into the heart of power, to become powerful himself, and to keep helping Milwaukee.

Attanasio had favored our city, and we felt lucky to be the ones he'd chosen. As owners go he's a good one, shrewd and earnest and passionate. But as I sought him with the binoculars, I couldn't help wishing for something else. Because what's an owner, anyway? We know who built Miller Park: the taxpayers, plus the buyers of tickets and jerseys—those same taxpayers. We know who builds all the parks, in all the cities, in all the sports. Wouldn't the whole world of professional sports be better, more transparent, less icky-feeling, if we recognized that it's the fans who put up the money and are, in fact, running the show?

And so I decided, late in the eighth, that the fans would go nowhere when the game was over, would stay put—would, in effect, occupy Miller Park. Would tailgate and tailgate, drink all the beer, organize a 4,000-team double-elimination softball tournament on the gorgeous green field, take turns wearing 10-foot-tall sausage costumes, sleep in the luxury suites until transparency was achieved and the current ownership agreed to sell to the people of Milwaukee—for a price that took into account all the money those fans had already poured into the project—the Brewers of Milwaukee. The roof was closed; we could stay all winter; it could only get so cold.

It was a fantasy, and yet only so far-fetched. Up in Green Bay, of course, there's an NFL team that's owned by its fans, and the method works. It plays in a city of 102,000 people, has a season-ticket waiting list of 83,000, and has won four Super Bowls. Beyond the bare numbers, there's a purity and intensity of devotion on the part of Packers fans that (I might be biased) seems unique in pro sports, and that can't be separated from their unique ownership of the team. No doubt there were hundreds of Packers stockholders in Miller Park at that moment. And didn't they prefer that directness, that clarity, that acknowledgment of the importance of their role? Didn't they prefer to live without the obfuscatory intervention of a single person with enough money to buy the team and sell it at a profit, but without enough money to house it in between? Of course they did. Anyone would. Selig could keep his statue; Attanasio could keep his seats. We would keep the team.

In the top of the ninth, John Axford entered the game. The Ax Man's excruciatingly dissonant entrance song, Refused's "New Noise," had been chosen by fans before the season, and ever since had served to trigger a celebration—the Brewers had gone 68–12 when he pitched. Today, down by six, it was merely excruciating, and it chased the fans from their chairs. By the time it ended, half the stadium's green seats were exposed. My dad and I stayed 'til the bitter end. The red shirts that had been scattered throughout the park collected behind the Cardinals dugout, like blood in the heel of a sock. The red shirts danced through the ninth, celebrating their team's 18th World Series berth.

That Series, thrilling as it was, seemed like a sad formality to Milwaukee fans—nobody believes in St. Louis like we do. Congratulations, Cardinals.

Originally published November 5, 2011

In 1967, Syracuse student Katherine Switzer registered for the Boston Marathon usng her first and middle initials K.V. Race officials attempted to tackle her when they realized she was a woman.

WOMEN ON
THE RUN

*Better runners, faster times, and a whole
lot of mid-'60's chauvinism*

by KATIE BAKER

"It takes getting used to, seeing young women run long distances, gasping and gagging and staggering around and going down on all fours at the finish line, pink foreheads in the mud," began an article in Sports Illustrated in 1966 about the National AAU Women's Cross-country Championship. "But they are young women, all right, make no mistake. The shaved legs, the singlets that actually do a service, all that symmetry, that fragrant hair." One athlete's coach, "a practical man, says it is good that she is trimmer, too, because she is going to be a woman much longer than she is going to be a runner."

So what exactly were the "long distances" writer John Underwood was referring to? A mile and a half. For even the most recreational of racers set to compete in this Sunday's 2011 ING New York City Marathon, that would barely even constitute a warm-up.

If seeing athletes later described as "pretty little dedicated things" compete in that race took some getting used to, imagine the reaction a few months earlier in 1966, when, to quote another *SI* piece, a "shapely blonde housewife" named Roberta "Bobbi" Gibb Bingay snuck onto the course of the venerated Boston Marathon and not only finished the whole damn thing, but did so ahead of nearly 70 percent of the field. Not officially, of course. "Mrs. Bingay did not run in the Boston Marathon," SI quoted the event's organizer as asserting. "She merely covered the same route as the official race while it was in progress."

The next year, a Syracuse student named Kathrine Switzer officially registered for Boston by filling out her entrant form as "K.V. Switzer." When race officials realized what was going on, they tried to tackle her, a move they later defended as a valiant attempt to enforce AAU rules that banned women—for their own good, of course—from competing in any race of more than those 1.5 miles.

I was born in 1983, something of a Title IX-driven sweet spot for a budding female athlete: While my fifth grade travel soccer team was the first all-girls team in our township, just about every other road had already been paved by women that came before, leaving girls my age to concentrate on breaking sweats, not breaking barriers. Which is why it was so surprising to me when I learned that I happen to be older than the women's marathon in the Olympics, which didn't become an event until 1984. It took that long?

What made this even more startling is the fact that these days, there may be no sport more democratic than distance running. Of all the tons of e-mails that come my way every fall from friends fund-raising for their marathon efforts (the surest way to make the race is to do so via charity, as otherwise you're at the whims of the lottery system), probably more than half come from my girlfriends, and when I've stood on First Avenue in Manhattan tracking my friends with newfangled iPhone apps so that I can briefly shout their name as they gazelle or straggle by, the paces between the men and women are largely indistinguishable.

But those are the hoi polloi, the people jogging alongside guys in chicken suits or Oprah. Surely at the elite end, there exists a much wider discrepancy, whether by function of biology or of being held out from distance running for so long. Right? Well, increasingly, not as much as one might think.

Grantland's ace infographer Alex Morrison was looking at the data for the top 100 finishes since the New York City Marathon was first held in 1970 (a low-key affair by today's standards, given that the male winner, Norman Higgins, had come in from Connecticut to run a 5K in the Bronx, entered the marathon on a whim, and won by over ten minutes, still the men's race's largest margin of victory). What Morrison noticed was that, while the top women's times have not necessarily changed substantially over the last several decades, the concentration of runners hovering around them has largely grown.

O ver 47,000 people are expected to participate in this year's New York City Marathon, and that is only a fraction of the number that wanted in: While the event grows yearly, it still shuts tens of thousands out each year. In fact, it has become so large that race organizers recently had to change their policies, grandfathering out or making stricter old rules around guaranteed entry. (The Boston Marathon also recently lowered its already stringent qualifying times.)

As more and more people have "caught the fever," even once-esoteric schools of running doctrine have grown more mainstream: Witness this weekend's *New York Times Magazine* story about the virtues of shoeless running by Christopher McDougall, whose book *Born To Run: A Hidden Tribe, Super Athletes, and the Greatest Race the World Has Never Seen* has become something of a manifesto to hard-core barefoot (or barely-covered-foot) enthusiasts.

While *Born to Run* is most widely cited and well known for its treatment of that topic, it also devotes plenty of space to another evolution-based theory that is just as grand: as distances increase, the gap between male and female performance not only disappears, it can reverse. "No woman ranked in the top fifty in the world in the mile (the female world record for the mile, 4:12, was achieved a century ago by men and rather routinely now by high school boys)," McDougall writes. "A woman might sneak into the top twenty in the marathon (in 2003, Paula Radcliffe's world-best 2:15:25 was just ten minutes off Paul Tergat's 2:04:55 men's record). But in ultras [ultramarathons, which can refer to races ranging from 50 kilometers to 100 miles], women were taking home the hardware."

Runner's World editor-at-large Amby Burfoot, who won the Boston Marathon in 1968, disputes this notion. "That's been a hot topic that's been out there for a millennia and has not been found to be true," he said, adding that the gap between men's and women's runners hovers around 10-11 percent in most races. ("You can bet on it and make a lot of money," he advised.) Still, he said that the sheer numbers of elite female entrants have helped account for more women cracking the top 100 in an event like New York. "Since there are more women and they're getting faster, there are more women at the top," he said. "Obviously women's running is exploding on our front."

New York organizers estimate that 38 percent of marathon entrants this year will be women, up from 32 percent in the early aughts and less than 20 percent a decade before that. Increased participation is not just happening in the marathon. In races of all sorts of lengths put on by the New York Road Runners (the organizing body that manages the marathon), more women than men are competing in the 20–24, 25–29, and 30–34 age groups.

On the elite level, there has been an increase in the number of competitors from two notable sources: traditional long-distance powerhouse nations like Kenya and Ethiopia, whose training programs have grown increasingly well organized and visible to young women—and, particularly domestically—the pool of female runners moving up to the marathon from middle distances.

American Kara Goucher is among the more notable of the latter type. After running World "A" Standard times in track events including 1,500 and

5,000-meter distances, Goucher ran a half marathon in 2007 that was the first race she'd ever competed in over 10,000 meters—and won. She qualified for the 2008 Olympics in the 5,000 and 10,000 meter races, finishing ninth and 10th respectively, and three months later made a stunning NYC Marathon debut, finishing third among women and 34th overall. Her time of 2:25:53 was both the fastest-ever marathon debut, and the fastest NYC time, recorded by an American woman.

"My coach really wanted me to try the marathon," she told the *New York Times*. "I wasn't convinced. The marathon is such a challenge. Just because you can run a 10K well doesn't mean it's going to transfer to the marathon. I kind of fought it … I was terrified of the distance and the pain."

Her training partner, Shalane Flanagan, who earned the bronze medal in the 10,000m in Beijing, made her own marathon debut in 2010 and finished second, the highest finish for a US woman in 20 years.

"It is true that the marathon is the flash point for a lot of women runners," Burfoot said, "Meaning that women who would have stayed on the track in the past in the 5 or 10K are now moving up to the marathon and proving they're very talented and very fast."

It's typical for runners to go up in distance as they move through the ranks of, say, the collegiate level—their natural speed, combined with the increased endurance that can come from more focused training, makes it a worthy strategy. "A lot of people try to resist that for some reason," said Catha Mullen, who ran the mile in high school and moved up to the 5K at Princeton. "I would never have imagined running a marathon as a youngster, or even in college." She finished 11th in New York in 2009 and is now training for the upcoming US Olympic Qualifiers in the event.

What's notable about runners like Goucher and Flanagan, in particular, is how dominant and flat-out athletic they are. Unlike some marathoners who got pushed up in distance because they were middling in strength and speed, those two, among others, are different: They're moving up almost despite being so freaking fast.

Burfoot cautioned that looking solely at the women's share of top 100 overall finishes can be misleading—"it's not a statistic we'd think of as having a lot of meaning," he warned, noting that every marathon is so unique, comprising such ever-changing fields of entrants, that it's not quite an apples-to-apples comparison. (The volatility between 2009 and 2010, for example, is partly a function of the fact that the USA Marathon Championships were hosted by New York those years for men and women, respectively.)

This year will have its own quirks: the US Olympic Qualifiers are being held this January in Houston, meaning most of the United States' top distance runners will be resting rather than running through the five boroughs. Top runners like Kenya's Mary Keitany, Ethiopia's Buzunesh Deba, and New Zealand's Kim Smith will all be competing, however. And the US will still have its own entrants, like Jen Rhines, a three-time Olympian in the 10,000m, the marathon, and the 5,000 who is returning after a five-year break from marathons, and Lauren Fleshman, another middle-distance standout who will be competing in the longer distance for the first time.

Fleshman has her worries. "I'm confident I can handle pain," she told espnW's Sarah Lorge Butler. "I'm confident I can handle the length of time. But my biggest fears come from things like, what happens if I have to, like, go poop? I mean, what do you do? Really. Do you stop or do you just do it?"

Statistics, world records, and "outliers of unfathomable magnitude" aside, it's things like this that show how far women's running has really come. Every pink dot on that chart—and all the ones found beyond the top 100 finishers—represents a new era of "pink forehead in the mud," women running fair and square in a race from which their own mothers were expressly banned. Less than half a century ago, coverage of the sport in major magazines included descriptions of "fragrant hair"—imagine how they'd react to this new kickass generation of fast and feisty ladies.

Originally published November 3, 2011.

ASSOCIATED PRESS

As a result of Switzer's 1967 run, AAU offically banned women from marathons until 1972. Switzer went on to win the New York Marathon in 1974.

THE LITERARY LIFE OF A HOME RUN

Remembering one of baseball's most famous
home runs and the novel that memorialized it

an interview with DON DeLILLO

In honor of the sixtieth anniversary of Bobby Thomson's "Shot Heard 'Round the World," National Book Award-winning author Don DeLillo answered some of Grantland's *questions about writing, baseball, and the historic 1951 New York Giants-Brooklyn Dodgers Game 3 that ended with Thomson's home run. The prologue to DeLillo's novel* Underworld *is set at Game 3.* —Rafe Bartholomew

Rafe Bartholomew: Can you explain how *Underworld* came together? The prologue was first published as a novella, "Pafko at the Wall," in *Harper's Magazine* in 1992, but *Underworld* wasn't released until 1997. When you wrote "Pafko," were you already planning to use that scene as the beginning of a long novel?

Don DeLillo: One day in October 1991, I learned from a newspaper story that this day marked the fortieth anniversary of a famous baseball game played in New York, in the old Polo Grounds, Giants v.. Dodgers. The event was located somewhere at the far reaches of memory, mine and many other people's. But some lingering aura persisted and finally sent me to the library, where I discovered news that startled me: on that same October day, the U.S. government announced that the Soviet Union had recently exploded an atomic bomb. The two events seemed oddly matched, at least to me, two kinds of conflict, local and global rivalries. In time I went to work on what I believed would be a long story and at some point well into the enterprise I began to suspect that the narrative of the ballgame and the atomic test wanted to be extended—well into the last decades of the Twentieth Century. I was eager to make the leap.

When I was working on the novel, I decided that each part's title would derive from an already existing cultural artifact—painting, book, film, musical composition, etc. So I exchanged "Pafko at the Wall", now the novel's prologue, for the title of a Bruegel painting referred to in the text—"The Triumph of Death."

Bartholomew: Do you remember where you were on October 3, 1951, during Game 3? Were you a Dodgers or Giants fan (or Yankees, since you're from the Bronx)? What do you recall about the pennant race, that game, Bobby Thomson's home run, and the feeling in New York that day?

DeLillo: I was at the dentist's office. Dr. Fish. Crotona Avenue in the Bronx. I was a Yankees fan and since they had already won the American league race, the game at the Polo Grounds was simply, from my viewpoint, a method of determining the Yankees' opponent in the World Series. The radio was on in the dentist's office and when Bobby Thomson hit his historic home run—"the shot heard 'round the world"—there was cheering in the office and the waiting room. I sat in the dentist's chair trying to smile, my mouth tight with clamping devices.

Bartholomew: What made you choose that game as a moment to portray America on the cusp of the Cold War and the nuclear age?

DeLillo: That playoff game occurred only six years after the end of World War II and at the beginning of the era to be known as the Cold War. In retrospect, it seemed to me wedged between significant world events as one of the last times in which people's enormous joy brought them out into the streets to run and shout and climb lampposts (but not to set fire to automobiles or ransack appliance stores). The game, for Dodgers fans, constituted a wound so deep that it lingered through their lifetimes. Brooklyn's collective memory still bears the image of [Ralph] Branca's pitch to Thomson. The significance of baseball, more than other sports, lies in the very nature of the game—slow and spread out and rambling. It's a game of history and memory, a kind of living archive.

The game, for Dodgers fans, constituted a wound so deep that it lingered through their lifetimes.

Bartholomew: If you were going to write a novel of similar scope about post-Cold War America and begin it with a scene at a sporting event, what do you think it might be?

DeLillo: To portray America over the past twenty years or so, I would think immediately of football, probably the Super Bowl in its sumptuous suggestion of a national death wish.

Bartholomew: The prologue to *Underworld* contains some memorable appearances from historical figures such as Frank Sinatra, J. Edgar Hoover, Jackie Gleason, and Toots Shor. Which of these characters did you most enjoy writing about? How is it different to construct a character whose life is already partly defined by history as opposed to one who is completely fictional? Do you prefer one over the other?

DeLillo: Gleason, Hoover, Shor and Sinatra were vivid figures to set into the larger landscape of the ballgame and the nuclear test. But in the novel itself, it was Lenny Bruce who posed the serious challenge. His appearances of course are pure fiction and in the novel they served to trace the deep apprehensions of the Cuban Missile Crisis as experienced by one of society's more notorious individuals. The test for me, of course, was to be funny in the way he might have been funny, with the danger of missiles flying into range at any hour or minute. I enjoyed the challenge and felt that Lenny's voice was the urban and ethnic counterpart of the culture of the 1960s that was on the verge of being born.

To portray America over the past twenty years or so, I would think immediately of football.

Bartholomew: In your 1993 interview for *The Paris Review*, you described language this way: " ... the sheer pleasure of making it and bending it and seeing it form on the page and hearing it whistle in my head." This reminds me of sports, the feeling we get when we're absorbed in the game and really playing well. Do you think sports and writing have some common, creative core?

DeLillo: When the work is going well, it can reach a level of spontaneity and unpredictability that is exhilarating—but it doesn't make the writer (not this writer anyway) pound the tabletop. It's an interior sense of satisfaction that's often so fleeting it can't be relived (or even remembered) when the writer revisits the page in a more critical mood the next day or six months later.

Bartholomew: In the same interview, you say that writing "Pafko at the Wall" gave you more pleasure than any of your other writing until then. Was the process of writing the rest of *Underworld* as pleasurable? What made writing the prologue so enjoyable?

DeLillo: Much of the pleasure derived from the fact that I'd grown up playing ball in the street and then in the playground and then on a field in the East Bronx that represented a plea for urban renewal. Of course I'd also followed the game on a major league level. The language and customs were deeply ingrained—a language, baseball's, that is unique and detailed and native-born. This represents an interesting challenge for a fiction writer adapting the language to his particular contexts. When I spoke to a group of foreign translators about *Underworld*, I spent nearly a full day (of three days) exclusively on the idiom and syntax and rules of the game of baseball. They were interested but I think the language remained essentially Greek to them, except for the Greek translator; she didn't know what it was.

Bartholomew: Fourteen years after *Underworld* was published and roughly nineteen years after *Harper's* first ran "Pafko at the Wall," how has the way you look at both pieces of writing changed?

DeLillo: Every so often I am asked to answer questions from translators and these glimpses of the novel tell me that my feelings about the book have deepened through the years. It seems more ambitious to me now than it did when I was working day to day: five years that now seem compressed into the folds and bends of daily routine. It seems new to me, filled with passages that I'd forgotten. I guess it's the response of a man to the culture and literature of a country that never fails to be astonishing.

Originally published September 28, 2011.

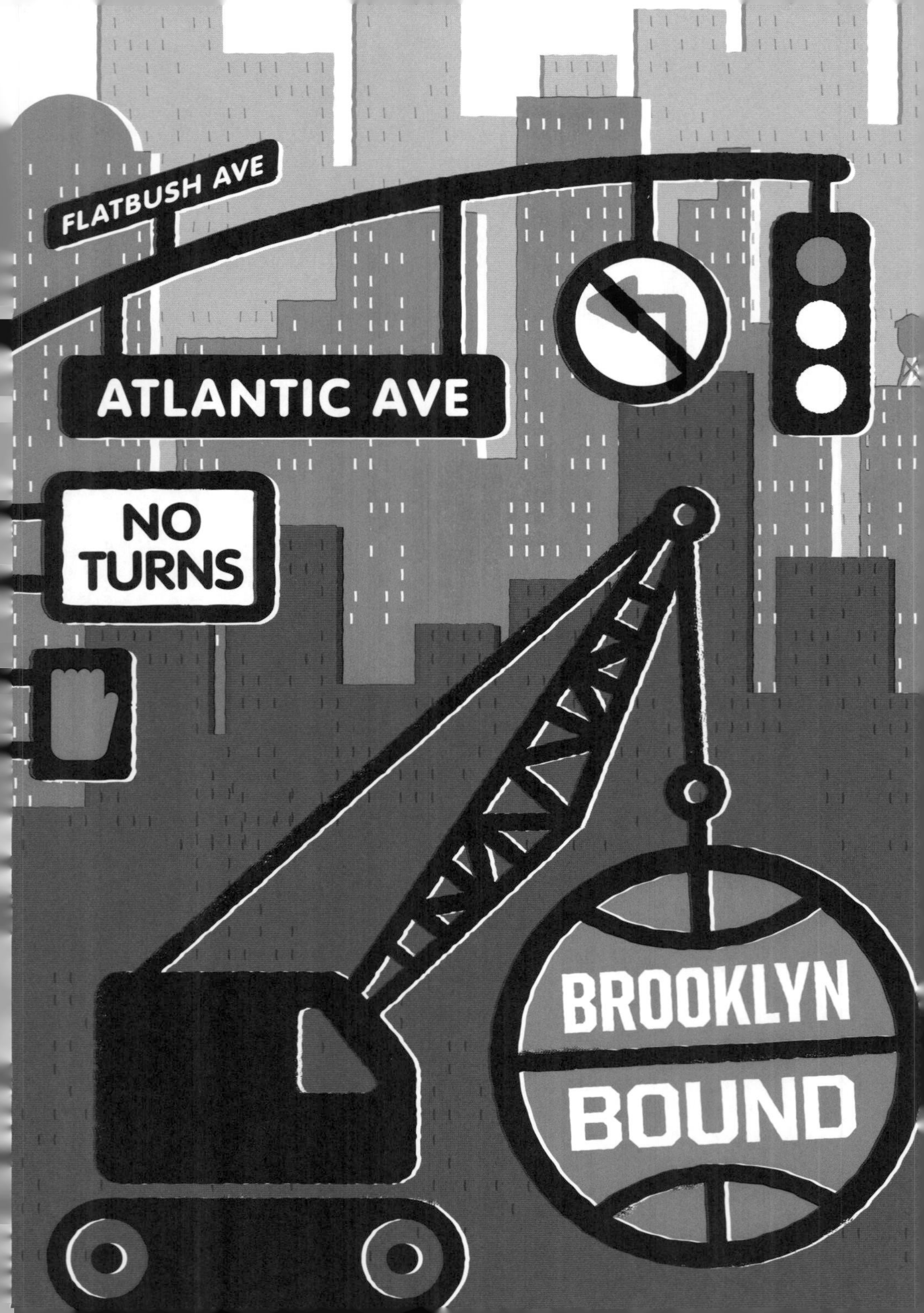
FLATBUSH AVE
ATLANTIC AVE
NO TURNS
BROOKLYN BOUND

THE FALLACY
OF THE NETS

*David Stern would have you believe the franchise
embodies the NBA's financial plight. It's not true.*

by MALCOLM GLADWELL

Ten years ago, a New York real estate developer named Bruce Ratner fell in love with a building site at the corner of Atlantic and Flatbush Avenues in Brooklyn. It was 22 acres, big by New York standards, and within walking distance of four of the most charming, recently gentrified neighborhoods in Brooklyn—Park Slope, Boerum Hill, Clinton Hill, and Fort Greene. A third of the site was above a railway yard, where the commuter trains from Long Island empty into Brooklyn, and that corner also happened to be where the 2, 3, 4, 5, D, N, R, B, Q, A, and C subway lines all magically converge. From Atlantic Yards—as it came to be known—almost all of midtown and downtown Manhattan, not to mention a huge swath of Long Island, was no more than a 20-minute train ride away. Ratner had found one of the choicest pieces of undeveloped real estate in the Northeast.

He gazed longingly at the corner of Atlantic and Flatbush, a light bulb went off inside his head.

But there was a problem. Only the portion of the site above the rail yard was vacant. The rest was occupied by an assortment of tenements, warehouses, and brownstones. To buy out each of those landlords and evict every one of their tenants would take years and millions of dollars, if it were possible at all. Ratner needed New York State to use its powers of "eminent domain" to condemn the existing buildings for him. But how could he do that? The most generous reading of what is possible under eminent domain came from the Supreme Court's ruling in the Kelo v. New London case. There the court held that it was permissible to seize private property in the name of economic development. But Kelo involved a chronically depressed city clearing out a few houses so that Pfizer could expand a research and development facility. Brooklyn wasn't New London. And Ratner wasn't Pfizer: All he wanted was to build luxury apartment buildings. In any case, the Court's opinion in Kelo was treacherous ground. Think about it: What the Court said was that the government can take your property from you and give it to someone else simply if it believes that someone else will make better use of it. The backlash to Kelo was such that many state legislatures passed laws making their condemnation procedures tougher, not easier. Ratner wanted no part of that controversy. He wanted an airtight condemnation, and for that it was far safer to rely on the traditional definition of eminent domain,

---

Know Your A-Holes: Bruce Ratner v. Brett Ratner

Ratner who publicly used an anti-gay slur: Brett

During the press tour for *Tower Heist*, Brett used derogatory language which led to him resigning his position as 2012 Oscars producer. Bruce has an openly gay sibling and is likely more sensitive to the topic.

Ratner most likely to turn up in the Hamptons: Bruce

Bruce recently downsized by selling a $10 million house in favor of a $5 million one. Maybe some of the displaced people of Brooklyn can rent a room in one of its five bedrooms, or in his third home in upstate New York.

which said that the state could only seize private property for a "public use." And what does that mean? The best definition is from a famous opinion written by former Justice Sandra Day O'Connor:

> Our cases have generally identified three categories of takings that comply with the public use requirement ... Two are relatively straightforward and uncontroversial. First, the sovereign may transfer private property to public ownership—such as for a road, a hospital, or a military base. See, e.g., Old Dominion Land Co. v. United States, 269 U.S. 55(1925); Rindge Co. v. County of Los Angeles, 262 U. S. 700 (1923). Second, the sovereign may transfer private property to private parties, often common carriers, who make the property available for the public's use—such as with a railroad, a public utility, or *a stadium.*

A stadium. The italics are mine—or rather, they are Ratner's. At a certain point, as he gazed longingly at the corner of Atlantic and Flatbush, a light bulb went off inside his head. And he bought the New Jersey Nets.

Earlier this year, NBA commissioner David Stern was interviewed by Bloomberg News. Stern was expounding on his favorite theme—that the business of basketball was in economic peril and that the players needed to take a pay cut—when he was asked about the New Jersey Nets. Ratner had just sold the franchise to a wealthy Russian businessman after

---

Ratner who attended NYU: Brett

Brett Ratner graduated from NYU's famous Tisch School in 1990. He was the school's youngest film major at age 16. Bruce Ratner was a law professor at NYU for four years in the early 1970s.

Ratner villified in a 2010 documentary: Bruce

Bruce Ratner is the villain of *Battle for Brooklyn,* which chronicles the Atlantic Yards saga over seven years. The film lays out its anti-Bruce politics by telling the story of a Brooklyn resident who becomes the lone of occupant of his apartment building. Brett Ratner was an executive producer of 2010's *Catfish*—the Facebook movie before *The Social Network*—which wasn't free from controversy. Critics questioned the movie's authenticity.

Ratner's genius was in understanding how beautifully the Nets could serve [his] purpose.

arranging to move the team to Brooklyn. "Is it a contradiction to say that the current model does not work," Stern was asked, "and yet franchises are being bought for huge sums by billionaires like Mikhail Prokhorov?"

"Stop there," Stern replied. "... the previous ownership lost several hundred million dollars on that transaction."

This is the argument that Stern has made again and again since the labor negotiations began. On Halloween, he and the owners will dress up like Oliver Twist and parade up and down Park Avenue, caps in hand, while their limousines idle discreetly on a side street. And at this point, even players seem like they believe him. If and when the lockout ends, they will almost certainly agree to take a smaller share of league revenues.

But Stern's success does not change how strange the NBA position is. There is first of all the hilarious assumption that owning a basketball franchise is a business—at least as that word is used outside of, say, the president's mansion in Pyongyang.[1] But beyond that is a second, equally ridiculous assumption, which is that the economics of basketball teams are principally about basketball. As it turns out, they are not.

Bruce Ratner's original plan for the Atlantic Yards site called for 16 separate commercial and residential towers and a basketball arena,

---

Ratner who is hated by his hometown: Brett

Everyone in Miami may not despise Brett, but the *Miami New Times* called him the "douchey embodiment of Miami's general sense of entitlement" and "a crude, loudmouth brat." Nonetheless, Brett keeps strong ties to Miami, and

Ratner whose family connections could rival a mafia family: Bruce

Bruce's grandfather started a lumber and construction company in the 1920s that has grown to today's Forest City Enterprises. FCE provided an infusion of cash to the Atlantic Yards project in 2006. The tentacles of FCE stretch across many states, though they are based in Cleveland.

all designed by the superstar architect Frank Gehry. The development would be home to roughly 15,000 people, cost in excess of $4 billion, total more than eight million square feet, and make his company—by some calculations—as much as $1 billion in profit. To put that in perspective, the original Rockefeller Center—one of the grandest urban developments in American history—was seven million square feet. Ratner wanted to out-Rockefeller the Rockefellers.

Ratner knew this would not be easy. The 14 acres he wanted to raze was a perfectly functional neighborhood, inhabited by taxpaying businesses and homeowners. He needed a political halo, and Ratner's genius was in understanding how beautifully the Nets could serve that purpose. The minute basketball was involved, Brooklyn's favorite son—Jay-Z—signed up as a part-owner and full-time booster. Brooklyn's borough president began publicly fantasizing about what a professional sports team would mean for his community. The Mayor's office, then actively pursuing an Olympic bid, loved the idea of a new arena in Brooklyn. Early on, another New York developer, Gary Barnett, made a competing play for the railway yard. Barnett's offer was, in many ways, superior to Ratner's. He didn't want the extra 14 acres, so no land would have to be expropriated from private

1. This was the point of my first Grantland piece. An NBA franchise is not really a business. It's a luxury good, like a piece of art, which means that making calculations about profits and losses makes no sense. Since then, TrueHoop's indefatigable Henry Abbott dug up this gem from Cleveland owner Dan Gilbert. It dates back to before the lockout. Gilbert, let us recall, has been one of the ringleaders of the players-are-greedy brigade.

"To me, NBA franchises are like pieces of art. There are only thirty of them. They aren't always on the market, especially a franchise that would have been such a natural fit. … If you just looked at the Cavaliers in terms of revenues, profits and balance sheets—and you paid this amount

---

Ratner who shares an ex-girlfriend with Common: Brett

Brett famously dated Serena Williams in 2004. The reason for their break up has never been confirmed, but rumors circulated blaming Brett's partying with Jermaine Dupri and Puff Daddy. Both Serena and Brett must have a fondness for rappers—she went on to date Common.

Ratner mired in litigation: Bruce

Bruce is being sued by construction workers who claim they were promised union jobs that have not panned out. Ratner is also tied to a New York state corruption case, though he is not officially charged with any wrongdoing. Arguably, though, both Bruce and Brett have already lost their cases with the general public.

owners. He wasn't going to plunk a small city down in the middle of an already crowded neighborhood. And he tripled the value of Ratner's offer. Barnett lost. He never had a chance. He wanted to build apartments. Ratner was restoring the sporting glory lost when the Dodgers fled for Los Angeles. As Michael Rikon, one of the attorneys who sued to stop the project, ruefully concluded when Ratner's victory was complete: "It is an aphorism in criminal law that a good prosecutor could get a grand jury to indict a ham sandwich. With regards to condemnations in New York, it can fairly be said that in New York a condemnor can condemn a Kasha Knish."[2] Especially if the kasha knish is being eaten to make way for a professional basketball arena.

Ratner has been vilified—both fairly and unfairly—by opponents of the Atlantic Yards project. But let's be clear: What he did has nothing whatsoever to do with basketball. Ratner didn't buy the Nets as a stand-alone commercial enterprise in the hopes that ticket sales and television revenue would exceed players' salaries and administration costs. Ratner was buying eminent domain insurance. Basketball also had very little to do with Ratner's sale of the Nets. Ratner got hit by the recession. Fighting the court challenges to his project took longer than he thought. He became dangerously overextended. His shareholders got restless. He realized he had to dump the fancy Frank Gehry design for something more along the lines of a Kleenex box. Prokhorov helped Ratner out by buying a controlling interest in the Nets. But he also paid off some of Ratner's debts, lent him $75 million, picked up some of his debt

This wasn't a fire sale of a distressed basketball franchise. It was a general-purpose real estate bailout.

for it—people would say 'You're insane! You're nuts.' But if you look at all the tentacles, the impact on our other venues, it makes tremendous sense. We have now opened a Cleveland office [of Quicken Loans] and that's tremendously successful. Our employees love it that we're associated with the Cavs and can come to games—that helps us attract and keep better people. There are a lot of nonprofit things that can be done with pro sports. It brings an unbelievable amount of excitement."

What's the matter, Danny? Don't like your Rembrandt any more?

2. Kasha is whole-grain buckwheat—Jewish soul food—and some would argue the only appropriate filling for a knish. Curious? Try Knish Nosh on Queens Boulevard and 67th Road in Queens—if for no other reason than that is the best restaurant name *ever.*

service, acquired a small stake in the arena, and bought an option on 20 percent of the entire Atlantic Yards project. This wasn't a fire sale of a distressed basketball franchise. It was a general-purpose real estate bailout.

Did Ratner even care that he lost the Nets? Once he won his eminent domain case, the team had served its purpose. He's not a basketball fan. He's a real estate developer. The asset he wanted to hang on to was the arena, and with good reason. According to Ratner, the Barclays Center (the naming right of which, by the way, earned him a cool $400 million) is going to bring in somewhere around $120 million in revenue a year. Operating costs will be $30 million. The mortgage comes to $50 million. That leaves $35 million in profit on Ratner's $350 million up-front investment, for an annual return of 10 percent.[3] "That is pretty good out of the box," Ratner said in a recent interview. "It will increase as time goes on." Not to mention that the rental market in Brooklyn is heating up, the first of Ratner's residential towers is about to break ground, and his company also happens to own two large retail properties directly adjacent to Atlantic Yards, which can only appreciate now that there's a small city going up next door. When David Stern says that the "previous ownership" of the Nets lost "several million dollars" on the sale of the team, he is apparently not counting the profits on the arena, the eminent domain victory, the long-term value of that extra 14 acres, or the appreciation of Ratner's adjoining properties. That is not a lie, exactly. It is an artful misrepresentation. It is like looking at a perfectly respectable kasha knish and pretending it is a ham sandwich.

And let's not forget Mikhail Prokhorov. How does he feel about buying into the financial sinkhole that is professional basketball? The blog NetsDaily[4] recently dug up the follow-

3. The economics of stadiums, of course, deserves its own separate article. But here's a small point, courtesy of my friend David Goldhill. Most stadiums—the Barclays Center included—are subsidized in some way by local government. The logic is this. An arena will bring a certain level of new economic activity to a neighborhood, which will generate tax revenues. So it makes sense for a city to put some portion of those expected revenues toward the construction of an arena. NBA owners love these deals. If there's no basketball season, however, then the tax revenue cities bank on to pay for their investment disappears. Goldhill says that in that case, owners really ought to reimburse the municipalities that gave them money. But has anyone even mentioned this possibility? The NBA plutocracy voted not to play basketball right after taking money from local taxpayers on the

ing quotation from a 2010 interview Prokhorov did with the Russian business newspaper Vedomosti:

> *We have a team, we're building the arena, we've hired professional management, we have the option to buy into another large project, the building of an office center. For me, this is a project with explosive profit potential. The capitalization of the team will be $700 million after we move to Brooklyn. It will earn approximately 30 [million]. And the arena will be worth around $1 billion.*

Let us recap. At the very moment the commissioner of the NBA is holding up the New Jersey Nets as a case study of basketball's impoverishment, the former owner of the team is crowing about 10 percent returns and the new owner is boasting of "explosive" profits. After the end of last season, one imagines that David Stern gathered together the league's membership for a crash course on lockout etiquette: stash the yacht in St. Bart's until things blow over, dress off the rack, insist on the '93 and '94 Château Lafite Rothschilds, not the earlier, flashier, vintages. For rich white men to plead poverty, a certain self-discipline is necessary. Good idea, except next time he should remember to invite the Nets.

O ne of the great forgotten facts about the United States is that not very long ago the wealthy weren't all that wealthy. Up until the 1960s, the gap between rich and poor in the United States was relatively narrow. In fact, in that era marginal tax rates in the highest income bracket were in excess of 90 percent. For every dollar you made above $250,000, you gave the government 90 cents. Today—with

promise that they would play basketball. How do these guys sleep at night?

4. NetsDaily is really very good. Even better is the brilliantly obsessive coverage of the Atlantic Yards project at Norman Oder's Atlantic Yards Report, in which every twist and turn in the entire story has been faithfully and astutely chronicled. I could not have written this without Oder's help.

good reason—we regard tax rates that high as punitive and economically self-defeating. It is worth noting, though, that in the social and political commentary of the 1950s and 1960s there is scant evidence of wealthy people complaining about their situation. They paid their taxes and went about their business. Perhaps they saw the logic of the government's policy: There was a huge debt from World War II to be paid off, and interstates, public universities, and other public infrastructure projects to be built for the children of the baby boom. Or perhaps they were simply bashful. Wealth, after all, is as often the gift of good fortune as it is of design. For whatever reason, the wealthy of that era could have pushed for a world that more closely conformed to their self-interest and they chose not to. Today the wealthy have no such qualms. We have moved from a country of relative economic equality to a place where the gap between rich and poor is exceeded by only Singapore and Hong Kong. The rich have gone from being grateful for what they have to pushing for everything they can get. They have mastered the arts of whining and predation, without regard to logic or shame. In the end, this is the lesson of the NBA lockout. A man buys a basketball team as insurance on a real estate project, flips the franchise to a Russian billionaire when he wins the deal, and then—as both parties happily count their winnings—what lesson are we asked to draw? The players are greedy.

Originally published September 25, 2011.

UN ROBO!
UN ROBO!

Pacquiao fights Marquez,
and no one wins

by JAY CASPIAN KANG

The night before the third fight between Juan Manuel Marquez and Manny Pacquiao on November 13, I went to visit the world's oldest tree. A stout, white church stood in the tree's considerable shadow, and up in the belfry, a man in a nylon parka was pounding out a crazy, incoherent rhythm on the three bells. In a nearby garden populated with hedge animals (fake), a young man was lying on his back on a patch of turf (also fake). At random intervals, he would flap his arms and legs, as if to make imaginary snow angels. The bells kept banging, and it occurred to me that the person up in the belfry must be insane. For the next 10 minutes, I waited for the man to stop. He did not stop. I began to wonder if I might have died in some car wreck and if maybe my soul had been transported into a Mexican purgatory where the tree is old, massive, and elegant, but where the bells won't stop clanging and never fall into any pleasant or, at least, predictable rhythm.

Right when I was about to admit my confusion to my tourmates, the clanging stopped, the young man stood up from his turf angels, and everyone calmly walked toward the garden's gate.

Twenty-four hours later, I was in a taxi headed to a bar where they had promised to show the fight. I had never met the couple in the cab with me, but both were nice and tried their best to speak to me in English. The guy, who looked exactly like a young Paul Giamatti, was telling me about how he didn't like Canelo Alvarez because "Canelo is TV creation," and how true Mexican boxing fans identified more with Juan Manuel Marquez. One thing I've always loved about boxing is how its fans, without malice, can sit and talk in ethnic and racial absolutes. You can describe a fighter as truly Mexican, load it up with a lot of implications, and not have to worry about the fallout. Which is to say, I was agreeing that Juan Manuel Marquez was a true Mexican warrior, and even though Manny Pacquiao and I are both Asian, I told my new friends that I hoped that Marquez would make a good showing for his home country. My new friend said, "Marquez, if he wins tonight, he is the best Mexican fighter of his generation. It is so hard right now to pick between him, [Marco Antonio] Barrera, and [Erik] Morales, but if Marquez can beat Manny, it will be clear."

We arrived at the bar at the end of the first round. Two hundred people were scattered around long, banquet-style tables. There were bottles of mezcal in the center of each of these tables, and everyone seemed to be in a good mood. When we sat down, the TV was showing Marquez on his stool. Nacho Beristain was saying something encouraging. The scorecard flashed and read: Marquez 10, Pacquiao 9. And although we would all come to learn that there was nothing official about that scorecard, everyone in the crowd roared with approval. Without much warning, the coverage quickly cut to a buxom, scantily clad girl, who, after mouthing the word "Tecate" (or, at least, that's what I assume she said, as she was wearing a Tecate T-shirt), poured water all over her breasts. This ad ran between every other round, alternating with an ad for Mexico City's Marxist newspaper.

With about a minute left in the second round, I turned to my new friend and asked what the hell was going on. Earlier that day, I had predicted that Manny would stop Marquez in the sixth because I thought Manny would be too fast and that at some point he would pivot or hop to the side and land the same punch he used to drop Ricky Hatton. Marquez had not looked particularly sharp in his past two major fights and hadn't carried the weight well in his fight against Floyd Mayweather. Manny, as everyone knew, got better as he got bigger. He had also become a smarter and more balanced boxer. It was difficult to imagine that he would fall into the same lunging patterns that had played into Marquez's hands in their first two fights.

But from the opening bell to the late-middle rounds, Manny seemed stuck in the past. Every time he went forward, Marquez answered with precision counterpunching. At the end of the seventh round, the Mexican TV scorecard read: Marquez 69, Pacquiao 64. It made sense. Manny was clearly frustrated, confused. Marquez had whipped himself into a rare focus. I asked my friend if he had ever seen Marquez this good, this sharp, this strong. He shook his head and said, "He is ready, I think, to be Mexico's champion."

It must be said that Mexican boxing television is about as impartial as U.S. Olympic coverage. Because the producers had to make time for the Tecate girl and the Communist newspaper, there were only a few seconds for the requisite super-slo-mo, face-melting replay. Every big punch that made it to replay was thrown by Marquez. But even if the TV bias had gone the other way and the crowd of 200 had been cheering for Pacquiao, all the promotional bluster in Manila couldn't have covered up what was becoming obvious: Marquez was not intimidated. He was landing harder punches, and although Manny was throwing more punches, Marquez was either picking them off or ducking his head into Manny's midsection to slow him down.

For the first six rounds, Manny kept lunging forward and Marquez kept tagging him in the forehead and the torso with counterpunches. After the fight, Freddie Roach would say, "I asked Manny to move to the right and he didn't." Maybe this was related to foot cramps that bothered Manny throughout the fight, but I took Manny's refusal to adapt as evidence of a hard truth about boxing: Fighters are mostly set in their styles. Manny did not step to the side because he became one of the all-time greats by lunging straight at his opponent.

Why would he have thought that fighting a 38-year-old he has already beaten would be any different?

M aybe it's because I read too many silly novels as a child, or maybe it's because I had been drinking too much mezcal that weekend, or maybe it's because of the world's oldest tree and the discordant, random bells and the young man making turf angels, but everything about Saturday night's fight felt surreal. As the rounds went on and Marquez kept pounding Manny with counterpunches, I began to accept that the invincible Manny Pacquiao was going to lose. But what I was witnessing bore no resemblance to what I had expected—perhaps, more than anything, the measure of a sports superstar is that when he struggles, and struggles badly, you feel as if the natural order of the world has been upended. And yet, there was also something inevitable and machine-like about Marquez's domination. By the sixth round, I had given up on the knockout. By the eighth, I wondered again if I had died in a car wreck on some Oaxacan freeway and had awoken into some drunken stereotype of a Mexican dream state. My friend felt similarly. He asked, "What the fuck is going on?"

It occurred to me that the uneasy, floaty feeling might have been a side effect of the brainwashing I was receiving from Mexican boxing television. But then I wondered if maybe I was just being un-brainwashed about Manny Pacquiao, who achieved his invincible status by fighting a broken Oscar De La Hoya, a pretender in Ricky Hatton, a possibly broken Miguel Cotto, a thoroughly uninterested Joshua Clottey, a possibly broken Antonio Margarito, and a shot-to-all-hell Shane Mosley. After Saturday night, the angle on Manny's past three years should shift a bit—is he the all-time great who moved up in weight or is he the smiling, marketable star of a desperate sport? Maybe he's both? I certainly couldn't tell—all I knew was that when HBO wasn't carrying the fight and when I wasn't hearing Manny Steward talk about all-time greats, Pac-Man didn't look the same.

As the fight moved into the ninth round, my head was in my hands. I kept picturing the press conference after the fight. Manny somberly saying, "I tried very hard, and I am sorry to my people and all my fans. He is a great fighter, and I am hoping I can fight him again so I can prove myself." Then Marquez saying, in Spanish, "Justice is finally mine. I beat him twice before and nobody gave me my credit. Today, I proved to everyone who is the better fighter." I even felt a little bad for Floyd—after this fight, he would clearly be considered the great fighter of his generation, but only because Manny had fought poorly against a man he had dominated just two years before.

Manny began his comeback in the ninth round. He finally stepped to the side and hit Marquez with a couple of combinations. The focus of the early rounds appeared to be breaking up. But Marquez wasn't done, either—he fought back gamely and landed a few of his own power shots. Given the score at the time, which, by my count, was six rounds for Marquez, two rounds for Manny, it didn't feel as if there was enough clock left for Manny to stage a comeback on the scorecards. It didn't really look like Manny thought much differently. The 200 in the bar started muttering about how all Marquez needed to do was not get knocked out. He could lose the next three rounds and still be far enough ahead on the cards to win by decision.

Instead, Marquez kept each of the last three rounds close while mostly avoiding the big shot. By the 11th, both fighters looked exhausted and the prospect for a knockout seemed far-fetched. The crowd began shouting, "Marquez! Marquez!" in anticipation. And when the final bell sounded after the bizarre 12th, in which Manny seemed to understand that he needed the knockout but couldn't quite gather himself to go after it, the bar erupted into cheers. As we watched each fighter's reaction— Marquez ecstatic and proud, Manny clearly crestfallen—the cheering continued. Because I was still confused, I began complaining: What the hell was Manny doing the entire fight, and why didn't Freddie Roach tell Manny to stop lunging straight into Marquez's counterpunches, and what the hell fight we were going to see next. The decision felt like a formality. After flashing a 117–111 score for Marquez, the footage on the TV switched over to the four Mexican ringside announcers. They looked beside themselves—the unthinkable had happened. Juan Manuel Marquez, the fighter most emblematic of the country's fighting spirit, had finally broken through.

As the footage switched over to a split screen that showed both men awaiting the official decision, my friend said, "Manny looks depressed. This is great."

And then Manny was jubilant, jumping up in the air like Rod Roddy just told him to come on down and be the next contestant on The Price Is Right. The bar filled with a chorus of boos and chants of "Un Robo!" I was in shock. I had scored the fight 116–112 for Marquez. I felt awful for Marquez, who fought a perfect fight. I felt awful for the people in the bar who had been ready to crown Marquez as the great fighter of his generation. But mostly I felt awful for myself and all the time I have spent over the past years trying to make sense of this corrupted, dying sport. The bout I watched was a dominating win by the fighter who was willing to make adjustments and outsmart his faster, stronger opponent. Manny threw more punches, but they reminded me of the "more punches" Oscar De La Hoya threw in his bout against Floyd Mayweather.

In that fight, the defensive, precision puncher clearly won on the cards. This, from what I had seen, was a similar victory. As some of the crowd shuffled angrily toward the exits, a stranger grabbed me by the arm and said, "Fucking Bob Arum, man. Fucking Bob Arum. He would not give Marquez a chance. That is why Marquez was so big and strong for this fight, because he knew he would have no justice unless he knocked out Pacquiao. Fucking Bob Arum, man."

I couldn't have said it better. Fucking Bob Arum. Fucking boxing. For 12 rounds, Marquez and Pacquiao put on a show. Marquez clearly emerged the better man. Even Manny, who slunk off to his corner after the final bell, seemed to understand that.

My friend said he never wanted to watch boxing again. He said he had always loved Manny but hated him now. I agreed with never wanting to watch boxing again and pointed out that in the States, idiots like me routinely shell out $60 to watch this garbage. As I was walking out of the bar, I looked up at the TV and saw Bob Arum with Marquez, who was having his gloves cut off.

Arum looked like he was apologizing.

When I got back to my hotel, I was shocked to find that a number of boxing writers whose work I admire had scored the fight much differently. One scored it a draw. The other scored it 115–113 for Marquez. Another had the fight 115–113 for Manny. And so I did what very stupid people on the Internet do when they're upset: I took my anger to Twitter. Before long, someone had tweeted back at me that neither side had lost the fight. Marquez would get paid off huge in the rematch, and Manny would get to continue his reign at the top of boxing.

I have no idea what fight the judges watched, but before the decision was announced in that bar in Oaxaca, the fight had one clear winner and one massive loser. The winner would have a redefined role in boxing history—he would now be considered one of the smartest and toughest fighters of all time. The loser's role in history would also change, albeit not as badly as some might have thought. Manny's first two bouts against Marquez would be reexamined, but for the most part, the story of Manny Pacquiao would be of a great champion who had just one guy he couldn't quite figure out.

Wouldn't that have been a pretty good ending?

Instead, both sides lost. But the biggest loser on Saturday night was the sport of boxing. No matter what HBO says over the next few months, Manny has been diminished. And Marquez, understandably devastated, has hinted at retirement. Who can blame him? He has nothing to gain in the ring anymore—the sport won't give him a fair shake against the one opponent who can change his legacy. I wouldn't be surprised if he beat up Erik Morales and never fought again. His legacy is secure in Mexico. He has more money than he'll ever be able to spend. Why would he submit himself to all the bloated pageantry of another Las Vegas PPV fight?

To say that both sides won because Manny, Marquez, and Bob Arum will get paid stinks of the rampant cynicism that has spread across the sports landscape. To be a fan these days, you have to pretend to be able to adjudicate TV deals, salary caps, contracts, advanced statistics, and whatever else makes one dude look smarter than the other guy at the bar. Who cares what Manny and Marquez might get paid for a rematch? Is it somehow worthwhile to humiliate the sport so that two people you will never meet can make even more money? It is exactly this sort of cynicism that allows for farces like a 116–112 scorecard in favor of Pacquiao.

People are already looking forward to the next fight and speculating about the payday.

Let's stop talking about the power of the almighty dollar and call the fight for what it was: a robbery. The almighty dollar isn't even ours.

Un robo! Un robo! Un robo!

Originally published November 14, 2011.

"WHEN YOU'RE TALKING ABOUT DATING AN ATHLETE, IT'S MORE THAN JUST THE MONEY."

(Jalen Rose and David Jacoby, continued from 117)

JACOBY: Carolina Panthers quarterback Cam Newton is allegedly dating Ciara. Why do so many women in the spotlight gravitate toward athletes, especially basketball players?

ROSE: Wow, strong. This is what makes our podcast special, huh? We give the people what they want, huh? I think Ciara is a different case—and I know Ciara by the way, I spent time with her, we have mutual friends in the industry. So we've been in the same place at the same time.

JACOBY: Are you name-dropping right now? You're name-dropping!

ROSE: You brought her up!

JACOBY: Okay, okay, pick that name up off the floor again and continue.

ROSE: She's a different case because she has a name on her own. So, for example, somebody like Cam Newton was a high school kid watching Ciara sing, "My goodies, my goodies, my goodies, oh my goodies!" He says, "Yum! If I'm able to meet her, I would holler at her in a minute!"

JACOBY: Yes, he wanted goodies.

ROSE: Just so happened he was the number one pick in the draft, doing his thing. Now he's in a position to meet her. So, allegedly, they met, and they've been seen in the same place at the same time, in Atlanta. But other women who don't have the platinum-selling status of a Ciara that seem to gravitate toward basketball players in particular: Football plays once a week.

JACOBY: Sixteen weeks a season.

ROSE: The NBA is eighty-two games, plus the play-offs. The stage is bigger. It becomes a bigger opportunity.

ROSE: So you're telling me if you're Kim Kardashian, for example, that your reason for dating a basketball player is because of the exposure of being at the game in the front row.

ROSE: Remember, when you're talking about dating an athlete, it's more than just the money that he makes. He has a platform that he is responsible for. He has some type of professional team that monitors that he's living up to a certain standard. There are some built-in safety nets that come with a professional athlete. And you get eighty-two games, plus play-offs. The stage can be bigger.

A HAUNTED HOUSE FOR THE RECESSION ERA

The real estate conundrum of American Horror Story
goes beyond your standard foreclosure

by TESS LYNCH

The problem with haunted-house stories are that the solution seems so obvious: just leave the house. Put it on Craigslist and find a good real estate agent sometime between after the faucet starts leaking blood and before you ever explore the screams coming from the basement. Sell your car and move into a beige condo with one bathroom. Leave while you have your life, and figure the rest out later.

American Horror Story, however—the everything bagel of haunted-house sagas—seems a more relevant and less impossible scenario now than it ever would have before: it is more difficult to leave a house, if you're lucky enough to be in the shrinking group of people who have the money and confidence to buy one in the first place, than it was before the housing crisis began. Selling your home, especially one with jars of babies in the basement and constant solicitations from a disfigured man who needs money for his acting head shots, is difficult; finding another place while your haunted mansion sits on the market makes the reluctance to leave even more forceful. The Harmons, the family around which *AHS* revolves, are struggling financially, and of course, like many supernaturally staged homes with kitchen islands of horror, the house has an additional psychological pull on them that makes them stay. Dylan McDermott's character Ben runs his psychiatric practice from the house, no longer able to afford an office, and it would be understandably difficult to see patients in a tiny corporate apartment. They're stuck—stuck in a modern way.

American Horror Story, besides being a sometimes over-the-top buffet of gore, is one of the most chilling television shows I've seen. The Harmon family—Ben, his wife Vivien (Connie Britton) and daughter Violet (Taissa Farmiga)—move into their new digs after a cross-country relocation, an attempt to outrun the effects of Vivien's miscarriage and Ben's adultery. It doesn't work, of course. His mistress knocks on the door of their new house, and Vivien becomes pregnant again under questionable circumstances, yielding ultrasounds that must look something like an uncut Aphex Twin video. The link between a new home and a new start is as unrealistic as it is comfortingly familiar, especially since the mortgage crisis proved that not as many of us owned our homes as we thought we did. Instead of being afforded a chance at reinventing themselves, the house reveals the Harmons' secrets to a network of gossipy neighbors, former occupants of the Tiffany-lamp Victorian, even more so than it divulges its own ghostly past. Those secrets tend to push the envelope further than television usually dares: Last week's installment featured a high school massacre scene, and each week's episode is an unpredictable event. Subjects like miscarriage— rarely touched on as frankly as it is in *American Horror Story* —infidelity, and psychotic maniacs dating your teenage daughter are threaded throughout each episode, less afterthoughts to the blood-and-guts violence than the real source of fear.

One thing you never do, if you live in a haunted house, is open the door. In the episode "Home Invasion," *American Horror Story* proved why: Not opening the door doesn't ensure you won't be murdered, but it drastically reduces your chances. Since 2007, many homeowners in arrears have found the same advice to hold true when it comes to answering a knock: a woman named Nancy Jacobini told Business Insider in 2010 that she called 911 when she thought she heard someone breaking into her house. It was a man sent from her bank to change her locks after three months' delinquency in mortgage payments. Banks and ghosts exert the same kind of force on the occupants of their property. If they really want to, they can get you out. The Chicago Tribune claimed in July that people feared foreclosure almost as much as they feared death, and since *American Horror Story* has been picked up for a second season, we must assume that in at least some cases, they fear it even more.

It is, in many ways, scarier to think about the idea of death of the nuclear family than of the home-ownership wing of the American Dream. I prefer to think that the American Dream has more to do with choice and equality than having your own carport and being able to paint the walls without asking permission, and that people can enjoy this dream even if they have to have a landlord. But though nuclear-family formats aren't appealing to everybody, its fans are getting a little frightened, finding themselves unable to afford housing and moving back in with their parents or other relatives. Besides the feeling that this lands us back in a mopey adolescent state, lazily throwing laundry onto the floor out of habit and sleeping in rooms that still carry the fug of angst and slammed doors, reclaiming your cubicle in your childhood home as an adult can feel like being stripped of your privacy and independence. The time needed to prepare a face to meet the faces that you meet is rarely afforded a person who shares walls and a roof with four other people; whether under duress or in a moment of carelessness, you may forget to conceal the evidentiary clues that spell out your private problems to your parents, grandparents, or children. The more guarded you are, or the more you have to hide, the more this can make you feel like a hermit crab robbed of its shell, looking very small and easy to squish.

The superstition of keeping a pregnancy secret for the first twelve weeks is rooted in medical fact: That's when a woman is most likely to experience a miscarriage. You are advised not to go public, even to close family or friends, because in the event of a miscarriage, they would know. And it's so intimate: It involves blood details too personal and biological to share. We don't often see it on television, perhaps, because we don't often discuss it in our lives; moving home, accepting its occupants as part of your everyday family, means that some of the gore of human life is intruded upon and requires explanation. The dark things that live within your relationships—the cheating, your teen's self-abuse, the loud arguments—creep into the shadows of the kitchen as your retired dad stands in front of the refrigerator looking for cold cuts. Sometimes it's just a shadow, other times you see the face.

The Harmons' neighbors—especially Jessica Lange as nosy and diabolical Constance from down the block—are so well-acquainted with the spookiness of the house that they become instrumental in its bummer trips on the Harmon clan. There's a reason for this: At some point, they've all lived in the house, which we now know has the power to sublet itself to past owners vacationing in Los Angeles on a break from the afterlife (if this perk were included in the MLS page, I think a lot of Los Angelenos would go for it. Most of us would be happy to put up with some carnage in order to come back from beyond to get some In-N-Out).

There are no secrets in this haunted house: The histories of past domestic shames are graffitied all over it, like the creepy pentagrams and missing toilets in vandalized foreclosed properties. The crimes (locking your kid in a closet, shooting your husband, blackmail) and arguments about the wallpaper (Zachary Quinto appears as half of a bickersome undead couple to mumble, zombie-like, "I feel like I'm doomed for all of eternity to be trapped in an unhappy, adulterous relationship, working on this goddamn house. Which will never be just the way I want it"), accumulated over the course of a century of hopeful residents, are made worse when they are discovered by the strangers linked by having shared an address. It's the addition of shame and guilt to these actions that happens when they meet the air, after the house has stopped magnetically attracting your finger to the trigger. Keeping secrets in a house that contains more souls than you expected is impossible. There are bloodstains, and someone's always lingering in a doorway offering his or her opinion or catching you in the act. Even in an unhaunted home, grandma is not olfactorily impaired enough that she can't smell the cigarette you blew out the bathroom window. It is generally not as catastrophic as, say, being impregnated by an evil apparition, but it involves an acceptance of the fact that your least flattering dimensions may become public to the strangers who make up your extended family, your genetic roommates.

L ast week, pregnant Vivien was cajoled into eating plate after plate of raw offal by her shape-shifting housekeeper (Frances Conroy). She sat at the table and cautiously but politely dug into some pancreas and a glistening brain while listening to her maid explain its prenatal benefits. It is hard not to relate this to the oft-repeated legendary parental tale of having to eat everything on the plate to avoid embarrassing the martyr-like family cook, usually your grandpa or grandma. The housekeeper appears to Vivien as a motherly, somewhat stern figure, doing more than is required of her with a steely old-fashioned work ethic; to Ben, she looks like a vacant-eyed sexual panther who's always scrubbing the floor in lacy underpants, which is a complicated psychological horror story in itself (Boardwalk Empire's Jimmy Darmody knows this, as does Stacy, immortalized by Fountains of Wayne). The tension created by this maid dual-personality is not unlike the tension that arises when a grown married couple moves back in with one set of parents: the redefinition of roles, the assertions of adultness, the misinterpretations of intent. Exposing your parents' inherent weirdness, which you always accepted as normal, to people who might not find it so but who are equally important to you. The natural passive-aggression of multiple cohabitation: I made you this brain. Eat, eat.

The Harmons' teenage daughter, Violet, is an interesting foil to Constance's daughter Addy (Jamie Brewer), a grown woman with Down syndrome who lives with Constance and often escapes to the Harmons' house, usually appearing to giggle in the basement and deliver cryptic news. While tormented Violet is staying out past curfew and exploring her sexuality with an evil floppy-haired suitor, Addy is stuck in the grip of her controlling mother, who locks her in closets and tells her she'll never be pretty. Constance stops short of wire hangers, but that's presumably due to the fact that Addy becomes indisposed a few episodes in. She's in a place where wire hangers can't hurt her anymore. Being a teenager is equal parts vulnerability (acne, not being able to make a decent grilled cheese sandwich, submitting to being grounded) and rebellion (sad experiments in self-mutilation, screaming at people to leave your room so loudly that they do so, accepting in advance the consequences of staying out late in order to continue to make out with a senior on the beach), and emerging as an adult on the other end requires learning to balance your responsibility to other people with gratifying yourself as an individual. What frightens us the most about being labeled as "extended adolescents": the vulnerability or the renewed need to clothe our vices and private indulgences in whispery secrecy? Even if the door on your old bedroom has a lock, you're likely to remember how your parents urged you, three feet tall, to never, never lock it.

Why is it so gratifying to see these characters sucked up in a cyclone of misery? Maybe because for the first time in a long time it doesn't seem so improbable. It hints at newly recognizable anxieties, not just the stranger knocking on the door after dark but the stranger knocking on the door and demanding a thousand dollars that don't exist (whether for head shots or the cable company); Vivien and Ben are as frightened, as desperate in the meeting with a Realtor about putting their house on the market, as they are when a recently bludgeoned corpse shows up in the bathtub. People are almost as afraid of foreclosure as they are of death. Maybe it's because sometimes it's the house that haunts you, but more often it's you who haunts the house.

Originally published November 17, 2011.

AL MICHAELS
in conversation with
BILL SIMMONS

On October 14, legendary Sunday Night Football *announcer Al Michaels returned to Bill Simmons's podcast. They discussed, among many other things, what makes a strong broadcasting team.*

BILL SIMMONS: You must have been a little worried that you weren't going to find the same rhythm with [partner] Chris Collinsworth that you had with John Madden. I feel like you've been better with Collinsworth. That's a little bit controversial. He has invigorated you about 15 percent, and I thought you did a good job with Madden.

MICHAELS: I've said this before, and I'll say it again: I had seven years with John, four at *Monday Night Football.*

SIMMONS: You have to be a tiny bit deferential with him because it's John Madden. You have to, even if you don't know you're doing it.

MICHAELS: I had DiMaggio, and then I got Mantle when DiMaggio retired. That's how I look at these guys. The great thing about John Madden is that when we started together in '02, we knew it was going to work. The first game we did was the Hall of Fame game in Canton, OH. We got to the first commercial and I felt like I had been working with John

for fifteen years. When you have a great on-air relationship with a partner, you don't think about the mechanics of who is going to talk when.

SIMMONS: It sounds like a real life relationship.

MICHAELS: Exactly.

SIMMONS: If you're analyzing what's happening in your relationship all the time, it's probably not going well.

MICHAELS: I had seven years with John. They were fantastic. It shocked me when John retired after the Super Bowl in January '09, which may have been my favorite game ever to do. Arizona v. Pittsburgh. You could make a case for it being the best Super Bowl.

SIMMONS: Two of the best plays in Super Bowl history.

MICHAELS: I thought our production crew had a phenomenal night. Every picture was perfect. Our guys in the truck were singing. I thought John had a tremendous game. I never had a greater feeling walking out of a booth than after that game Everybody was on the same page. So it shocked the hell out of me when John retired.

Then I got Chris. I found Chris by watching a game, maybe 17 years ago. He was doing a college game. I said to my wife, "That guy's good!"

(Continued on page 203.)

SPOELSTRA IN THE PHILIPPINES

The Miami Heat coach invigorates
a nation of basketball fanatics

by RAFE BARTHOLOMEW

Somewhere north of the U.S. Embassy in Manila the white charter bus carrying Miami Heat coach Erik Spoelstra made a wrong turn. The group, which included Spoelstra, two NBA employees, a handful of bodyguards, and a driver, was headed toward Torres High School, where Spoelstra planned to lead a basketball clinic. For now, however, they found themselves crawling through the cramped alleyways of Tondo, the most densely packed district of the world's most densely populated city, where more than 600,000 people scrape out a living in three square miles along the banks of Manila Bay. While the panicked driver jabbered into his cell phone about a missed stoplight, Spoelstra and company stared through the windows at Manila street life: pedicabs zipping around the lumbering bus; children being bathed in plastic basins along the sidewalk; and freelance trash collectors pushing wooden wheelbarrows, beseeching anyone in earshot to donate "diyaryo't bote"—newspapers and bottles. Block after block, the coach saw homemade basketball hoops, some with rims bent out of repurposed rebar and others with plywood bed frames serving as backboards, hanging over street corners and tucked away in narrow walkways. The game was everywhere.

A couple of miles away, another bus sat parked in a courtyard within Torres High School. Inside were Heat assistant coaches David Fizdale and Chad Kammerer, two NBA Asia employees, and Spoelstra's sister, Monica Spoelstra Metz. Outside the van were more than a thousand restless teenagers eager to see the NBA's only half-Filipino head coach. Actually, the students were excited to see pretty much anyone foreign. I made it three steps past the school's gates when a swarm of young girls and boys spotted me and started shrieking. A few kids screamed "Younghusband!"—a reference to Phil Younghusband, the Filipino-British star of the men's national soccer team who dates a famous actress and appears topless on canned-tuna billboards. No one actually believed I was Younghusband; they only meant that I looked foreign enough to be someone worth squealing over, that I must have come from somewhere far away from Tondo. And they were right—I had arrived earlier that morning on a Philippine Airlines flight from Los Angeles. I had dropped in on the middle of Spoelstra's weeklong trip to the country, and would be spending the next four days following him around to basketball clinics, mall appearances, and family gatherings.

That morning, I walked to Torres from an elevated train stop near Manila's Chinese cemetery. A block from the school, a hearse drove by me, blasting what sounded like an '80s Peter Cetera ballad. The name JHEREMIAH was stenciled in the window in yellow bubble letters, and I wondered if Jheremiah was the name of the undertaker's son or the deceased. My guess: the former. This, among other things, is what I love about the Philippines. The country keeps you guessing, and I hoped that somehow, in the midst of a stage-managed NBA tour or Manila, I'd get a chance to see Spoelstra interact with this side of the country.

Spoelstra's trip to Manila was part of the NBA FIT program, the league's initiative to promote healthy lifestyles, and his visit to Torres was cosponsored by the Philippine Department of Health. Until the coach arrived (Spoelstra's bus had lost its way and would arrive 20 minutes late), however, the students would have to settle for his assistants. As it turned out, this was not a problem. When Fizdale and Kammerer stepped down from the bus, a crowd of schoolgirls in uniform orange blouses and ankle-length maroon skirts erupted in applause, cheers, and shrieks.

The initial frenzy wore off just as Spoelstra arrived. The coach said a word of thanks and swiftly began coaching. "Stance!" he shouted, and the kids bent their knees and stretched their arms in a defensive position. "Good!" Then a five-second pause. "Up!" The pattern—"Stance! Good! Up!"—continued for five minutes. A few of the students looked up; their black bangs were sweat-plastered to their foreheads and a hint of panic was in their eyes. Usually, these visits from basketball royalty involve little more than high-fives, layup lines, and pats on the back. NBA Asia's Ed Winkle crept behind me and whispered in my ear, "Once he gets going, I don't think he can differentiate between these kids and his players."

S poelstra, whose mother hails from San Pablo, a midsize city about two hours south of Manila in Laguna province, has traveled to the Philippines in each of the past three summers. Spoelstra spent two of his afternoons during this year's trip at the Mall of Asia's activity center, an open-air atrium looking out on Manila Bay. The NBA lined up an array of demonstrations and workshops, all highlighting exercise and proper nutrition under the NBA FIT banner. When called upon, Spoelstra dutifully extolled the virtues of eating right and regular exercise. NBA FIT's cause was a worthy one, and especially necessary in the Philippines, where a typical diet might consist of little more than white rice and pork or—if you're on a budget—white rice and canned sardines. Close to 12 million Filipinos suffer from high blood pressure, and local pharmacies sell glucose-regulating dietary supplements in designated areas called "Diabetics Corner." Among the several hundred mall-goers who stopped to watch Spoelstra, dozens probably would do well

to heed the NBA's advice—"go for a jog; eat a salad"—but it was easy to see how that message could get lost amidst the slate of restaurants surrounding the activity center. They included fast-food staples such as Burger King, Chowking, and Jollibee; Dennis the Grill Boy, whose window signage promised UNLIMITED RICE; a pork-rind emporium called Guby's Chicharon Espesyal (they also sold fried chicken skin and chicharon bulaklak, which are deep-fried pork intestines); and the Spam Jam kiosk.

Spoelstra may not be able to single-handedly save the Philippines from its love of fried pork fat, but he certainly managed to connect with his heritage and Filipinos' affection for basketball. At an event at the Mall of Asia in Manila, he delivered a version of the spiel he closed almost all of his appearances with: "Remember, there is nothing better than being here in this open air with this ball and this basket. That's life right there. Respect this game, and it will respect you back." Coming from almost anyone else, that line might ring false—just another boilerplate-gilded sports cliché. But coming from the mouth of an NBA head coach, and hearing it in the Philippines, where millions of people really do plan their days around afternoon pickup games, neighborhood tournaments, and broadcasts of the local college league, it sounded simply golden. Throughout the mall people stopped chattering, pocketed their cell phones, and nodded along with Spoelstra's words.

S ince 2009, Spoelstra has been making up for the years he never got to spend in the Philippines. If he was initially worried about how people would receive him, he's grown more comfortable with each successive visit. "I don't think he really felt Filipino until he went there," said Fizdale, who has accompanied Spoelstra on all three trips. "Then he got to the country and saw his upbringing reflected in everything."

That process started with a clinic in Zamboanga City, a regional hub in the Philippines' far south, a frequent battleground in the ongoing armed conflict between the Philippine government and Muslim separatists. "ZAMBOANGA CITY" is the dateline you see when bombs explode in a public market or a couple of Westerners get kidnapped; it is not typically the first place sports luminaries are brought when they visit the Philippines. But the 2009 tour was sponsored by the U.S. Department of State, which is always keen to send something other than military aid to Southern Mindanao, so Spoelstra and his assistants were enlisted as basketball envoys to win some hearts and minds.

When they arrived at the gym, they found an entire neighborhood gathered inside—not just the players slated to participate in the clinic, but also their younger siblings, mothers, fathers, uncles, and grandmothers. Security guards holding machine guns and assault rifles surrounded the court and guarded the doors. About 200 kids and teenagers stood on a single full court. As Fizdale remembered it, some wore basketball sneakers, some had on dress shoes, many sported flip-flops, and others were barefoot. All were ready to play, but the clinic's organizers brought only a handful of basketballs. To make the coaches' job even more challenging, many of the young *Zamboangueños* spoke very little English and not even that much Tagalog, the Manila-centric basis for the Philippines' national language. The predominant language in Zamboanga is Chavacano, a kind of Spanish Creole, so Spoelstra and his assistants ended up developing a crude hoops sign language and relying on jump-stop-pivot drills and defensive slides to occupy the throng of players.

"The kids picked things up just by watching," Spoelstra said. "We would demonstrate and they would just mimic it right away with such athleticism and coordination. It was incredible." After the workout the players sat down for a question-and-answer session. "We were like, 'Come on, they don't speak English. What are they gonna ask?'" Spoelstra said. Then, with help from a Chavacano interpreter, the kids started *rattling* off questions about Dwyane Wade's contract situation heading into the 2009–10 season and answering trivia questions about Bill Russell's career. "That blew us away," Fizdale said. "When you realize that these kids have nothing and they live in these circumstances and they still know Dwyane Wade's scoring average over the last three years? That's how we could tell what a big deal hoops was."

This story is an excerpt from a longer essay originally published September 27, 2011. The complete text can be found on Grantland.com.

John Brandon Presents:

THE HUNKS

OF COLLEGE

FOOTBALL

Stephen Garcia

SENIOR QUARTERBACK, SOUTH CAROLINA

HEIGHT 6'2" | **WEIGHT** 232 | **HAIR** Was rocker, now gym coach
EYES Mischievous | **HOMETOWN** Tampa, FL | **OFFENSE STYLE** Late-life spurrier
PERSONAL STYLE Devil-may-care casual

Ladies,

Enough of these goody-goodies timidly toeing the straight and narrow, putting pie-in-the-sky team goals ahead of the clear and present aspiration of getting mad fucked-up. You're young, ladies. You're in college. No children to rear or mortgages to keep pace with. A sense of humor is fine and dandy, as is the earning potential attached to a snooty degree from that book-readin' geekery Vanderbilt University, but admit it: There's nothing like a bad boy. There's nothing like a Dylan McKay. There's nothing like a Jordan Catalano. And there's nothing like a Stephen Garcia. Nobody understands him—not the cops, not those alumni who don't deserve him, not even the Ol' Ball Coach, who used to flout a little convention himself. They're all old, Stephen is young. They'll never change him no matter how short they cut his hair. He's got an NFL receiver to throw to, an NFL tailback to hand off to, and a seeming desire to watch them from your cuddly couch for the next ten years of Sundays. Like Randall "Pink" Floyd before him, your Stephen will never sign that paper. He's too busy L-I-V-I-N. And don't you hate that brown-nosing Connor Shaw, waiting for Stephen to screw up so he can jump in and save the day? Doing every little thing he's told. Getting named the opening week starter. He makes you sick, that, that … game-manager! Connor Shaw is the type of guy your parents are always nagging you to date, but you want a guy who does what he wants when he wants, who doesn't let a leadership seminar get in the way of a bitchin' day-buzz. You're only young once, ladies, and Stephen's only got one more shot at an SEC crown.

Justin Blackmon

JUNIOR WIDE RECEIVER, OKLAHOMA STATE

HEIGHT 6' 1" (maybe still growing because he seems taller than that, doesn't he?) | **WEIGHT** 215 | **HAIR** Faux hawk | **EYES** Brown | **HOMETOWN** Ardmore, OK
OFFENSE STYLE Effective | **PERSONAL STYLE** Loose-limbed alertness

Ladies,

I know I'm always full of pep, always filling you with hope and esteem, but there's also something to be said for choosing your battles. There are lots of fish in the sea and lots of receivers on the gridiron. Justin won't be in the League for another year, but he's already way out of your league. Scout and Rivals missed on this stud, but you won't have to regret missing out on him because you never had a shot. They gave him three stars, sweetie, but for you he might as well be in another galaxy. Don't cry. I don't mean to be harsh. You've got your charms, especially all gussied up in that orange dress you found the last time you went into Tulsa, standing on the porch with your hands clasped behind your back, mock-shy, spinning a toe into the varnished planks. You're sure pretty, just not as pretty as the Ardmore Assassin as he glides effortlessly under a fade pass in the back corner of the end zone, holding a defensive back off like a little brother—smooth stride, soft hands, six more points. Corralling this Cowboy is too big a job for the DBs of the Big 12, and it's too big a job for you. I just don't want you to get hurt. His coach is a man and so is Justin, and, after all, you're just a little girl, a tiny-town girl with a spunky streak and a tight-in-the-waist baby doll dress you got at the Promenade Mall. Justin's season can only end with Bedlam, and the best place for you when that sort of chaos hits is near the hearth in Daddy's living room.

John Brantley

SENIOR QUARTERBACK, FLORIDA GATORS

HEIGHT 6'3" | **WEIGHT** 219 | **HAIR** Brown | **EYES** Deer-in-headlights
HOMETOWN Ocala, FL | **OFFENSE STYLE** Pro-style this year, thank Jesus
PERSONAL STYLE Bangs-tossing country casual

Ladies,

You've had enough of spending whole days at the salon, of picking up salads at Panera instead of sitting down and enjoying the Alice Springs Chicken and a Foster's, of burning away afternoons in the tanning bed and then picking out that perfect sexy-but-not-slutty ensemble, only to go out on the town with your man and have him check out every other girl in sight. None of that with John Brantley. If you're his primary, he'll lock onto you and stare, stare, stare, come hell or high water. It'll be like those other gals don't even exist. John needs confidence, ladies, and between your stand-by-your-man ways and Charlie Weis' pro-style offense, he'll have quite the support system. Nab this bruised beefcake while he's low, like a stock with solid fundamentals, before he shows why he was once chosen as Gatorade Player of the Year. He's got a golden arm, an orange helmet, vanilla quotes for the media, and a heart full of red, American blood. Be the gal to get that blood pumping, something Urban Meyer could never manage to do, and you just might find yourself in the dreamiest two-person huddle in Gainesville.

RISE OF THE BLUR OFFENSE

How do you call a play
without calling a play?

by CHUCK KLOSTERMAN

JOEL KIMMEL

The NFL is complicated. In fact, the NFL is so complicated that it almost looks simple.

Every team is trying to trick whoever it's playing on virtually every down on both sides of the ball (in a recent *Sports Illustrated* article, Saints coach Sean Payton suggested the single most important word in modern pro football is confusion). The game has become so internally sophisticated that even the semiserious fan has no chance of really understanding what's happening on the field. Yet this sophistication has a paradoxically static impact on how the sport looks: To the casual eye, most NFL offenses seem more similar than different. The various formations are not identical, but they're all relatively close (only the Wildcat is totally dissimilar, and that's mostly a gimmick). In 2010, the club that passed the most (Indianapolis) threw only

13 more times a game than the team that was dead last in attempts (Chicago). A platitude endlessly parroted by broadcasters is that the NFL is "a copycat league," but it's one of those platitudes that's true: Because the level of athleticism is so high, there are only certain things that work. The smartest guys and the dumbest guys know all the same secrets, and it pushes the whole game toward a virtual singularity.

But move down one level, and things start to change.

Watch a major college game, and the action gets weird. You immediately see plays that simply can't happen[1] in a pro game. At the subdivision and Division II tiers, things get stranger still. And by the time you hit Division III, you begin to see football games that are more philosophical than technical. With no athletic scholarships and extremely limited resources, football becomes a game in which the system matters more than the play calling or the personnel. The polarities become acute. This is where you find the most extreme versions of contemporary football: This is where you find teams that still live in the 1950s and teams trying to play basketball on grass. This is the level where football changes—and also where it doesn't change at all.

L ast October, Maine Maritime Academy defeated Westfield State University, 42–21. That score was probably mentioned in a few newspapers, but that doesn't make it news; this was a Division III game between two members of the New England Football Conference, hosted by a town with a population of 1,300 and a community aesthetic matching Cujo. But there's one detail about this contest that made it unlike almost every other college football game from 2010: Maritime won by three touchdowns while passing for exactly 0 yards.

1. Easy example: When Baylor played TCU in the opening week of the season, Baylor quarterback Robert Griffin III threw a lateral bubble screen to the right side of the field—and then he broke into the secondary and ran a post pattern. As a QB, Griffin caught a pass 15 yards downfield, in traffic, on third down. This couldn't happen in the NFL for two reasons. For one, no one would ever try it. For another, NFL quarterbacks are eligible to catch passes only when they line up in the shotgun (and Griffin started the play under center, making the play even more visually unorthodox than it already was).

They rushed for 435, but they passed for none (they threw the ball just five times, and the only one that didn't hit the ground was an interception). Even weirder, the Mariners managed to win without controlling the clock—Westfield had a greater time of possession. Yet as unorthodox and lopsided as those numbers seem, they were only slightly crazier than most of Maritime's 2010 schedule: The Mariners went 6–1 in their conference, scored more than 46 points a contest, and somehow averaged 16 passing yards a game. The week after beating Westfield, Maritime defeated Framingham State 50–26, again throwing for 0 yards. The week after that, they knocked off Massachusetts Maritime by a single point—and here, again, they won without a single passing yard. They went 5–0 in October with 63 total passing yards (not 63 per game, but 63 for October). Half their team stats seem like misprints; last season, the Mariners' starting quarterback appeared in 11 games and completed a total of 17 passes. But this is how the Mariners want it. This is the design. This is the most reactionary offense in America.

"I don't care what everyone else is doing. I've never been like that." Mariners coach Chris McKenney tells me this while sitting in his office. McKenney is like a football coach from a 1970s Afterschool Special: He's got short hair and a walrus mustache. He wears khaki shorts and a blue polo shirt. He'll turn 50 this fall. He's built like the small college linebacker he used to be. He still says all the things football coaches used to say when LBJ was president. "I don't care how many passing yards we get. I love to run the football. And this kind of option attack is as much finesse as it is physical. The mentality we use is to just keep running the ball and running the ball and hammering away, and eventually things will pop open."

The option attack Maine Maritime employs is a hyperquick adaptation of what you see from Georgia Tech or at any of the service academies: the "modern" version of the Wishbone, with the two tailbacks lined up at each wing. A skeptic would argue that no Division 1 team could succeed by being this extreme, and that's probably true; even Paul Johnson's run-obsessed Yellow Jackets threw for more than 1,000 yards in 2010 and attempted almost 13 passes a game. But Maritime is a special case: It's a Division III school with 900 (mostly male) students and some inherent recruiting limitations, most notably the fact that almost all the academic majors are focused on nautical careers (it's not a military school, but the students still take regimen training and wear uniforms). Part of the reason this option scheme exists is because it works so well within those parameters— you can succeed with undersized linemen and "untraditional" athletes at the various skill positions. And Maritime's success has been remarkable, at least numerically: Last year, it rolled up 5,538 yards of total offense, 94 percent of which came on the ground.[2] There really isn't a corollary for this kind of one-sided assault; McKenney doesn't seem particularly influenced by anyone. Over lunch in the Maritime cafeteria, I ask him if he recruits kicking specialists or just tries to find someone on the roster who can handle PATs. He tells me that the Mariners' placekicker is technically a nose guard. A few years ago, Maritime went for two points after almost every touchdown. The Mariners would just stay on the field and run the option again.

"I haven't attempted a field goal in the 10 years I've been here," he says. "Why kick a field goal?"

2. That equates to 5,189 rushing yards, which was just seven fewer than the most statistically efficient option team ever—the 1971 Oklahoma Sooners. "The guys on the team all knew that. They were disappointed we didn't beat Oklahoma," says McKenney. "Personally, I had no idea we were that close. But that's the Internet."

W hen LSU hammered Oregon on the first Saturday of the 2011 season, it did so by making the Ducks play in a manner they despise: They made them play slow. This is pretty much the only way Oregon loses anymore—if a physical team can consistently contain the Ducks on first down, they need time to think about what they want to run on second and third down, and that deliberation makes them no different from any other team in the country. But Oregon absolutely kills people when it plays fast. The Ducks' Chip

Kelly is the architect of the "Blur Offense," which is not so much a play-calling scheme as a design for life. The concept of using a nonstop, no-huddle offense is not new (Sam Wyche did it in the 1980s with the Cincinnati Bengals), but that tactic was originally employed to stop the defense from making situational substitutions. It was pragmatic. The Blur is more like a psychological weapon. Its premise is that a simple offense snapping the ball every 15 seconds is more effective than a complicated offense running at regular speed, because an accelerated tempo manufactures its own momentum. It's the reason so many of the Ducks' opponents seem to tire and collapse (in 2010, they outscored opponents by an average of three touchdowns in the second half).

Even after its 40-27 loss to the Tigers, nobody disputes Oregon's status as the fastest team in the country. But it's not the only team that plays like that—it's just the one people want to copy. Amherst College[3] is one of those programs. The Lord Jeffs'[4] 2010 statistics aren't as mind-warping as Maine Maritime's, but they're almost as dominant: They outscored their opponents by about 16 points a game (they put 70 on the board versus Tufts University). What's especially intriguing about Amherst is its rapid evolution from the past to the future, skipping the present almost entirely. When Amherst coach E.J. Mills took over the program in 1997, they ran a two-back, pro-style offense that mostly involved handing the ball to the tailback and eating the clock. It was almost an "anti-Blur" posture, and it was fairly successful. But one mediocre autumn was all it took to scrap everything.

"In '07, we went 4–4. It was not a good season," says Mills, a man who looks and talks like a noncrazy Les Miles. "I felt we'd become too easy to defend. If we couldn't knock the snot out of people, we didn't have much to offer. We had

3. Dedicated ESPN readers may remember this passing mention of Amherst by Gregg Easterbrook in a 2010 story about the Ducks.

4. This is really their nickname. "Lord Jeff" was Jeffrey Amherst, an 18th-century British military commander who conquered Montreal (among other things). It's also the title of a 1938 movie about a loathsome orphan, but this is probably a coincidence.

to spread things out. And that evolved into what we do now."

What the Lord Jeffs now do is orchestrated by Don Faulstick, the team's offensive coordinator. He designs and calls all of Amherst's plays (Mills is primarily a defensive specialist). A former college quarterback with a master's degree in criminal justice, Faulstick is exceptionally good at explaining how the details of football work—unlike most coaches, he does not avoid questions or speak in empty clichés. He's straightforward. What the Jeffs run on offense seems most akin to Oregon, but the genesis for their system actually comes from Troy University: In 2006, coaching svengali Tony Franklin[5] took over an anemic Troy offense and immediately led the Sun Belt conference in passing. Faulstick was curious as to how this happened, so he called the coaching staff and directly asked them how they did it.

"I just went to Troy and said, `You guys are really good. What is the key to this passing game? What's makes you so good at this?'" Faulstick says. "And they were like—listen, it's not about the plays. It's about the tempo. It's about lining up and pressuring the defense and wearing them out. You don't need a perfect play in this offense. You just need a good play."

What this means is that Amherst is not concerned with how defenses intend to stop them, almost to the point of ignoring what the opponent is doing—if the Jeffs offense is worrying about the defensive scheme, it means they're playing too slow. This is not how things worked in the past; 10 years ago, Faulstick focused on picking the ideal play for whatever specific situation he happened to be facing. He responded to whatever look the defense presented. Now he mostly worries about the speed of play. Amherst huddles fewer than five times a game (usually only in goal-line situations). It essentially has three running plays that can go in

5. Franklin has made a cottage industry out of his offensive philosophy: He's now a well paid consultant who sells "The Tony Franklin System" (as well as his views of life) on the lecture and clinic circuit.

either direction (an inside run, an outside run, and a power with a pulling guard). Like the University of Nevada, the base set is the pistol. The Jeffs' offensive lineman stay in a two-point stance. When they're on a hash mark, they go into an automatic formation called "Cheetah" (which sets three receivers to the wide side); if the ball's in the middle of the field, the automatic formation is called "Queens" (a balanced attack with two receivers on each side). The intent of every detail is to make things happen faster, because that's when things seem to work—or vice versa.

"I suppose it's kind of a chicken-or-the-egg situation," Faulstick admits. "Do you play better when you play fast, or do you need to play well in order to play fast? That's the question."

T he wishbone has been around forever," McKenney constantly reminds me, and—though not technically true—it's at least as old as the modern age of football. The wishbone was created by Texas high school coach Charles Carson in the mid-'50s and became the dominant collegiate offense by 1970. It's almost never seen anymore (Air Force[6] was the last team to succeed with the classic wishbone as its base formation in 1985), but just about every program built around a triple option attack is still using a modern variation called the "flexbone": Instead of keeping the two halfbacks in the backfield, they are flanked just outside the offensive tackles. The fullback is still lined up directly behind the quarterback and serves as the dive back (he's the first option). The QB keeper is the second option, and the wingback swinging around from the weak side is the pitch back (he's the third option). When you watch a team like Navy or I-AA Georgia Southern, you'll

6. Air Force managed to get as high as no. 2 in the country that year, as late as the 13th week of the 1985 season. It finished no. 5 in the final coaches poll.

notice that the pitch back sometimes goes in motion just before the snap to get depth and create separation from the quarterback. Obviously, this motion telegraphs the direction of the play. But that barely matters. When the triple option succeeds, it's not because the defense is fooled; it's because the defense is forced to make difficult decisions about a something it fully anticipates.

McKenney uses the flexbone as Maine Maritime's base set. However, he's made a couple of adjustments that appear unique to this program. The first is that his fullback is lined up extremely close to the quarterback—instead of being three yards behind the line of scrimmage, he's right on the QB's tail. And unlike most of his option peers, McKenney almost never puts the wingback in motion before the snap. Instead, the wingback flies straight down the line (without much depth). As a result, the quarterback is sometimes forced to pitch the ball to a running back who's uncomfortably close to him. This is all done for the sake of speed—a Maritime option play unspools quickly and with a high degree of risk. But the rewards are massive: In 2010, senior fullback Jim Bower led the nation in rushing with 1,915 yards and scored 20 touchdowns. Quarterback Matt Rende ran for another 1,333, and the two halfbacks combined for 1,600 while averaging 10 yards a carry.

"The personal keys for me are the center, the quarterback, and the fullback," says McKenney. "It's those three guys, right down the middle. And if I can't find the kind of guy I need, I'll build one." Bower (who graduated with more than 6,000 career rushing yards) had been an oversized tailback before McKenney turned him into a fullback. Rende was a skinny wide receiver until his last year in high school and had never run the option; he's now a 190-pound All-American candidate, even though McKenney admits that, "Rende would be a defensive back anywhere else."

Maritime's style is defined by the things it doesn't do. It has a handful of shotgun formations in the playbook, but McKenney has never used the shotgun in a game. The Mariners don't have a single pass play in which the quarterback takes a seven-step drop. They use the I-formation maybe

10 times a season, and McKenney can remember only two plays involving trap blocks in all of 2010. They don't punt very often—when faced with third-and-long, they typically run the option and try to create a fourth-and-short situation, and then they just go for it. "I go into a game thinking we have four or five running plays and maybe two or three passing plays," McKenney says flatly. Those five running plays are as follows:

1. The true triple option. (This is Maritime's bread and butter—it's the fullback running off the guard, with the QB-RB pitch option to the outside.)

2. The midline option. (This involves the fullback diving straight over the center—and because of his lack of depth, the fullback hits the hole almost immediately. The rest of the play is the same as the triple option.)

3. The veer option, which Maritime refers to as the "wide dive." (In this scenario, the fullback is running over the offensive tackle—it's a little tougher than usual because of the fullback's tight alignment.)

4. The counter option. (The fullback goes to the left while the QB and the pitch back go to the right, or vice versa.)

5. The wingback counter. (As the triple option flows in one direction, the playside wing breaks against the flow and takes a handoff the other way.)

Part of what makes this offense so atypical is the gap between how hard it is to execute and how easy it is to learn.[7] Running the triple option requires an insane amount of repetition: Maritime practices those five core plays over and over and over, constantly perfecting the "mesh"[8] between the

7. "My playing calling in high school was much more complicated than my play calling is

quarterback and the fullback and striving to make all aspects of the option look identical on every play. It requires intense discipline and endless, mechanical rehearsal. However, learning this offense is amazingly easy. A typical Mariner play is "Shoot 48." The word "shoot" is the name of the formation (it's the standard Maritime flexbone, with a wing on each side and two split ends). The number "4" is the play itself (the triple option). The number "8" represents the play's direction (in this case, it means the play is going left). That—in four syllables—tells everyone in the huddle everything they need to know, because the blocking schemes are dictated by how the defense aligns itself. A play like "Shoot 42 Counter" is a little more complicated, but not by much: "Shoot" is same formation as before. The "4" describes the action of the play (here, again, it's a triple option—and to the defense, it should look exactly like Shoot 48). But the number "2" dictates that the play is coming back to the right,[9] and the inclusion of the word "counter" means the wingback is taking the handoff and running against the grain.

I'm informed of all this verbiage while watching film with McKenney in the Maritime football office with two assistant coaches. Since I'm writing down the names and numbers of everything he's showing me, McKenney half-jokingly asks if I'm going to publish the literal names of his plays. "Does it matter if I do?" I ask in response, and he just laughs and says nothing. Because here's the thing: It doesn't matter. Most of the time, it wouldn't matter if Rende texted whatever they were running directly to the opponent's middle linebacker. Maine Maritime runs the same five plays 80 percent of the time; if you're aware that this football program exists, it might be the only thing you know about it. And that's to its advantage.

"It's OK if teams know what we're doing," McKenney

here," says QB Rende, who attended a high school (Cony, in Augusta) with a larger student population than Maritime's. "We had all this pro-style language. It's actually easier at this level. I don't know how many other college quarterbacks could say that."

8. The "mesh point" (sometimes called "the ride") is when the quarterback places the ball into the stomach of the fullback and looks at the hole where the fullback is headed. What the QB wants to see is whatever defender the offensive line has consciously not blocked. This unblocked defender is then forced to make a decision— does he go after the fullback, or does he wait to see what happens? If he waits, the QB leaves the ball with the fullback and the play becomes a dive. If the unblocked defender remains disciplined, the QB keeps the ball and attacks the corner (with the pitch back trailing the play from the weak side). "We don't really read defenses as much as we read perimeters," Rende says. "This is

says, and that's an understatement. The fact that everyone knows exactly what Maritime does is better than OK, because every team that plays them spends the entire week trying to teach its defenders what they'll see, what their individual responsibility is, and which assignments they need to accept. And that's completely antithetical to how modern defenses want to operate. Instead of reacting and hitting, defenders end up reading and thinking. It stops opposing players from being themselves, and that's half the battle.

T he first obstruction to running The Blur is basic: How do you call a play without "calling a play?" Oregon gets a lot of attention for using a bizarre collection of symbols on a piece of tag board—if you watch the Ducks sideline during dead balls, you'll sometimes see an assistant coach a backup quarterback holding a mammoth four-quadrant tag board featuring the mug shot of an ESPN broadcaster, a random number, a caricature of a lynx, and a photograph of an F-14 fighter jet. Nobody knows exactly[10] what these symbols represent (and Oregon is obviously not going to tell). Much of it might be window dressing. Instead of signage, Amherst prefers to do everything through hand signals. But because the Lord Jeffs want to play fast, this communication system creates its own unique hurdle: Traditionally, the only guy on the field who needed to memorize all the hand signals was the quarterback (who would then translate those gestures for everyone else in the huddle). But Amherst has no huddle. It had to figure out its own way to make this work.

"Two years ago, the plan was that the whole team would watch the hand signals and everyone would get the play that way," Faulstick says. "That was how we were going to play fast. But in reality, we did not play fast, or at least not fast

kind of hard to explain, but it's not like I come to the line of scrimmage and say, 'OK, they're in a 4-3. I'm facing a 4-3.' It's more like I look at the side we're running toward and count how many guys they have on the perimeter. I don't really care what defense they're running."

9. Here again, Maine Maritime employs a numbering system that is older (or maybe just weirder) than most other programs in the country. Typically, teams set up their offense through a right-hand/ left-hand hole system: The gap between the center and the left guard is the "1 hole," the gap between the center and the right guard is the "2 hole," the gap between the left guard and left tackle is the "3 hole," the gap between the right guard and right tackle is the "4 hole," etc. Even at the high school level, this is how it usually works—even numbers go the right and odd numbers go to the left. But not at Maritime. At Maritime, they just number the gaps in succession from 1 to 9, but—for whatever reason—they start on the far right and move

enough. The lineman were always looking back at the sideline, trying to pick up the hand signals instead of getting to the line of scrimmage. That killed the tempo. The quarterback was always repeating the whole play at the line for all the guys who missed it. So last year we changed."

What Amherst does now is somewhere in-between everyone learning the hand signals and the quarterback calling an audible at the line of scrimmage. The skill position players look to the sideline and read the hand signals themselves; the lineman are vocally informed of the play through a series of "tags." What this means is that specific plays are represented by a key word that can be disguised through imperfect synonyms. In their old system, an inside run for the Lord Jeffs was called "24" (this is the classic way to name a running play—it's the "2" back running through the "4" hole). But if you're vocalizing plays at the line of scrimmage, you can't keep saying "24" over and over again; eventually, defenses will figure it out. Instead, Amherst calls this play "Texas."[11] But that can be disguised by using a variety of words associated with Texas—"Dallas," "Waco," "Longhorn," or "Cowboy." All those different words mean the same thing. The Jeffs use a similar code when informing the lineman about pass protection: If they're blocking the pass rush with six players, they use code words associated with hockey (because hockey is played with six guys on the ice). If they're blocking the rush with only five players, they use code words connected to basketball.

For Division III schools like Amherst, implementing the Blur as a system isn't as complicated as actually operating it, simply because they don't have athletic scholarships (and therefore can't fill positions with precisely what they need). Their roster includes players who run the entire spectrum of athletic ability, and that throws things out of balance. They

left. A sprint option to the far left is a "49." The "2" in "42" counter means the ball carrier is going just inside the right tackle. The "5 hole" is straight up the gut. (Also, if you're in eighth grade, I'm sure this explanation of various holes was absolutely hilarious.)

10. "Chip Kelly's philosophy is based around McDonalds," explains Mills. "When you go to McDonalds, you look at the big board and say, 'I'll have a number two.' The quarter pounder with cheese, or whatever. It's an easy way to memorize things. So the idea is that everybody on the team will know what the board signifies, just because they're used to McDonalds. The hand signals tell them what board is live and what quadrant is the play. So if you see a picture of Kirk Herbstreit, that probably signifies the word 'Ohio,' and that might be the name of their basic set. Usually, if Oregon is using the boards, it means they're kicking somebody's butt. The board only shows the base plays. They're probably

can't be as symmetrical as a Division 1 team. For example, one of their current wide receivers (senior Ben Kettering) is 6-foot-6, mobile, coordinated, and abundantly confident. For a Division III receiver, he's a beast. There might be certain pass plays that work only with his specific skill set. "Our problem is that in major college football, the guys who get recruited as wideouts all tend to be pretty similar," says Faulstick. "They're all big and fast and dynamic. They're interchangeable. But at our level, it's likely the one receiver is going to better than the other. So we have to deal with the fact that certain plays might only work in one direction, because not everything works the same both ways."

Yet limitations sometimes spur innovation. One thing Amherst does that's particularly forward-thinking is the way it calls the cadence—instead of by the QB, it's called by the center. Once the quarterback has informed the lineman of the play, his only presnap responsibility is making sure everyone is lined up correctly and "mentally visualizing" what he needs to do next; he doesn't have to worry about getting the ball snapped. Now, does this actually allow the Jeffs to play faster than other teams? That's unclear. But it does create other advantages that will probably be copied by other coaches over time.

"When the center calls the cadence, your offside penalties go way down," Faulstick says. "Plus, your center gets a jump on who he's blocking. It was a great idea. We immediately went from being a team that would jump offside and kills drives to a team that almost never does. That just ended. But I don't think a lot of teams are doing this anywhere else."

Basically, there is no magic about a game plan," offensive supergenius Sid Gillman said 20 years before his

running the simplest plays and just ramming the ball down people's throat."

11. This is not the actual name of the play. The one thing I had to promise Faulstick was that I wouldn't use the real names for these tags.

2003 death. "There is no way you can sit behind a projector for 185 hours and, presto, come up with an idea that's going to make people disappear." This is, of course, true: There's nothing any football team can devise that will win them games without talent. It does not matter how much Maine Maritime practices the option or how fast Amherst run its offense—you can't design something that reinvents the wheel (or the wheel route). It's possible to overthink things. But thinking is what makes life interesting. It's why pure talent isn't necessarily as entertaining as doing more with less. Maritime and Amherst exist within limitations, but they're stretching those limitations in ways you won't see in other places. Big-time football is great because the players are great (and everybody knows it). Small-time football is great because the players are not (and nobody knows anyone).

We live in a celebrity culture, and that collective ideology drives sport as much as anything else. When we turn on the TV, we want to see famous people. Yet every athletic superstar is just another stand-in (both for the player who came before him and the player who'll come after). Life is a game, and we are the pawns. The only thing that matters is how the pieces move.

Originally published September 9, 2011.

"WE'RE NOT IN THE EX-JOCK BUSINESS."

(Bill Simmons and Al Michaels, continued from 175)

SIMMONS: NBC had Collinsworth do play-by-play before they knew they could get you, right?

MICHAELS: Yeah, there was a moment in time.

SIMMONS: That wouldn't have worked.

MICHAELS: Chris was thrilled to death because the roles are different. The play-by-play announcer has to watch the actual game. Why are the analysts so good sometimes? Because they're watching the left guard taking on the inside linebacker. If you start watching that when you're doing play-by-play, next thing you know there's a guy running seventy yards for a touchdown.

SIMMONS: It's two different skill sets. It's only worked once with two color guys—when the McEnroe brothers did it together. It was great! I think it could work with baseball potentially, too, just because there is so little action. Football—no way.

MICHAELS: Tennis is almost all analysis.

SIMMONS: Let me ask you this: Terry Francona replaced Tim McCarver for a couple of baseball games, and he was great. He was a natural. He had

been so immersed in the season and he had insight that I just wasn't going to get from McCarver. Do you think that color guys should be recently retired or between jobs? How hard is it to combat being out of the game for that long?

MICHAELS: I think the key, Bill, for any analyst who wants to be great is to understand you're in the broadcasting business. You're not in the ex-jock or ex-manager business.

SIMMONS: You can't just carry the weight of "Oh, when I played … "

MICHAELS: You come off the field and you go "Well the quarterback thinks … " Does every quarterback think the same thing in every circumstance? Of course not. You can also get too much into the vernacular. When I hear an announcer talk about a three-technique tackle? Collinsworth and I laugh about this.

SIMMONS: I don't know what it is and I write about sports for a living.

MICHAELS: I hear this and think, What are you talking about? You're not doing a high school clinic. We're in the entertainment business. The great analysts know how to entertain you, they know how to make it fun. People want to hear you have some humor. John Madden was the first guy to have the sound effects, and people loved that!

WAITING FOR RADIOHEAD

The occupation of Wall Street, the concert in New York, and the political vagaries of one of the world's most famous bands

by HUA HSU

It was raining when I arrived at Wall Street last Thursday. The streets were empty, as though this vicious, sudden storm had washed everyone— good, bad, and nonpartisan—away. But there was a muffled din; between the street's unkind acoustics and the fierce rains, I couldn't tell where it was coming from. As I ducked under the awning of a deli to study the design flaws of my umbrella, a bearded man marched by, then one whose face was covered by a bandana, then a woman in a suit with the word "CRIMINAL" stenciled on her back. They had come to occupy Wall Street. Dozens filed by, pointing their signs toward a waylaid delivery-man and me and cheerfully encouraging us to join them. The entire day, someone seemed to be holding a sign to my face. Sharpie on cardboard: the typeface of the desperate.

"WAKE UP!" a sign read—one of many that opted for a kind of forceful vagueness. Barricades restricted movement to Wall Street's sidewalks. The closing bell had long since sounded; it was early evening. There were no wealthy bankers sipping champagne, watching from their thrones, and scoffing at the unwashed masses, save the one who had merged with the mob only to break away at the door of the nearby gym. About 50 people chanted and sang, cheerfully beckoning those on the sidelines to join them, and then they politely filed back to their base at nearby Zuccotti Park. The protesters who had brought musical instruments huddled at the edge near Broadway and began jamming. On the far side of the park stood a mobile police tower, its intentions hidden behind a tinted pane.

That evening, about 80 blocks north on Broadway, Radiohead played the Roseland Ballroom. The set pieces were familiar: those same barricades, segregating those with tickets from those without; more cardboard signs, this time offering large sums of money (and more) for any spare tickets; some nameless, shapeless feeling in the air that we were living within someone else's matrix. But the preponderance of shoulder laptop bags and tucked-in shirts suggested this was more of an after-work crowd than one frothing for change. This was the second and final show of Radiohead's brief visit to New York, where they also featured as the musical guest on *Saturday Night Live* and taped a special episode of *The Colbert Report*.

Their appearance on Colbert was notable for highlighting the English

A Brief History of American Protest Music	1900-'20: World War I and the Labor Movement	'30s-'40s: The Great Depression
	Joe Hill, "The Preacher and the Slave." Mocked the Salvation Army and urged worker solidarity.	Aunt Molly Jackson, "Kentucky Miner's Wife (Hungry Ragged Blues)." Exposed the poverty of Appalachian mining families.
	James Oppenheim and Caroline Kohlsaat, "Bread and Roses." Commemorated the nine-week textile mill strike of 1912.	Yip Harburg, "Brother, Can You Spare A Dime?" Articulated the great shift from rich to poor.

band's political enthusiasms, particularly their keen interest in climate policy and their stance against corporate sponsorship. As is the show's conceit, Stephen Colbert lampooned this stance, offering Dr. Pepper as the band's "official soft drink" and pressing them on their use of electricity—did this not compromise their stance on emissions? For their part, the band met Colbert's

> Their protest was confined to a knowing arching of the brow or an exaggerated burst of agreement with Colbert.

irony with some of their own, although theirs was subtle to the point of inscrutability. In between platitudes about their children's futures and the hijacking of participatory politics by corporate interests, their protest was confined to a knowing arching of the brow or an exaggerated burst of agreement with Colbert.

When Radiohead first emerged with the 1992 hit "Creep" there was little evidence they would evolve into a daring, formidable, and forward-thinking band. Evolution always seems inevitable and obvious in hindsight, but in the case of Radiohead, it seemed most natural that "Creep" would both make and extinguish them. In the shadow of Nirvana's *Nevermind*, a paradigm shift in the music industry's sense of marketplaces, the early 1990s was filled with many momentarily intriguing one-hit wonders and buzz bands. The intense pressures exerted upon the band, the constant materialization of label representatives checking in on the new product, none of this broke them; instead, it became a subject for their music, and a reason for each album to be more

---

'50s: Nuclear War and McCarthyism

Woody Guthrie, "Union Made." A Pro-union folk song.

Vern Partlow, "Old Man Atom." Explicitly expressed the extreme volatility of the atom bomb.

Pete Seeger and Lee Hays, "If I Had A Hammer." Written in 1949 to support the anti-war progressive movement.

'50-'70s: Civil Rights and Vietnam War

Bob Dylan, "Only A Pawn in Their Game." Sung at 1963 March on Washington to protest the death of Medgar Evers.

James Brown, "Say It Loud—I'm Black and I'm Proud." Called for black empowerment.

The Doors, "The Unknown Soldier." A reaction to how American media represented the war.

challenging than the last. They began to compose songs that described the sort of alienation one might experience if everyone needed to speak to you but rarely about anything that truly mattered.

All of this came about in the mid-1990s, that boom era when it wasn't so strange for a college graduate with wits to land a decent job. The Internet had yet to fuse with our lives with such totality and finality—at least it seemed this way—and suddenly there were new kinds of jobs and ways to make money. For listeners of a certain age, even casual ones who had discovered them through "Creep," Radiohead offered some semblance of critique, a reason to temper hopes about the abundant jobs available for the choosing and a warning not to misread the dizzying pace of global change as inevitability. Their 1997 album, OK Computer, contained oblique barbs about consumerism, our pre-millennial numbness, the mantra of productivity. But the malaise was never named, as though this hidden transcript still required decrypting.

This sense grew more pronounced on 2000's Kid A, which managed to feel both paranoid and comfortable with the future and its possibilities. The opening moments of its lead track, "Everything in Its Right Place," captured the band's newfound ambivalence toward traditional rock aesthetics: Singer Thom Yorke's vocals arrived as a scrambled blur, and instead of guitars or drums there was an electric piano and little more. The album wore the influences of ambient electronic and modern classical music proudly, denying the back-to-nature catharsis that is the engine of so much popular music.

'80s: Iran Contra, Anti-Government

Public Enemy, "Fight the Power."Spoke out against the law and government abusing power.

10,000 Maniacs, "Please Forgive Us." Written to dissociate the American people from government actions in Nicaragua.

Dead Kennedys. "Stars and Stripes of Corruption." Criticized government for putting war before domestic issues.

'90s: Anti-Corporation, Women's Rights

Rage Against the Machine, "Bullet in the Head." Anti-corporation, anti-greed and anti-government-brainwashing.

Sonic Youth, "Swimsuit Issue." Furious with American media for objectifying women.

Pennywise, "Homeless." Wagged its finger at government for ignoring problems at home.

All of this helps explain how Radiohead came to be understood as a thinking person's band—by toying with their fan base's expectations, but still giving them the feeling that they were sharers of a secret. At Roseland that night, I began to wonder: Is this music that, per the sign I had seen earlier in the day, awakens us to our surroundings? This was clearly one of their intentions, from the late 1990s up through today. And yet Radiohead's music has never enunciated their convictions clearly or offered any legible rage. Its sense of dissatisfaction feels profound yet vague. What if this is what it looks likes to be bright-eyed and present in 2011?

R adiohead's set drew largely from their past two albums, 2007's *In Rainbows* and this year's *The King of Limbs*. The band's performances have always brought attention to their fine rhythm section, something one barely notices on their records. Even though their new songs are largely guitar-based, their sense of repetition—a haphazard pluck or a hypnotic arpeggio replayed over and over—feels inspired by the stuttering, hiccupping electronic dance music Yorke often champions. The older material sounded less strange, which perhaps illustrates Radiohead's influence: It is no longer unusual for a band to aspire toward a guitar-free sound. They are a book about Marx or existentialism that challenged you in college, the "USED" sticker still prominent on its spine.

The following day, rumors persisted that Radiohead were to play a surprise show down on Wall Street, in support of its occupation, or rather, the occupation of a small park near Wall Street. Representatives of the movement insisted this show was happening, even as the band's management denied it. Maybe, some suspected, the band had agreed to play an unannounced show for the protesters but backed out the moment the protesters went public with the news. Perhaps, others accused, the protesters had floated this rumor merely to drum up support for their cause. Conspiracy is the intoxicant of the fringe. In any event, interest in what was going on surged that day as a result of this rumor, just as it had when Michael Moore, Russell Simmons, Cornel West, and hundreds of uniformed airline pilots had come by at various points earlier in the week to lend solidarity. Best of luck to the occupation, the band eventually explained, but we never had any intention of playing.

As you grow older, you begin to worry about the coming revolution's logistics. It's likely that such a concert would have brought an immediate end to the occupation. A few hundred would have become many thousand, and there finally would have been a reason for the police to descend in the name of crowd control, codes governing amplified noise or some other potentially arbitrary reason.

I wondered what they might have played, had they showed up. One of Radiohead's working titles for *Kid A* was *No Logo*, in homage to Naomi Klein's influential 2000 book on the new classes of consumers and activists whom the globalized economy of the 1980s and 1990s had produced. I'm sure it was buried deep within some of those overstuffed, water bottle-laden backpacks in Zuccotti Park. *No Logo* has had a strange career these past 10 years, for it clarified, in an almost prophetic way, the possibilities of both advertising (whose attempts at branding have grown remarkably sophisticated) and activism.

To isolate this contradiction—the way Klein herself became a "brand," or the various compromises Colbert pointed out in the Radiohead platform—is not to defuse the idea or save us from having to ponder it. Even as I stood at Roseland, wondering when Radiohead's fans had grown this muscular and professional, I was reminded of how powerful their elusiveness of meaning had once been—how it had been enabled by their desire to step outside of the timelines, schedules, and external demands that dictated their lives. This is an old story, the reluctant superstars who have earned the privilege to be deliberative and experimental. But in many ways, this is also what makes the Wall Street occupation so enchanting from afar. This isn't a brick

This is a meandering deliberation, an attempt at democracy in slow motion, a motley assortment of people who share a sense but little more.

through the window of the nearest Starbucks or a limousine in flames; this is a meandering deliberation, an attempt at democracy in slow motion, a motley assortment of people who share a sense but little more. The mellow, holding-pattern pace of it all against the logic that time is money.

There was something faintly sad about this Radiohead gig that wasn't. The protesters weren't ready for their close-up. Someone posing as the band's manager had pranked them, and if you couldn't trust their ability to figure this one out before it was too late, then how could you take any of the rest of their manifestos and demands seriously? Those on the sideline had turned their attention to this cause and the promise of a free concert, but the incentive never materialized. The media finally sought out the organizers, but it was so they could comment on this embarrassing hoax. That day, the protesters had finally issued their declaration of grievances, which ranged from the tyranny of student debt to the protection of animal rights to the status of corporations as "people." At the bottom of this list, a tiny note: "These grievances are not all-inclusive."

Originally published October 5, 2011.

THE META PROBLEMS OF GAMIFICATION

The storytelling techniques of Dead Island
beget its narrative problems

by TOM BISSELL

Earlier this year, the trailer for a video game called *Dead Island* caused quite a stir, so much so that even a few of my non-video-game-playing friends were linking to it on their Facebook pages. With its (mostly) backwards-running account of a happy family's horrific introduction to the zombies in their tropical-vacation midst, the *Dead Island* trailer stood out as a troublingly beautiful little fillip of digital filmmaking. Now that *Dead Island* has been released, a lot of people are complaining that the trailer is deceptively unrepresentative of the game it was designed to advertise. I confess to finding this complaint a little odd—unless, that is, you expect a string quartet to be playing while you present your girl with her De Beers engagement ring or a bathykolpian hottie to whip off your trousers at the first whiff of Axe's Dark Temptation body spray.

It has been a tough year for Techland, the Polish developer behind *Dead Island*. In July, the company released the miserable Call of Juarez: The Cartel, which is, ethical questions aside, roughly as invigorating as taking a tranquilizer dart to the jugular. I came to *Dead Island* with considerable wariness, then. I also came to *Dead Island* wanting very much to love it. Two of my favorite video games are *Left 4 Dead* and *Dead Rising*,[1] both of which, like *Dead Island*, involve zombies. Neither *Left 4 Dead* nor *Dead Rising* has much of a story, and neither game needs one. There is, anyway, only one story worth telling in a zombie game, and here it is: See those zombies over there? You should probably get away from them.

Left 4 Dead and *Dead Rising* are very different games. The almost perfect simplicity of *Left 4 Dead* allows the player to charge through environments dynamically designed for multiplayer experiences, with the added fun of an internal A.I. "director" tweaking the environmental variables so that no two runs through*Left 4 Dead* are ever exactly the same. The game is all about the pure adrenaline thrill of first-person-shooting your way through bad odds. Conversely, the third person and more RPG-ish *Dead Rising* is harder, weirder, and far more challenging, with weapons that degrade so quickly they seem made of chalk and an absolutely uncompromising mission structure. The clock is always running in *Dead Rising*. If you fail to finish certain important story-furthering missions within the time the game gives you, too bad, and the game just ends. Unlike nearly every video game manufactured in the past decade, it is quite possible to spend six or seven hours playing *Dead Rising* and be forced by some time-management blunder to start all over again. That does not sound like much fun, I know, and it wasn't much fun, truth be told. So what was it? Absorbing. Upsetting. Tense.

1. An imminent shortage of zombie titles that include the word "dead" is, I fear, on the horizon. Oh, wait: Dead Horizon! You're welcome, video-game developers.

Scary. Everything, in other words, a zombie game should be.

Left 4 Dead's weapons don't degrade, but the game can be positively miserly when it comes to ammunition and health packets, which is what gives *Left 4 Dead* a large part of its inimitable jolt. *Dead Rising*'s combat is based upon the fact that just about every object found in the game can be used as a weapon. All of this is to say that scarcity is an important aspect of the apocalyptic zombie game. If the player feels too well equipped, the apocalyptic aspect recedes. If the player feels too powerful, the zombie aspect recedes. In *Left 4 Dead* and *Dead Rising*, we see two underlying gameplay systems—one simple, one complicated—achieving a similar emotional effect through different though equally appropriate means. They are games that know exactly what they are about and exactly the type of experience they want to give you.

In this respect, *Dead Island* is a goddamned mess. Know that I was not expecting *Dead Island* to have an involving story (it does not) or any interesting characters (they are vile), though I was worried—accurately, it turns out—that it would try its hand at providing both. What I did expect from *Dead Island*, at the very least, was a viscerally diverting few hours of chopping up and running from zombies. And it did give me that, to some extent. What I did not expect from *Dead Island* —and what it doggedly, depressingly, and finally infuriatingly provides—is an experience woefully bound up in a concept that only recently leapt the transom of academic gamer discourse and is now being pondered in corporate boardrooms around the world. I speak of Gamification.

"**G**amification" is a little like postmodernism in that no one really knows whether it is primarily a practice, a stance, an era, or a diagnosis.

Equally uncertain is whether it is a perilous thing, a potentially positive thing, or a drear and lamentable thing. Gamification, most basically, involves the constant, subtle incentivizing of everyday life, often in a digital or technological manner. If you go for a jog in your Nikes, say, a chip in your shoe posts how many calories you burned on your Facebook page. Obviously, some version of this shit has been around for a long time. Happy Hour is a primitive form of Gamification. (So are, for that matter, paychecks and military rankings.) But the specific use of numbers and seemingly actionable data in modern Gamification schemes is quite a bit younger. It turns up as early as the founding of Weight Watchers in 1963 and the launching of Dungeons & Dragons—which Gamified the ancient art of campfire storytelling—a decade later. (And now I am wondering if there is not some connection to be made between the two. Never trust a slender Dungeon Master, as I have always said.)

The writer, academic, and game designer Jesse Schell gave a talk at a 2010 game-industry conference in which he laid out the many ways in which Gamification is poised to invade modern life, largely through Facebook and other social-media platforms. In the talk, Schell imagined a future world in which we might get achievement points for doing things like brushing our teeth or working out. A lot of people, including the esteemed game thinker Ian Bogost, have since recoiled in horror from this future,[2] but others have proved more enthusiastic proponents of Gamification. Probably the most prominent of these is Jane McGonigal, whose book Reality Is Broken makes the argument that games have become so enticing precisely because real life is so comparatively drab. Anyone who finds real life lacking when compared to video games has basically given on

2. Even Schell himself lightly backed away from the apparent optimism of his talk, calling it a Huxleyan vision of what could be rather than an endorsement of what would be.

life. (Believe me: I know.) That is certainly sad. What it is not is any kind of a solution.

So what does Gamification have to do with *Dead Island*? A lot. *Dead Island* is a video game that essentially destroys itself through the devices and enticements of Gamification. You might ask, "How can a video game be ruined by the kinds of systems video games are primarily responsible for unleashing upon the world?" I realize this sounds paradoxical. But consider this: *World of Warcraft* is, by any measure, the most popular video game in history. The game is systemically based upon three pillars: customization, randomness, and looting. The more you customize, the better you can control the randomness. The more you loot (and then customize), the better you can control the randomness. In *WoW*, every player runs around, randomly initiating encounters, the outcomes of which they have looted and customized to better control. All the while the *WoW* motherbrain is rolling its internal 20-sided die and determining the fates of its players. Millions of people consider this fun. I am not one of them, but I have played enough lower-octane RPGs to know that there is some enjoyment to be had in customizing a character to mitigate video-game randomness. The part of me that enjoys this is also a part of me for which I have no real use.

Of course, we have Dungeons & Dragons to thank for these fictional experiences overtly governed by statistics, in which you roll to see if you hit the Quickling, evade the whirlpool, slay the Boalisk. The 20-sided die was what enabled those who played Dungeons & Dragons to trust one another. Not even the Dungeon Master him- or herself [sic] was as unimpeachable as the good old D20. This unquestioned trust in the D20 was profound—and profoundly shaped what eventually became video-game design. What the D20 hath wrought is, I believe, a big part of what is ruining many video games.

T echland, if I had to guess, was working away on what it hoped would be a riveting open-world zombie game when the RPG/first-person-shooter hybrid *Borderlands* came out. To be sure, *Borderlands* is a terrific game. It was also an unexpected hit. *Borderlands* is RPG-ish enough to encourage all the customization the average customization weenie could ask for, and it is shootery enough that the average shooter nut never gets bored with all the bullshit customization. In some games, a measure of customization is thematically and internally appropriate.[3] *Borderlands* is a game in which Mad Max savagery meets sci-fi weaponry, and its sheer amount of gun porn is amazing. Video-game guns are open to this kind of conceptualization, in that their real-world counterparts fire different ammo at different velocities and have sometimes drastically different effects on targets. So I get it, I get all this, and I accept that in some games it makes sense that the more you use a weapon, the more skilled you become with it. Where you begin to lose me is when I am shooting at someone in *Borderlands* and numbers begin to cascade off his body. These numbers represent the amount of health your enemy is losing, which is a pretty amazingly unnecessary bit of information to take in during a gunfight. How about you just shoot at each other until one of you is dead?

Someone at Techland, I suspect, played *Borderlands*, loved the hit-point cascades pouring off the enemies, loved the endless customization of weapons, loved the facile thrill of leveling up, and decided, "I think our riveting open-world zombie game needs all of this." If this is indeed what happened, I would like the party responsible to know that he made a terrible, terrible mistake. For one thing: "Leveling up." Why do this in a game with no naturally occurring RPG trappings? What

Why this useless Gamification of what are already games? Why do we tolerate it?

3. Like, say, the *Fallout* games or *Mass Effect* or the recent *Deus Ex: Human Revolution*. The last makes skill trees and leveling up central to the game's fiction, given that the controlled character is an augmented human learning how to use his newly androidal body.

purpose does it serve? If the goal is to ensure equal difficulty throughout a game experience, so that player strength and enemy strength are always rivalrous, why not, you know, just sort of design the game to do that invisibly? But why level up, anyway, if the game is going to stay equally difficult through-out? You leveled up and rolled the dice in Dungeons & Dragons because it was impossible to run such systems under the game's hood. You know why? Because there wasn't a hood. Video games not only have hoods but also engines, and all manner of delightfully invisible computation can be dealt with and handled there. So I ask: Why isn't it invisible more often? Why this useless Gamification of what are already games? Why do we tolerate it? What do we actually get out of it, other than some mouse-brain satisfaction of knowing exactly where we are in the maze?[4]

In *Dead Island*, your character progresses by gaining levels, which would be fine, I suppose, if these levels were not so deterministic. Every *Dead Island* zombie has a level, too, and, I have to say, running up to a zombie with LEVEL 7 floating above its head certainly makes for a weird experience. The weapons also have levels, and if you are not at the level needed to wield a weapon, you are unable to use it. This does not make a hell of a lot of sense when the weapon in question is a knife or a pipe or an axe, especially when you have been wielding all of the above quite adroitly for hours. What on earth does a Level 4 Pipe even mean, anyway? Worse yet, the weapons are all subclassed, so you are not just finding a Level 4 Pipe; you are finding a Flimsy Level 4 Pipe or a Homemade Level 4 Pipe, the differences of which are utterly unclear. Techland consulted some real geniuses of nomenclature in coming up with *Dead Island*'s weapons' subclass names: We have the Flimsy Cleaver, the Tiring Knife, the Frightening

4. I recently asked a game-designer friend if one of the reasons these skill-tree and leveling-up systems actually show up in games is due to the fact that some poor bastard actually had to work for months and sometimes years refining them and plan-ning them and gaming them out, so that everything made sense and demonstrably kept players from getting too powerful too quickly. He said, with a sigh, "Pretty much." Which means that one problem with game design today is the game designer's emotional inability to hide his or her hard work. Oh, the humanity.

Mace, the Spiteful Pistol. It all sounds like the work of two Poles with a big bag of weed and a thesaurus. What's next? I wrote in my notes. The Recalcitrant Hoe? Two minutes later, no joke, I found the Languid Pistol. It replaced my Weak Pistol, which was for some unfathomable reason more powerful than the Spiteful Pistol. Let's not even talk about the inventory system, or your character's carrying capacity, other than to say this: You have limited weapon space and unlimited item space. In a game like this, carrying capacity should be one unified, logical system, and that system should either be unlimited or severely limited. Anything else is arbitrary, stupid, and altogether bad game design.

Dead Island's *WoW*-ish or *Borderlands*-ish overlays make even less sense with regard to the game's setting, a resort community found somewhere in Papua New Guinea, which could not emit a less Magickal or techno-sci-fi pulsar if it tried. In addition, *Dead Island* claims to be an open-world game, but it most certainly is not, and the exploration-minded gamer will quite often find the following words on his or her screen: YOU ARE LEAVING THE PLAYABLE AREA. Here is a game that systemizes pipes and knives but has no comparatively complicated system in place for dealing with the player who wanders a few feet beyond *Dead Island*'s shore.

I did not finish *Dead Island*, and the reason I did not is instructive. For most of the game, the damage you inflict on your zombie enemies remains in effect when you die, and you do die, often, which is fine, because the game does not make player death overly punitive. At worst, you begin again a few meters from your point of expiry, and the visible health meter of the Level 10 zombie that killed you remains reassuringly chipped away. Your degrading weapons' overall condition does not reset, however, so if your Level 15 Punishing Axe was ruined by the encounter that killed you, it will stay ruined. A perfectly cromulent system, all in all. Until, that is, a late escort sequence in the game. The tribal chief (don't ask) I was escorting and I turned up in a village. I had plenty of ammunition for my guns, and my bladed weapons were all in top shape. In this village, we were, naturally, attacked by zombies, most of which I managed to kill, but my tribal chief pal died. I tried again, and noticed that all the absurdly powerful Level Whatever zombies I had just killed respawned. Meanwhile, I had half as much ammo. I tried once again, fought valiantly, and my tribal chief pal died. Again. And again the zombies respawned. Now I had no ammo and half of my bladed weapons were ruined. I tried again. Failed again. That son of a bitch tribal chief! Soon I had no usable weapons and also no quick way to opt out of this disastrous mission without the tribal chief dying and sending me back to the infuriating checkpoint. Ladies and gentlemen, there is a phrase to describe this kind of game design, but a part of this phrase involves a word that Grantland's grandparent company, Disney, will not permit me to use.

Here is what *Dead Island* should have been about: running from things that want to kill you and killing them by finding weapons hidden away in an interesting series of environments. It should have been scary and primitive and animal and savage. It should have involved weapons that visibly degrade in your hand rather than weapons tricked out with pointless little subscreen health meters. It should not have involved an in-game economy with duct tape you can sell for $3 and buy for $150.

The hell of it is, many gamers will probably love *Dead Island*. So many numbers. So many levels. No wonder such people turn to Metacritic for guidance. For these gamers I have one question. In a game about running from things that want to eat you, what is more important: the emotional experience of running from things that want to eat you, or knowing that the thing that wants to eat you is a Level 23 thing that wants to eat you? Knowing that the machete in your hand can take its head off, or knowing that the machete in your hand is capable of doing 320+ hit points of damage? On second thought, don't bother answering. That this game exists is answer enough.

Originally published September 13, 2011.

BLAME THE MOMAGER

*The saga of Kim Kardashian's divorce
has a clear villain—her mother*

by MOLLY LAMBERT

*The desire to get married is a basic and primal instinct in women. It's followed by
another basic and primal instinct: the desire to be single again.*   —Nora Ephron

Kim Kardashian is a professional athlete. We know this because she just
PLAYED US ALL. Now, I may have been cynical enough to know that this
was not a "real" wedding, but I believed they'd stick it out for a contractually
obligated year or two. At least through a couple of faux-pregnancy scares.
They didn't even wait for the split rumors to calm down to a dull roar before
rolling out this latest plot twist. Now come weeks of denials, conspiracy
theories (Danilo was Kim's first choice! Kris heard from TMZ! Everyone
was in on it the whole time!).

Let's look at the real monster: Kris Kardashian. One moment of actual
gravitas in the Kardashians' E! show came during the "should Kim pose for

Playboy?" plotline, when Kris all but ripped Kim's clothes off for the cameras. No, just kidding, Kim is an adult and makes her own decisions (OR DOES SHE?). But the episode played up Kim's discomfort with being photographed naked for a national magazine, as well as Kris's horrifying insistence that mother knew best, and the idea that what all twentysomething girls from L.A. want is to be on the cover of Playboy. The character of the "momager" has really caught on in the past decade as a kind of horrific Lady Macbeth who uses her daughter as a conduit for her own ambitions. Because of cultural stereotypes that all moms are "good" and the fact that most kids are of course predisposed to listen to mom, the momager seems particularly evil. Like a thought experiment conducted in the setting of a family. Other stereotypes about women that say they are more empathetic and emotionally attuned make this seem especially cruel and heartless. Exploiting the parent-child bond to further your own financial aims conveys total lack of regard for your child's emotional well-being.

The only thing scarier than momagers are dadagers (looking at you, Joe Simpson and Matthew Knowles). The idea of using your child like a product to make money for yourself is so tremendously fucked up, even if the kid has bought into it. Self-objectification is one thing, but objectifying kids makes people very uncomfortable and fascinates them. The Thylane Lena-Rose Blondeau scandal and the popularity of shows like Toddlers & Tiaras and Dance Moms reflect this phenomenon. Kim is not a kid, but her relationship with her mom on Keeping Up With the Kardashians shows that she has been groomed for stardom her entire life. The rumor was that Kris urged Kim to leak the sex tape in order to become famous. "How could these moms do this to their daughters?" we wonder without looking away. (Kris seems to have no qualms about putting youngest daughters Kendall and Kylie into bikinis and then manufacturing a controversy over whether they are being too sexy too soon.) The answers reveal themselves.

Just as parents project their own hopes onto their children, they also project their own failed aspirations: In this case, the will to fame. In a culture that values women as sexual objects above all else, what could be more awesome than being nationally validated as a sexual object? (I dunno, a Pulitzer?) Because they never fully achieved this aspiration, they never thought beyond the plausible positives. In Kim's case, she is the butt (sorry) of endless public jokes. Her life itself is treated like a joke, because she seemingly treats it like one. On-camera she mimics a pure sex object: giggling, talking in a baby voice, seemingly having few to no strong opinions about anything except what is "cute" and "not cute," pouting sometimes but never really getting mad. Jessica Simpson displayed more emotional depth on Newlyweds.

Even more profitable for Kim than a quickie courtship and a lavish televised wedding is a quickie divorce and lavish televised heartbreak. We should have listened more carefully to her interview with her hero Elizabeth Taylor. What Kim clearly admires most about La Liz is not her acting talent or way with a quip, but ability to remain in the spotlight for decades. Everything is potentially convertible capital: your body, your face, the way you feel about your body and face, your taste in jewelry, perfume, makeup, and men. Kim is hardly the first person to embody this lifestyle (in the UK it's a veritable culture cottage industry involving WAGs and Page 3 Girls), but she is the most current.

What Paris Hilton, Kim Kardashian, and Lindsay Lohan did in the aughts was reinvent the kind of celebrity for the TMZ age that Marilyn Monroe perfected and Madonna tried hard to empower. The celebrity as sexual athlete. Lohan's case is saddest because she showed a lot of promise as an actress that she seemed intent on compulsively squandering, but considering her mother's public lying about being a Rockette it makes sense that she would learn to consider being a cultural showgirl the ultimate prize. Accordingly, she is doing a full-frontal pictorial in Playboy.

For a public sex object, Kim Kardashian's sex tape is tremendously underwhelming. If we're going to make celebrities out of girls from the valley with great asses that have on-camera sex, why not just put Naomi in the tabloids too? Her backstory is much more interesting. Her dad's a rabbi. Kanye has name-checked both in song and named the line of slutwear he recently designed after his mother, Donda. Kanye semi-processes the potential conflict between seeing women as sex objects and seeing them as people with dreams, bills, and backstories because Kanye's relationship with women is "it's complicated."

What Kim and Kris and all the Kardashians are doing that is so spiritually questionable is exploiting the notion of romance so cynically that even Don Draper would wince. Taylor Swift (God bless her) may have unrealistically naive ideas about what constitutes heteRosexuality, but what she peddles so popularly to tweens is a pure fantasy and she doesn't pretend it's not. She may wear a wedding dress in concert (and Jesus Christ we hope she'll outgrow that), but I don't think she would ever wear one in a wedding for sheer publicity. The Kardashians aim to sell a cartoonish super-fantasy version of what "real life" is like for the rich and famous, but what kind of a person aims to stay famous by setting a world record for quickie divorces? It's the ultimate expression of superficiality. It says "fuck you, emotional intimacy! I love diamonds." They should have dedicated the wedding to Nate Dogg (RIP). That Kim had her "fantasy wedding" to a groom she barely knew is sad. That he was relentlessly emasculated in the tabloids for supposedly spending her money during the NBA lockout and being less famous than Reggie Bush is stupid. That they got divorced is not very surprising. Who wants to have Kim Kardashian's life? Does Kim?

People will get sick of Kim Kardashian eventually, because her career is predicated on novelty and her primary talent (being hot, which she is) is transitory. After one possibly staged marriage fails, she becomes the Kim who cried wolf. E! is not exactly in the business of building lasting careers. Rumors that Kris H. was "cast" in order to ensure Kim underwent her first marriage before the dreaded age of 30 have yet to prove true or false, but faked relationships are as old as Hollywood itself (they are as old as 1853). The endless Kardashian family spectacle serves to take focus off the real issues by distracting us with shiny ass-shaped lures. And as long as we continue to pay attention, we lose. Because we all tuned in to her stupid wedding special and allowed her to be a star, Kim Kardashian is the 1 percent and we are all bottom-feeders.

Originally published November 1, 2011.

BILLY HUNTER
in conversation with
BILL SIMMONS

After mentioning it in his columns and podcast, Bill Simmons finally got Billy Hunter, executive director of the National Basketball Players Association, on the BS Report on October 24. They discussed the NBA lockout, which at the time, seemed poised to wreck the entire NBA season.

BILL SIMMONS: Last week Bryant Gumbel compared Stern to a modern-day plantation owner, and that took this whole thing in a direction that I'm not sure it needed to go. Did you feel any obligation to stand up and stick up for David Stern? Why didn't you speak up on that?

BILLY HUNTER: I really didn't think it was going to get any traction, it was Bryant Gumbel's opinion. David is a hard-charger, and David pretty much treats everybody the same. Obviously when you've got this set-up that we currently have—when you've got a league that's predominantly black and then you've got a group of white owners—it may take on a different color or appearance, but no, no I don't think David is racist at all.

SIMMONS: But why does it have to take on a different appearance? I mean the NFL—obviously they don't have as many African American players as the NBA.

HUNTER: I think it's simply because of people like Bryant and others. You're left to draw the conclusions that they wish to draw.

SIMMONS: Right, but that's not healthy for this whole thing, I don't think.

HUNTER: It's not healthy, it's not healthy, but that's just the nature of life in America, that's all. I mean people make those assumptions every day. The difference is that we're on Front St because we're very visible, we're professional sports. People will make comments and render opinions that they think move their own agenda.

SIMMONS: I have to ask you about the salary structure. Are we rewarding mediocre players too much and are we not taking care of the superstars enough?

HUNTER: What we tend to do is over-emphasize and we paint the picture, give the impression, that it's endemic within the league! There's about ten guys who fall within that top class. No team is required to give a player a guaranteed contract, no team is required to sign a guy for five or six years. When it comes to the parity and the competition, the players know more about what it takes to put together a winning team than most of the people that run these franchises.

(Continued on 287.)

HAUTE COUTURE OF THE 1990s

*An appreciation of the
iconic Starter jacket*

by REMBERT BROWNE

It was exceptional to be a sports-obsessed child of the '90s (ages three to 13) for 10 main reasons:

1. *Sports Illustrated for Kids*
2. *NBA Inside Stuff*
3. *D2: The Mighty Ducks*
4. Ken Griffey Jr.
5. The naive belief that you had the only Ken Griffey Jr. rookie card
6. Matt Christopher books
7. *Space Jam*
8. Jordan Highlight VHS box sets
9. MTV Rock 'N' Jock Basketball (Dan Cortese, I SEE you).
10. Starter jackets

WALTER GREEN

With all due respect to the first nine items on this list, no. 10, Starter jackets, is to Julie "The Cat'" Gaffney what nos. 1 to 9 are to Team Iceland.

I have three two of those things in my room presently (Matt Christopher Books, Ken Griffey Jr. Ken Griffey Jr. rookie card). The fact that a Starter jacket isn't on that list sickens and embarrasses me. Why is it, though, when I envision a starter jacket hanging up in my closet, there's no hesitation as to what kind it would be: Charlotte Hornets, teal and purple.

When I initially thought this, it made sense, because I once owned a Charlotte Hornets Starter jacket and wear a Charlotte Hornets T-shirt on a weekly basis. But there were other Starter styles around in the '90s. I turned to Google in an attempt to remember what they were. That didn't help too much.

Five of the first 20 Google image search results that were returned for me were Charlotte Hornets Starter jackets. To steal a phrase from Grantland's Katie Baker, I mustn't be the only one who thinks the Hornets getup is the "Starteriest Starter jacket." But why?

How did the Hornets Starter jacket ultimately become synonymous with the Starter jacket look? Why was it the ultimate jacket to have in the '90s, and why does it currently carry with it the more nostalgia than, say, the Chicago Bulls or Oakland Raiders versions? Can we explain its meteoric rise?

TOP 5 REASONS THE HORNETS STARTER IS NO. 1

5. Charlotte, N.C. Charlotte would be in last place if this was a "Top 10 Reasons," "Top 15 Reasons," or "Top 200 Reasons" list. Fact: The popularity of this jacket has nothing to do with the city of Charlotte. Call this South-on-South hate, but as an Atlantan, I wouldn't live in Charlotte if you promised me a $1,000 a day and a lifetime supply of teal and purple color contacts. If there's one thing I know, it's that zero percent of this jacket's success should be attributed to the quasi-decent city of Charlotte, North Carolina.

4. Hugo. Before there was Blake Griffin, there was Hugo. We all know the clip of Blake posterizing poor Timothy Mozgov by handballing it into the

basket. Yes, Blake was doing this in 2010, but Hugo was pioneering it in '91. Here are a few quick stats:

- Three-time NBA Mascot Dunk Contest Winner: 1991, 1992, 1993

- Two-time *Inside Stuff* magazine "Best NBA Mascot" award recipient

- Only known mascot to wear Jordans on a trading card

Sure it's hard for kids and teenagers to truly connect with an insect and/or mythical creature that wears a teal bag over its entire body, but there's no denying the excitement it brought to the franchise. (A word of warning, should you ever cross Hugo, NEVER bring up the New Orleans Hornets mascots, Air Hugo and Mini Air Hugo, in passing conversation. He took a lot of the blame for the collapsing of the franchise and slumped into a dark depression, but has been clean for two weeks now. We wouldn't want to trigger any harmful behavior.) There were definitely a few kids led to the Hornets Starter by way of the flyness that was Hugo.

3. A New Franchise. Franchise teams are like freshman girls in college: They bring a level of excitement to the scene, they go out of their way to stand out, and they get a comically large amount of positive attention, even when they publicly embarrass themselves on a consistent basis. (Yes, in this analogy, we, the consumers = senior guys.) The way the Hornets began their history (and ended the '80s) was abysmal, but based on the masses of senior guys that came out to watch these freshman girls miss layups, turn the ball over, and lose at an alarming rate, you would think they were playoff bound. It was apparent that newness was more important to popularity than success, and the groundwork laid in the late '80s launched the Hornets' fan-favoriteness into the stratosphere in the '90s, once they actually started becoming a good team. There's no surprise that the newness of the gear made the Hornets Starter extremely desirable, but at a much higher rate than the three other late '80s expansion teams (Miami Heat, Orlando Magic, Minnesota Timberwolves). What separated the Hornets from the other three? Keep reading.

2. The Players. Kendall Gill. Muggsy Bogues. Larry Johnson. Alonzo Mourning. Glen Rice. Anthony Mason. Dell Curry. All great basketball players, but for a few of them, their star power often went beyond the basketball court. Do you remember that episode of My Brother and Me with Gill? What about the fact that in *Space Jam*, two of the five NBA players who get their abilities stolen by the Monstars are Hornets (Bogues, LJ). The dilemma that consumers initially had with the Hornets was, "I need like six Hornets jerseys. What am I to do?" Enter Starter jackets, allowing you to simply show your love for an entire franchise. Yes, seeing a Gill jersey for sale would probably send me into anaphylactic shock, but the long-term decision to invest in a Hornets Starter jacket was easily the way to go. Based on their laughable start as a franchise, there's no way anyone could have predicted the players on this team to practically reach cult-athlete status, but I'm certain the rag-tagness of the Hornets contributed to their popularity, and to the popularity of the jacket.

1. Teal & Purple. The outfit of the '90s, without question, is a Charlotte Hornets Starter jacket with a Mighty Ducks snapback. There isn't even a close second. The common thread between the two teams and their apparel: teal and purple. In the '90s, these two colors were markedly different from some of the other popular Starter jackets (the Raiders' black and silver, the Bulls' red and black, the Cowboys' blue and silver). Full gangs can (and have) mobilized around these Starter jackets. Never really heard much about teal-and-purple gangs terrorizing residential communities. You know why? It's impossible to be in a bad mood when you are wearing teal and purple, especially when that teal and purple manifests itself in a Hornets Starter jacket. No one could have predicted the way in which the color scheme took off, but it was and still the main reason the Hornets jacket is the Starteriest Starter Jacket.

* * *

If you used to have one and have managed to hold on to it, bravo to you. If you're like me and outgrew yours some years back, maybe today is the day you go and find one online, as to regain that happy feeling you had years ago. And if you've never owned a Charlotte Hornets Starter jacket, stop what you're doing and go buy two, but only if you're OK with being heavily complimented, being revered by your peers, pupils, and elders, and looking better than ever before.

Originally published September 20, 2011.

Muggsey Bogues was integral to the 1990s Charlotte Hornets teams that turned their Starter jacket into an icon.

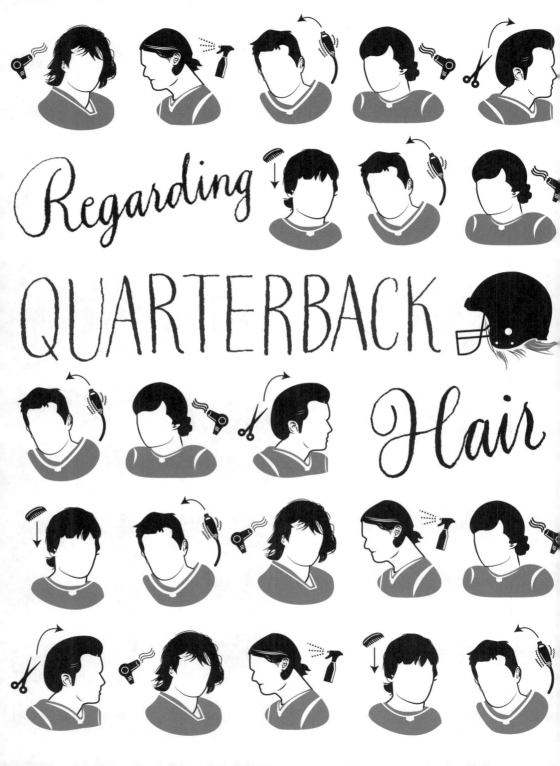

Regarding QUARTERBACK *Hair*

The Patriots QB pulls
a reverse Samson

by WESLEY MORRIS

For some men, throwing an uncharacteristic four interceptions in one game would necessitate a real gut-check moment. They'd review film, talk to their receivers, go to Jesus. They'd ask, "What's wrong with me?" Tom Brady knew what was wrong. He threw four interceptions, then HE cut his hair. Anyone who noticed sang "Hallelujah." People wrote obituaries and burned scrunchies. Last Wednesday was a great day for people who hate ostentation, uniqueness, or style, for people who believe Brady had become too fancy for serious football. Lots of athletes get their hair cut in a salon. Brady's crime was that he looked like he did. Last Wednesday, those people—people who love Tom Brady the quarterback, but bristle at Tom Brady the spokesmodel—celebrated an early Christmas.

But that hair—The Hair—was an exciting moment for the National Football League. When Brady arrived at training camp two summers ago, he came with a haircut that matched his risky approach to football: He was taking a chance. It was hair that said to men, "Guys, I'm not sure where this is headed, but let's just see where it goes." And so we took a journey that, more than a year later, ended unceremoniously. For a man who really doesn't say a lot, the haircut said everything. It said, "I'm sorry." It said, "You were right." It said, "Gisele uses both blow dryers." Brady asked the world to read nothing into it, which then allowed the world to read further while grumbling that he should also run for office.

You can see Brady's point. Really, the new hair is just the old hair: a 3 on top, 2 on the sides; a Supercut. But it's the hair of three Super Bowl rings and numerous Sports Illustrated covers. It's the haircut of the Man Who Got Gisele. Brady was equally blasé in deciding to grow it out. During the preseason, he told reporters it was more or less an accident. "We've had two-a-days for the last three weeks. ... This is what happens," he said. "I passed that uncomfortable stage with it. Now, I'm just like, 'Screw it, let's just keep going.'" But it was always a little uncomfortable. Some days its fullness made him look like a cross between a Redgrave and Mrs. Doubtfire. Eventually, the pop star Justin Bieber went on the attack, all but crying copyright infringement.

The hair had volume. It had charisma. There were reasons to feel it deserved an agent. But it was never popular and frequently misunderstood. In a few men it had aroused traumatic discomfort. This is the hair that smacked your tray onto the cafeteria floor. It was the hair into whose locker your girlfriend not-that-secretly slipped "I like you" notes. How many hearts had that hair broken? How many wedgies had it given? How many times had you tried to have that hair only to wind up looking like a Santa Monica pot dealer or Shaggy after too many Scooby Snacks? The hair, in that sense, was an affront. How you felt about it also depended on the lens through which it was viewed. On the one hand, you could perceive Gisele's influence. She had turned an All-American quarterback into a Brazilian beach bum, from Tom Brady to Gustavo Kuerten. On the other hand, as time went on, Brady's hair had become loosely commonplace. On a bad day it was a poor man's Clay Matthews or an elegant one's Jeremy Shockey.

In deciding to grow it at all, there might have been a degree of calculation. Two years ago Mark Sanchez arrived in the league, and America began passing out. Even before he'd thrown his first football, he was the most drooled-over player in the NFL. Sanchez has a breathtaking handsomeness that's both antique and of-the-moment—part 1930s movie star, part Bachelor Season 17—and he has real, confident style. You couldn't help but feel for guys who wanted a piece of Sanchez's action. Perhaps without quite fully realizing what he'd done, Brady had entered the fray of grooming and personal style. For instance, he and a slicked-back incarnation of the hair are currently starring in ads for UGG for Men, a move that, however momentarily, manages to unite those who despise the Madison Avenue sideshow of American sports and those who despise the UGG Australia brand. But the company is determined to make inroads with American dudes, and choosing Brady to help blaze that trail is shrewd. Of course, Wednesday feels a bit like rejection of that Tom Brady.

It was increasingly unclear what exactly it was Brady wanted that hair to do, what he wanted it to say. It was statement hair, and the message, the adventure, the fun had all gotten away from him. Sports people whispered it wasn't a leader's haircut. Complaints that it was unmanly allegedly came from Randy Moss, whose cornrows turn into a Pam Grier Afro with impossible ease. That blown-lead loss against the Bills might not have been the reason Brady had his hair cut. Yet that he did at least suggests that the last year might have been frivolous—even the ferociousness he occasionally unleashed during the regular season now feels somehow experimental. In cutting his hair, he cut away the UGG campaign, the Bieber jokes, the insulting, paranoid idea that his wife is some kind of reverse Delilah. Sunday, against the Oakland Raiders, was his first game with the new hair, and Brady gave a routinely clean performance. He might not like us to talk about any corollaries. But this is back-to-business hair that denies us the right to speculate that Brady's business is anything other than football. "Go long" can now apply only to his passing game.

Originally published October 3, 2011.

Tayshana Murphy's death reverberated widely throughout New York City. Crowds gathered outside the funeral home where her wake was held, with friends and family waiting to pay their respects.

THE MURDER OF TAYSHANA MURPHY

*A conflict no one can explain
claims a player no one can forget.*

by JONATHAN ABRAMS

Mention a court in New York City—West 4th, Rucker, Orchard Beach—they don't just know of Tayshana "Chicken" Murphy. They know her. She possessed that killer crossover and played "man strong," as Taylonn Murphy, her father, likes to say. Tayshana loved contact. "Babies," she called the girls who helplessly bounced off of her when she drove to the rim. She played taller than her 5-foot-7 and with a fierceness that contrasted against her gentle, hazel eyes. Now, Taylonn sits by the phone, waiting. "I still wait for my phone to ring and her to say, 'Pops, come pick me up from the gym.'" A family mourns, a basketball team is struggling to regroup, and a community is struggling to understand the senseless death of Tayshana Murphy.

Before her senior year at Murray Bergtraum High School for Business Careers, Tayshana was ranked the 16th-best point guard in the nation by ESPN. She always tried to stand out instead of blending in. She carried her own style and often wore boys' clothes. Sometimes she walked into the gym wearing a perm and curls. Other times, she wore her hair in braids. Tayshana would soon be part of the same lineage as Shannon Bobbitt of the WNBA's Indiana Fever at Murray Bergtraum. Ed Grezinsky, the same coach who had Bobbitt, would now give Murphy the reins. Tayshana hoped to stretch that run to a 14th straight Public Schools Athletic League championship.

Taylonn and Kasim Alston, Tayshana's godfather and often coach, laid out the blueprint. Together, they were the primary members of Team Chicken. Taylonn told her to shoot for the stars because it would be OK if she landed on the moon. They often talked about professional basketball.

"WNBA?" she once told her father. "I ain't talking about the WNBA. I think I can play in the NBA."

"Yo, Chicken, you bugging," Taylonn responded.

"No, I think I can," Tayshana said.

T he details of the early morning of September 11, 2011 are still unraveling and may not fully be explained for months, if ever. Tayshana lived in the General Ulysses S. Grant Houses. Youth residents in her project and a nearby project, the Manhattanville Houses, had sparred for years. The group in Grant is known as a gang called "3 Stacks." An hours-long brawl between residents of the two houses erupted at the Grant Houses on September 10, according to several people who witnessed it. The same people are divided on whether Tayshana or any of her relatives participated.

Robert Cartagena, 20 (at the time of the shooting), and Tyshawn "Ta-Ta" Brockington, 21, allegedly obtained a nine-millimeter handgun from 24-year-old Terique Collins. A witness reported seeing Collins possess the weapon at the Manhattanville Houses at around 3 a.m., according to a criminal complaint against Collins. A second complaint states that Cartagena and Brockington were spotted about 45 minutes later and said they were going to "smoke" someone from the Grant Houses. From their apartment on the 15th floor, Tephanie watched the scene unfold. Tayshana had been dancing in a courtyard with a group of friends. Now, she darted into 3170 Broadway. She ran through the doors that were supposed to be locked, up the stairwell, and made it to the fourth floor

"I am not with them," a cornered Tayshana said, according to a witness in one of the complaints.

"I don't give a fuck," replied a male voice, the same witness told police.

Tayshana raised her arms in self-defense. On her forearm, there was a tattoo with a basketball and the inscription "It's not a game. It's life."

The assailants shot her three times with a nine-millimeter, according to the city's Office of Chief Medical Examiner.

Tephanie ran out of the apartment and was the first to locate Tayshana. "Why did no one open their door to help my daughter?" she cried out. When law enforcement arrived, the clothes of Tephanie and other relatives were soaked in Tayshana's blood.

N owadays, it is not just awkward when Taylonn Murphy and Kasim Alston see one another. It is painful. To see the other is to see Chicken and relive the nightmares of shattered dreams.

Taylonn has the frame of an every-down running back or a point guard who stopped growing. His head is shaved and he will remove his glasses several times over the next couple of hours to wipe away the tears. Kasim is thinner and wears a red sweater. He speaks in a low voice tinged with pain.

They meet at a barbecue joint a half block away from Central Park. While together, both will need to excuse themselves at separate times to recompose.

Alston thinks about the circumstances of the tragic weekend. Tayshana had scheduled a workout with him that Friday, but they never met up. A Friday practice could have led to another workout on Saturday. She often spent the night with Alston's family in Queens because the workouts were so rigorous. Maybe she would not have even been at Grant that Saturday night if they had stayed the course.

"You can't blame yourself," Taylonn says.

"I lost one of my first cousins like three or four years ago," Alston says as the tears swell in his eyes. "He got killed in Brooklyn at a basketball game. It wasn't a basketball player who killed him. But that really hurt me. It tore me up. I lost my father four years ago. I lost my aunt a week before Chicken. I don't want to say I want it to be all over, you know? That's not how I feel. But there are days when all you want to do is stay up or just not feel it anymore. I thought I knew death. But I thought death was a process. You get sick, you get old, you die."

"When you do stuff, you've got to be held accountable for it," Taylonn says. "All I can say about those guys is God have mercy on their souls. I pray for their families. It's a tragedy all the way around the board. What kind of justice is really going to be served if I reacted to violence with violence? It's like three or four families all screwed up by this whole thing. It's just senseless. You know what I mean?"

"In the beginning, if I was the type of person in the streets, like one that dealt with weapons, I'd probably have went up there and went crazy," Kasim responds. "But then as time went on, I really thought about it and I really wouldn't want to do nothing to those kids, really. Because I know what it felt like to lose a kid, and for their parents to get the news that we got, I know what it would do to them. I don't want anybody to ever feel that. I want justice served."

"But there is no justice," Taylonn solemnly states.

"Those children are going to jail," Kasim says. "Their parents are affected. They're grieving. Everybody is affected around the board."

"It takes more strength to have a forgiving spirit," Taylonn says, taking a long inhale. "It takes a whole lot more strength to forgive and look to make things better. Chicken left us here to actually make things better."

"I'm going to be honest," Kasim says bluntly. "Right now, I'm not forgiving them. I just wish no harm on them as far as their parents having to go through what we went through. But right now ... "

"I understand what you're saying," Taylonn says, cutting him off. "But understand what I'm saying. My thing is, you don't fight hate with hate. You know what I mean? You have to fight hate with the opposite, which is love. We might not be able to reach those dudes who did what they did. But maybe we can reach some other guys that's thinking about doing the same thing. Right now, it's all about how many people we can get to change their mindset. I've got to think about what Chicken would have wanted. Would Chicken have wanted me to run around and look for revenge and kill the people behind her being killed or would she want me to try to change things?

"Every right I think I have, I owe her something to feel this way and keep her name alive in a positive way. When you're trying to be positive, you can't be halfway positive. There's no gray area for that. I know what I want to do. I'm talking and trying to be sensible and not wanting to add fuel to what's going on. As a parent, I'm furious. There's times I'm furious and want to say, 'Give me 10 minutes with them cats.' But if you looking for change, how are we going to do the same thing they did? That's not change. That's just a cycle, and we've got to break the cycle."

Taylonn soon rises from the table. The pendant he wears around his neck is now fully visible. It is a picture of Tayshana smiling with an accompanying poem.

> *If tears could build a stairway*
> *and thoughts a memory lane*
> *I'd walk right up to heaven*
> *and bring you home again*

He wishes Kasim a good night's sleep and strength for the following day. He hops in a cab that goes north up Broadway and stops at the Grant Houses. He will sit in his daughter's room and pray for his own courage, his own Chicken.

This story is an excerpt from a longer article originally published November 14, 2011. The complete text can be found on Grantland.com.

TRAGIC COMEDY

Hard to believe, but at one point Eddie Murphy
was the funniest guy in America

by BILL SIMMONS

There's this little box that African-American actors have to work in, in the first
place, and I was able to rise above that box.

—Eddie Murphy, *Rolling Stone* (Nov. 10, 2011 issue)

We don't consider Eddie Murphy as a pioneer because he never overcame anything. Or so we thought. Bill Russell, Jackie Robinson and Oscar Robertson overcame the worst kind of prejudice imaginable. Muhammad Ali did the same and became part of the Vietnam movement. Sidney Poitier and Bill Cosby broke ground for African-Americans in their respective fields and paved the way for everyone who followed. Richard Pryor pushed racial boundaries while barely containing his seething anger about them. Eddie? He was just funnier than everyone else. That's it. His color mattered, but not as much as it could have. Eventually, he transcended race the way Ali and Jordan did, and Will Smith does right now. We came to think of him as Eddie and Eddie only.

Over the last 30 years, Eddie enjoyed too much success and made too much money; his career became governed by a higher degree of difficulty, almost like we collectively started squeezing his strike zone in 1989 and never stopped. Ask anyone under 35 what they think of Eddie and they'll probably say, "Hasn't been funny for 15 years." Ask anyone from 35 to 50 what they think and they'll say either, "One of the funniest ever" or "Loved that guy, wish he stopped making so many shitty movies." We don't argue about Eddie, we don't celebrate him, we don't really do anything. You're not exactly going out on a limb by praising Eddie Murphy. It's much more interesting to say he sucks, or that he isn't nearly as good as he once was.

Eddie could have shaped that discussion by giving more interviews, making a viral video or three, grabbing meaty supporting parts in indie movies, returning to stand-up clubs, or doing anything else to shed that "hasn't been funny in 15 years" rap. Even an occasional *Saturday Night Live* hosting gig—something he could have ripped off in his sleep—would have done the trick, but Eddie hasn't returned to 30 Rock since he left.[1] He swerved the other way publicly, taking seemingly safe roles and barely interacting with the media: partly to protect his privacy, and partly because of an embarrassing incident in 1997, when Eddie's car was pulled over in the wee hours, in a relatively seedy part of Hollywood, with a transvestite prostitute in the passenger's seat ... and Eddie driving. He claimed to be giving her a ride (the "Good Samaritan" defense), few believed him, and we never really heard from Eddie again. He just kept cranking out those kids' movies.

1. People blame David Spade's vicious cutdown of him in a 1995 "Weekend Update"— a picture of Eddie in *A Vampire in Brooklyn* along with the joke, "Look, kids, a falling star"—and even Eddie admits that he was so rankled that he refused to come to any subsequent anniversary show. But people forget,

Well, until this weekend. At age 50, Eddie Murphy is making a comeback of sorts by co-starring in Ben Stiller's new action comedy, *Tower Heist*. The consensus seems to be, "Fairly entertaining movie, but more importantly, Eddie is Eddie again." You know, the Eddie we loved (and in my case, revered), not the dude from the kids' movies. He even consented to a few interviews this time around, including a candid one in *Rolling Stone* that should have resonated more than it did. Let's dive into Eddie's IMDb page and figure out what happened to his career, why it happened, when things turned … and why we have so much trouble remembering it quite the right way.

Eddie left the show in 1984 and never hosted after that.

STAGE I: THE COMET

I bet you could figure out the combined grosses of people who came off Saturday Night Live *in the movies—me, Adam Sandler, Will Ferrell, Mike Myers, Bill Murray, Dan Aykroyd. I bet it's like $15 billion. That show's like Harvard for the comic actor. When you come off that show and get into the movie business, it's like you're moving into slow motion for a couple of years. You've been working like a crazy person in this pressure cooker, then you're in the movies, just sitting in your trailer.*[2]

2. All these quotes in italics come from Eddie's recent interview with *Rolling Stone*.

Saturday Night Live (1980–1984). Eddie came to *SNL* right when black TV characters were being marginalized as tokens and parodies. That wasn't always the case. In the mid-to-late 1970s, Fred Sanford (*Sanford and Son*), George Jefferson (*The Jeffersons*), James and J.J. Evans (*Good Times*), Benson (*Soap*), James Hayward (*The White Shadow*), and even wisecracking pipsqueak Arnold Jackson (*Diff'rent Strokes*) carried themselves with dignity, stood up for themselves, railed against prejudice, used humor to disarm uncomfortable situations, talked frankly about the plight of poor people and, over and over again, handed some insensitive white person his comeuppance. By 1981, that spirit had faded away. George and Arnold had been neutered. James, Fred and JJ were long gone. Benson had been defanged and spun off into his own show. The White Shadow was getting canceled, and only after CBS' deplorable effort to rescue it by making it whiter.

You know which black characters got to stick around? People like *The Love Boat's* Isaac, a good-natured bartender who happily pointed at the camera in the opening credits. *Heyyyyyyyyyyyy! I'm the token black guy! Would anyone like a piña colada?* You always knew what you were getting from Isaac: He'd serve some drinks, laugh at everyone else's jokes, and on those rare occasions when a black actress came on the show (say, Lola Falana), you knew Isaac was stepping in because God forbid a white character talked to her. Of the top twenty shows from the 1981–82 season, only one revolved around black characters (*The Jeffersons*) and only one other even featured a black character (*The Love Boat*). Of the quality dramas that year, only *Hill Street Blues* bothered to incorporate black characters—police officers Bobby Hill and Neil Washington, both relegated to supporting roles because that's just how it went in the early '80s.

So on *Saturday Night Live* (and television in general), 19-year-old Eddie stood out … to say the least. For its first five years, Garrett Morris had been *SNL's* weak link, its least funny cast member, someone who seemed fifteen years older than everyone else, someone who never fit in … and, of course, someone who was black. Great. Viewers never latched onto any Garrett character except for his Chico Esquela; the show's writers never respected him, repeatedly making him dress in drag and even humiliating him by casting him as the monkey in a *Wizard of* Oz sketch (which would cause an Internet riot if it happened now). According to 1985's fantastic *SNL* book, *Saturday Night: A Backstage History of Saturday Night Live* by Doug Hill and Jeff Weingrad (now out of print, because God forbid we could read it), a deeply depressed Morris started freebasing to cope with his unseemly plight. That only caused their writers to bury him even more. For a cutting-edge comedy show that became such a pop-culture phenomenon in the late 1970s (and a ratings smash), it's kind of startling how white *SNL* really was. Only the show's diverse musical acts and Richard Pryor's electric hosting job in 1975—dead honky—saved it from any real criticism. During the show's first seven seasons (139 shows in all), only five blacks hosted the show: Pryor, Ray Charles, Cicely Tyson, O.J. Simpson, and Bill Russell. Five!

By sheer coincidence, a show that desperately needed diversity stumbled into one of the most talented young celebrities who ever lived ... and on top of that, someone created by God to appear on that show every weekend. I can't even think of an athletic parallel. He's the most talented *SNL* cast member ever, the only one to host the show when he was starring on it. Of the biggest stars in *SNL* history—Eddie, Ferrell, Myers, Dana Carvey, John Belushi, Chevy Chase, Gilda Radner, Sandler, Billy Crystal, Bill Murray, Aykroyd in some order—only Eddie broke into show business on the show.[3] He was a cast member at 19, the show's meal ticket by 20, a movie star by 21, and a full-fledged superduperstar by 22. Tell me when we'll see that again.

Eddie never catered to *SNL*'s mostly white audience, that's for sure. His most popular running sketch was "Mr. Robinson's Neighborhood," which was basically *Mr. Rogers* in the projects (and almost always ended up with him escaping the police). His most popular "Weekend Update" character was Raheem Abdul-Muhammed (who vented about various injustices while always finding a way to play the race card). His most popular running characters were

3. I can't count Robert Downey Jr. Sorry.

Mr. Robinson, Velvet Jones (a goofy pimp), and Dion (a gay hairdresser who wanted to sleep with various black celebs). His most popular celebrity imitations were Stevie Wonder (someone who had always been off-limits in the black community), James Brown, and Michael Jackson (two other black icons), Little Richard Simmons (just a genius creation) and Buckwheat (the retroactively offensive *Little Rascals* character). His edgiest sketches always involved Eddie tapping into the black/white thing: like "Images" by Tyrone Green (a poem by a convict about killing white people) or "Kill the White People" (Tyrone's rasta band singing that song in front of an all-white audience).

Watch these clips on Hulu or YouTube now and they won't feel groundbreaking. Back in the early 80s? You can't even imagine. With Pryor battling a career-killing drug problem[4] and *The Cosby Show* still just a pitch on a piece of paper, only Eddie kept America from relying on white people and British people for laughs. His second-finest moment: the watershed "Buckwheat's Been Shot" series (an inspired parody of the assassination attempt on Ronald Reagan), when Eddie played Buckwheat and his creepy assassin, John David Stutts. His finest moment: when Stevie Wonder hosted the show right as Eddie was doing a wicked (and slightly controversial) impression of him at comedy clubs. You watched that show live thinking, "There's no way Eddie will do Stevie in front of Stevie, right?" … while secretly hoping he would.

It happened in a sketch with Joe Piscopo (playing an agent) bringing Stevie (playing a celeb impersonator) to audition for Murphy (who was a music executive) … with the catch being that Stevie's character billed himself as the Stevie Wonder Experience. So Stevie does his Stevie "impersonation" and botches it horribly. Murphy interjects, "No, no,

4. From 1981 to 1985: *Bustin' Loose, Some Kind of Hero, The Toy, Superman III, Brewster's Millions.*

you're doing it all wrong," then proceeds to slip on a pair of sunglasses as the crowd goes batshit. And he does Stevie with Stevie standing right next to him.

I was 13 when this happened. You can think I'm crazy, I don't care, but the most exciting TV moments of the early '80s were (a) this sketch, (b) Letterman taking his show to L.A. and having Carson as a guest, (c) Michael Jackson singing "Billie Jean" and doing the moonwalk on the "Motown 25" special, (d) Reagan getting shot by Hinckley, (e) Roddy Piper smashing the coconut into Jimmy Snuka's head, and (f) the premiere of "Thriller" on MTV. No other arguments can be accepted. Anyway, Eddie brings the house down with an impression of Stevie singing My Cherie Amour. Unbelievable. Crushes it. With Stevie standing right there. The crowd settles down and Stevie "tries" his impersonation again … still terrible. Eddie's turn. He nails Stevie a second time. After the crowd settles down, the scene shifts back to Stevie for one last "attempt."

Only this time, Fake Stevie suddenly turns into Real Stevie and belts out an a cappella version of My Cherie Amour that was like … I mean, I can't possibly describe how good this was.[5] Nobody could bring it quite like Stevie in his prime. When he nails the last note, the crowd erupts like someone made a midcourt shot to win an NCAA Tournament game; if you watch the tape, even Piscopo breaks character and lets out a delighted yelp. That's how remarkable it was. I know he's a first-ballot Hall of Famer and a musical icon, but I can't imagine Stevie Wonder ever brought the house down quite like that. Eddie pushed him there.

Of course, Eddie never breaks character. He waits for the applause to die down, waits for an extra second and finally says, "No, man, it still sucks." Huge laugh. Perfect ending.

5. I hate that this isn't on the Internet except for Hulu Plus. It's criminal. Hulu needs to designate the best 25 *SNL* sketches and free them from behind the wall, if only for comedy's sake.

At that specific moment, you would have bet anything that Eddie Murphy would be one of the biggest stars in the world someday. Nobody had felt that way about a black entertainer before. Within two years, Eddie would flee the show, star in three smash-hit movies, become a millionaire, and even record a cutting-edge comedy special for HBO. We put Dwight Gooden's Mozart-like 1985 season on a pedestal because of his age (20). Same for a 19-year-old Magic jumping center in the 1980 finals and demolishing the Sixers, Mike Tyson winning the heavyweight title at 20, even 22-year-old LeBron dragging a crappy Cavs team to the 2007 finals. Eddie Murphy had an entire career before he turned 24. We should probably mention this every once in a while.

STAGE II: THE APEX

My significance in film—and again, I'm not going to be delusional—was that I'm the first black actor to take charge in a white world onscreen. That's why I became as popular as I became. People had never seen that before.

48 HRS (1982). One of the great movie experiences of my life. We went on opening weekend in December (me, my mother, my stepfather and a friend) to the old Avon Theater in Stamford, Connecticut. The crowd couldn't have been more jacked up—it was about 70 percent black and 100 percent pro-Eddie. If you remember, Eddie didn't appear on-screen for the first 15 minutes. When he finally showed up (the scene when Nick Nolte's character visits him in jail), there was an electricity within the theater unlike anything I can remember. People were hanging on every line, every joke, everything. At the end of the scene, when Nolte storms off and Eddie screams, "Jack! Jack! (Defiant pause.) FUCK YOU!," someone who had already caught a few showings stood up on cue and screamed "FUCK YOU!" with Eddie. And it went from there. The scene when Eddie rousts the redneck bar practically caused a riot. Bullshit, you're too fucking stupid to have a job. People were doubled over. People were cheering. I've never seen anything like it.

Look, I'm biased: I have watched *48 Hrs* more times than any other movie. (It's not close, actually.) I know every line. I love Reggie Hammond, I love Ganz and Billy Bear, I love the Bus Boys, and I even love that irascible racist with a heart of gold, Jack Cates. So it's tough for me to talk about it rationally—it's one of the most ripped-off movies of the last 30 years. (Think how many wisecracking buddy-cop movies or black/white-didn't-like-each-other-right-away movies have been made since 1982.) But this couldn't have been a smarter first movie for Eddie, and just when it couldn't get any better, fate intervened: Nick Nolte was supposed to host *SNL* on the movie's opening weekend, partied too hard, had to cancel … and Eddie hosted in his place … and crushed it. At that specific point, Eddie Murphy's stock was like Apple's right after the first iPad came out.

DELIRIOUS (1983). A crucial career move because of the salty language, the edgy content and the comedy itself (it's on the short list of "funniest stand-up specials ever"). Eddie taped this for HBO right as HBO was starting to become HBO—they played the show constantly, and really, I can't remember another reason to watch HBO in 1983 unless you were hoping for late-night nudity. I cannot defend Eddie's gay-bashing other than to say that, in 1983, nobody knew any better. I remember laughing at every one of those jokes without even a shred of guilt. When the gay community protested, I even remember thinking they needed to lighten up and get over themselves. Seven years later, when one of my family members came out, I thought differently. It's tough to re-watch those specific parts in 2011; there's no question. But in 1983? That may have been the funniest hour I ever spent. I remember going away for one holiday vacation, bringing the Delirious cassette with me and listening to it, James Brown, and Ice Cream Man dozens of times over the course of a week.

Something bigger was happening, of course: From 1982 to 1985, our "cutting-edge" comedy tastes undeniably shifted from the Carson/Pryor/

Carlin/Martin/Imus generation to Eddie, Howard Stern, Letterman, *SNL* (revived by Eddie, then by the Crystal/Short/Guest season) and every up-and-coming comedian on Letterman's show (Jerry Seinfeld, Jay Leno, Richard Lewis, etc.). By 1985, poor Carson was starting to feel like a dinosaur. Eddie was more responsible than anyone.

TRADING PLACES (1983). The movie that made it clear (a) Eddie wasn't a fluke, (b) Eddie would become Hollywood's biggest star sooner than we thought, (c) Dan Aykroyd could survive without John Belushi, and (d) the next time an actress feels pigeonholed by a specific genre (like Jamie Lee Curtis and horror films), she should just make a comedy and show off her fantastic boobs. And you know what? The movie holds up shockingly well 28 years later—there's absolutely no reason to remake it. One crucial point: *Trading Places* was released on June 8, 1983. Within a week, it became clear that Eddie needed to leave *SNL*. Like, as soon as possible.[6]

BEST DEFENSE (1984). You know someone became a giant star when they release a dogshit movie almost as a dare. You really like me that much? Well, I dare you to see this. You're only allowed one of these—you could call them Mulligan Movies. Julia Roberts in *Dying Young*. Leo in *The Beach*. Eddie in *Best Defense*. Cruise in *Legend*. Sandra Bullock in *The Net*. It's harder to make these now because of social media; if a movie stinks, the word gets out by Friday night. Not in 1984. I saw *Best Defense* on opening weekend and refused to believe these murky reports that it was secretly a terrible Dudley Moore movie with a few Eddie cameos. How could it suck? Eddie's in it! Well, it totally sucked. Even though it was marketed like an Eddie movie, he probably

6. This led to *SNL* changing its contract structure and making it so any cast member had to stay for five years no matter how well their career was going. Now it's six years.

254

appears in 15 percent of it. When he hosted *SNL* the following year, he joked about the movie, "What?! How dare you give me a script like this! Oh, THAT much money? Let's go!" It wouldn't be the last time that happened.

BEVERLY HILLS COP (1984). Apex Eddie. Total command. Killer premise, killer execution, more than a few laughs, everything you'd ever want from a cop movie. *Cop* completed the best three-year run by a funny person: from 1982–84, Eddie was the funniest person alive by any calculation, as well as our single most popular celebrity other than Michael Jackson. It also unleashed one of the better movie-related "What Ifs": *What if Beverly Hills Cop* had been made with the star who originally developed it … that's right, the one and only Sylvester Stallone?!?!?!? My head just exploded.[7]

SATURDAY NIGHT LIVE (1984). Eddie's much-ballyhooed return as host delivers the goods. "White Like Me" becomes the piece everyone remembers … yes, Eddie poking fun at the race thing again. Still holds up. And just like that, he never came back. I still say this was his single biggest career mistake—every two or three years, no matter how many crappy the movies he was making, he should have been showing up at 30 Rock specifically to remind everyone that Eddie Murphy was still a funny motherfucker. Not taking advantage of that was a bigger mistake than *Pluto Nash*, *Vampire in Brooklyn*, *I Spy*, and *Imagine That* combined.

PARTY ALL THE TIME (1985). OK, here's where things start to get a little goofy. Eddie had just spent the past four years becoming America's second-most popular celebrity (trailing only Michael Jackson). He still hadn't turned 24.

7. Three years ago, I was watching *Cop* on one of the HD channels, and maybe it was seeing Jenny Summers' come-hither smirk in high definition for the first time, but how did I never notice the smoldering sexual tension in the scene when Axel brings his old friend Jenny back to his Beverly Hills hotel room and she lays down on his bed and bats her eyelashes at him for a couple of minutes? For God's sake, she did everything but take her clothes off and assume the missionary position, and yet Axel was more interested in ordering room service for Taggart and Rosewood. I don't

Eddie Murphy returned to Saturday Night Live as host in 1984. This was technically his second time hosting, though the first was in 1982 when he was still a cast member. He filled in at the last minute for Nick Nolte.

Naturally, he thought he could do anything ... you know, like make a no. 1 pop album. That's how *Party All the Time* happened. America indulged it the same way that Seth MacFarlane's party guests indulge his Sinatra songs. *That's great, Eddie! We love it! Um ... You think you're going to make a movie again soon?* Only one thing redeemed this song: Rick James' epic performance in the video.[8] They need to make a provision in the NBA lockout settlement that three players per year have to play an 82-game season while wearing Rick James' hair from the "Party All the Time" video.

2nd *MTV VIDEO AWARDS* (1985). Why didn't Eddie make a movie in 1985? I don't know. This turned out to be his best achievement: hosting a relevant-at-the-time show (while wearing a terrible sweater) to protect his "funniest person alive" title, even introducing Run-DMC at one point, a moment that turned out to have a little more meaning than we thought. I remember thinking Eddie and Bernard King were the two coolest people alive in 1984 ... and within a few years, people like the Run-DMC guys and the NWA guys started popping up, rap took off and Eddie suddenly didn't seem so cool anymore. It happens.

get it. Leading me to my $64,000 question: Was Axel Foley secretly gay?

In the first two *Cop* movies (*Cop 3* never happened), Axel didn't have a girlfriend, and we never saw him hook up with a single girl. In *Cop 1*, he convincingly pretended to be Victor Maitlin's lover in a public restaurant. In *Cop 2*, he ruined what could have been a fantastic time for his buddies at the Playboy Mansion by starting a fight for no real reason with a suspected bank robber. In *Cop 1*, he made Taggart and Rosewood follow him to a strip joint, almost like he was overcompensating, then spent more time looking around the club than looking at the girls. In both *Cop* movies, he ably served as a platonic friend for Jenny and

Bill Simmons's Funniest Person of the Year Rankings (Updated from a 2010 "Mailbag")	1975	1979	1981	1987
	Richard Pryor	Robin Williams, Steve Martin (tie)	Bill Murray	Jay Leno, Howard Stern (tie)
	1976		1982-84	
	Chevy Chase	1980	Eddie Murphy	1988
	1977-78	Rodney	1985-86:	Eddie Murphy
	John Belushi	Dangerfield	David Letterman	

THE GOLDEN CHILD (1986). This might be a terrible movie and I've been in denial for 25 years. Here's my defense: Eddie hadn't made a film for two years, so by the time this came out, we were ready to laugh at anything. You know on *Survivor* when they haven't eaten for days, then somebody wins a challenge and gets to eat a meal, and they're just stuffing their face like animals? That was every Eddie fan with *The Golden Child*. It was Eddie food. We didn't care about the quality.

BEVERLY HILLS COP II and *RAW* (1987). *Cop II* ended up being the third-best movie Eddie ever made. Totally underrated. Still holds up. One of the few sequels that actually exceeded the original. (In particular, Rosewood and Taggart were fantastic.) And by the way, comedy sequels almost always fail ... as Eddie would find out three years later. Can you name three comedy sequels that you liked? Meanwhile, *Raw* remains the no. 1 stand-up comedy film of all time even all these years later ($9.1 million opening weekend, $50 million domestically). I didn't like it quite as much as *Delirious*, but only because it wasn't quite as much fun—it's a little angrier, a little more full of itself, a little less funny, and as far as vanity projects go, the opening credits of *Raw* make *Party All the Time* look like child's play. I think Eddie was pretty

Lt. Bogomil's daughter (without ever making a move on either of them); he clicked with two obviously gay characters (the ones played by Damon Wayans and Bronson Pinchot); and he loved playing a perverse cat-and-mouse game with Taggart and Rosewood (two guys). And he was willing to risk his job and his life to avenge the murder of his old "buddy" Mikey, who just happened to be coming back to "crash" at Axel's apartment on the night he was murdered. We're sure Axel Foley was straight? We're sure?

When I brought this up in 2008, I settled this debate by saying that we'd have an official answer when Logo starts running either *Cop* movie. (That's how we settled the "Was *Bull Durham* a chick flick?" argument years ago, when it

1989	1992	1994	1997
Dana Carvey	Jerry Seinfeld, Mike Myers (tie)	Jim Carrey	Garry Shandling
1990		1995	1998
Billy Crystal	1993	Chris Farley	Adam Sandler
	Mike Myers		
1991		1996	1999
Jerry Seinfeld		Chris Rock	Mike Myers, Chris Rock (tie)

much convinced he was the Black Elvis at this point. And why not? What evidence did we have that he wasn't?

COMING TO AMERICA (1988). Eddie's last great movie, as well as his first foray into the whole "playing multiple characters" routine … and a really smart career choice. *Coming to America* feels different than any Eddie movie before it—a little softer, a little smarter, a little more family-friendly. When lumped with *The Cosby Show*, *A Different World*, Arsenio Hall's talk show, Spike Lee's movies, Michael Jordan's Nike commercials and Magic Johnson's swelling popularity, the message was pretty clear: Black people could make successful family movies, carry smash-hit sitcoms, take chances cinematically and sell shoes just like white people could. (In other words, farewell to the days of Isaac the Bartender.) And by the way, we just ended the most successful/funny/creative/original seven-year movie run any comedian ever had. Will Ferrell, Steve Martin, Chevy Chase, Bill Murray, Adam Sandler, Mike Myers, Pryor … nobody can touch Eddie's stretch from 1982 to 1988. It's morbid, but if you applied the Kurt Cobain Test here (in other words, what would have been the optimal time for an athlete or artist to drop dead as a career move?), had Eddie died in an airplane crash four

started running on Lifetime. As far as I'm concerned, the ball is in Logo's hands. They would know better than me.) Then the readers weighed in and repeatedly made the same point: In 1984, America wasn't ready to see Axel Foley bang Jenny Summers in the Beverly Hills Wilshire. It's the same reason they cut out Eddie's sex scene with Charlotte Lewis in *The Golden Child* two years later, right? The whole interracial sex angle was too racy for a big-market movie in the mid-1980s. In 2011? There's a 90 percent chance that Axel bangs Jenny in the Beverly Hills Wilshire … and a 10 percent chance he bangs Rosewood. But he's definitely banging somebody. Anyway …

8. My illegitimate son Rembert Browne wrote on Grantland this

---

2000	2003	2006	2009
Will Ferrell	Dave Chappelle	Sacha Baron Cohen	Zach Galifianiakis
2001	2004		2010
Matt Stone and Trey Parker (tie)	Dave Chappelle, Jon Stewart (tie)	2007 Larry David	Stephen Colbert
2002	2005	2008	2011 Larry David and
Larry David	Steve Carell	Tina Fey	Louis CK (tie)

weeks after *Coming to America* came out, we would have forever discussed him in reverential tones, cried that he was taken too soon, and bemoaned every Eddie movie we never got to see (with every hypothetical movie being fantastic, of course). Real life doesn't work that way. As we were about to find out.

STAGE 3: THE INEVITABLE SWOON

You have to remember, there was no hip-hop back then, or hip-hop was just novelty music, and for years, I'm the whipping boy. Anybody that wanted to vent, I was the one. I got a lot of shit that wasn't fair. The root of it was racist. If I was rubbing you the wrong way, at the core of it was some racist shit: "look at this arrogant nigger, two thumbs waaaaaay down." Then I wasn't helping either. I wasn't giving no humble pie: "Fuck y'all, suck my dick, motherfucker."

HARLEM NIGHTS (1989). During Eddie's ascension and peak, the man lacked any haters other than the gay community (who had rightfully turned on him). Even cynical dickheads loved him. At the height of his fame, Eddie always joked about how people worried about him burning through his money or throwing his career away.[9] His success eventually derailed Eddie from a pure "funny" standpoint, but not for the typical reasons: Funny people need to be around people to stay funny. Poor Eddie was too famous. By 1989, Eddie was either holed up in his New Jersey mansion (surrounded by friends and family) or partying in Hollywood with Arsenio Hall and Magic Johnson (the self-proclaimed "Black Pack"). How can you notice funny things, pick up goofy quirks or find humor in various situations if you're trapped in your mansion,

week: "They should have retitled the video 'Rick James Will Party All the Time With You, Whether Eddie Is Around or Not.' Calling Rick James' performance a 'cameo' is like referring to Brandy as 'Ray-J's sister.' Rude Rude Rude. Rick is the star of this production and there's nothing Eddie Murphy can do about it. Every time he's on-camera, with that supersize curly fry mop shag of a hairdo, I think to myself, 'This might very well be the greatest man alive.'"

9. The inherent racism tied to that concern was always implied, but never fully said. That was the difference between Eddie and someone like Pryor—he did everything with a smile on his face, but if you read between the lines, you knew.

protected in a club by bodyguards or dealing with an endless onslaught of ingratiating ass-kissers?[10] Wouldn't you lose perspective on anything and everything?

My buddy Gus believes that movie comedians have a "funny" shelf life of seven years, almost like a carton of milk. When you look at what happened to Sandler, Carrey, Myers, Ferrell, and everyone else over the years, it's hard to disagree. You almost have to reinvent yourself at that seven-year mark and turn into something else (like Tom Hanks did). Maybe Eddie realized that, and maybe that's why he thought it would be a good idea to star in and direct the unwatchable *Harlem Nights*. His intentions were noble: share a screen with two other African-American comedy icons (Redd Foxx and Pryor), branch out by directing it, make a period piece, take a career chance ... I just know that I limped out of the theater afterwards and haven't seen a frame since. The movie got skewered and it affected every choice Eddie made from that point on, despite what Eddie claimed in *Rolling Stone*.

"I'm never gonna go, 'I want to do this role because it's a challenge. I might not be able to pull it off, that's why I'm excited about doing it.' For someone to sit on the outside, talking about, 'They need to push themselves,' it's so ridiculous. Push myself? I've had a whole fucking career already, these are the gravy years. I have more than distinguished myself in the movie business."

Bullshit. Once upon a time, I think he wanted to push himself: That's why *Coming to America* happened (a good push), and that's why *Harlem Nights* happened (a bad push). He never totally gambled with another movie.

ANOTHER 48 HRS (1990). Tough year for me: *Rocky 5*, *Another 48 Hrs*, *Godfather 3* and Larry Bird missing a dunk

10. One of Eddie's Rolling Stone quotes was inadvertently illuminating: "Michael sat in the same hot seat as Elvis was in, the biggest star in the world ... how can I put it? It's like you're not a person, your human-beingness is compromised. The stuff that everybody had to deal with, take that and magnify it by 1,000—that's where Michael and Elvis are sitting. It's madness swirling around them at all times. On the surface, you're coming off like you have it all together, and behind the scenes, you're completely unraveling."

during a series-deciding loss to the Knicks in the Boston Garden. My whole childhood fell apart in 1990. And by the way, I will never forgive them for screwing up the *48 Hrs* sequel so badly that it actually affects how you watch the first movie. Wait, Kehoe from the first movie was the bad guy all along? What? It's inexplicable. I despise this movie. Eddie didn't do himself any favors by plodding through it while carrying an extra 15 pounds; it was like watching his fat brother doing a Reggie Hammond impersonation. Let's just move on.

BOOMERANG (1992). Eddie's first "comeback" movie. I'm a total *Boomerang* defender—Eddie felt like Eddie again, the story was funny, it's an adult comedy (with sex scenes and everything), it's one of the better "here's what happened when you get whipped" premises, and most important, it features young Halle Berry and an in-her-prime Robin Givens. Robin Givens is so hot in this movie that, after you watch it, Mike Tyson's abrupt downfall, eventual prison sentence and subsequent bankruptcy make total sense. Anyway, I would have bought Eddie stock in 1992. He had seemingly righted the ship. Or so we thought.

THE DISTINGUISHED GENTLEMAN (1993). Not as bad as you remember ... but not good, either. This one felt cheap, like they used all their money for Eddie and saved everywhere else on little things like the cast, director and production crew. Meanwhile, Michael Jordan had quietly grabbed the "Most Famous/Successful/Revered Black Guy" championship belt from Eddie and his friend Michael Jackson, and rap artists like Dr. Dre, Snoop Dogg, and 2Pac were collectively hoisting the "Coolest Black Celebrities" belt. Eddie and Michael Jackson didn't totally fit in anymore. Only they didn't totally know it yet. Which led to ...

"WHATZUPWITU" (1993). Ahhhhhhhhhh! AHHHHHHHHHHHHH-HHHHHHHHH!

BEVERLY HILLS COP III (1994). The ultimate desperation move: running Axel Foley back a third time. I tried to watch this one recently, had one of those, "Wait, this is better than I remembered, was I too harsh on this movie?" moments about six minutes in … and 10 minutes later, I was shaking my head and flipping channels. I'm actually shaking my head as I'm typing this.

A VAMPIRE IN BROOKLYN (1995). Eddie explains: "The only way I was able to do *Nutty Professor* and to get out of my Paramount deal, I had to do *Vampire in Brooklyn*. But you know what ruined that movie? The wig. I walked out in that longhaired wig and people said, "Oh get the fuck out of here! What the hell is this?" I wish he had told me that before I paid for the movie.

Vampire concluded a seven-year run that undid much of the cache of the previous seven-year run … which, again, was the greatest run by any comedian ever. How does that make sense? We certainly don't approach sports this way. If Albert Pujols signs with the Angels for $250 million next month and doesn't live up to that deal—an inevitable statistical swoon, followed by a few DL trips, the slowing of his bat speed and whispers that he's three years older than he claims—it won't change the fact that Albert's first decade ranks up there with anything that's ever happened in baseball. When the Rolling Stones released 30 straight years of forgettable albums from 1982 on, it didn't change how we felt about everything before 1982. Why wouldn't Eddie get the same leeway?

STAGE 4: THE NOT-SO-SUBTLE SHIFT

I've been making movies for so long that now it's all just one body of work. If you have a flop movie, so what? And if you have a hit movie, it's 'so what,' too, it's on to the next movie. If I do something and I die in it, at least I took a chance.

THE NUTTY PROFESSOR (1996). Smart career choice, terrific use of Eddie (the "multiple characters" thing again) … oh, and it made almost

$274 million worldwide. So much for Eddie being washed up.

We'll let Eddie explain (via *Rolling Stone*): "I had a bunch of movies that didn't work. People were saying, 'Eddie's not good,' so I was like, 'Not good? Let me show you what I can fucking do. I'll do something where I play all these different characters.' It's a trip, it seems like every five or six years, you have to do something to remind them that they like you. Then you get offered a bunch of stuff, because you were in a hit, and some of the movies might be shitty, but they throw so much paper at you that you can't say no to it. The problem when you're doing those flicks for a lot of paper, though, is on TV they show your hit right next to your flop, on there forever."[11]

METRO (1997). Just to be sure it's gone, Eddie tries the "wisecracking cop in an R-rated action movie" ploy one last time. And fails. His career strategy falls into place: stop trying to relive the '80s, start cranking out kids' movies for a lot of paper.

DOCTOR DOOLITTLE (1998). IMDb's description: "A Doctor finds out that he can understand what animals are saying. And the animals find out that he understands." (Grimly nodding.) This movie made $294 million worldwide.

HOLY MAN (1998). IMDb again: "Eddie Murphy stars as an over-the-top television evangelist who finds a way to turn television home shopping into a religious experience, and takes America by storm." Yikes. This one bombed ($12 million U.S. gross) and might be more unwatchable than any of Adam Sandler's most dreadful movies with the possible exception of *Little Nicky*. Even worse, Eddie had disappeared from the public eye because of the transvestite incident—we

11. I can't tell you how much I loved this interview. The lights were on these past 15 years but I never knew if Eddie was home, or if he understood everything that had happened to him. Clearly, he did. I almost got the feeling he wanted to say more than he did.

could only judge him movie by movie, so when he released one this bad? You couldn't shake the stink.

LIFE (1998) and *BOWFINGER* (1999). Eddie in *Rolling Stone*: "I could have done a bunch of movies when I stayed as the Axel Foley or Reggie Hammond persona. But I didn't want to be doing the same thing every time. Every now and then, you crash and burn, but that's part of it."

Post-1988 Eddie took more chances than you think, even if it didn't totally seem like it. *Life* didn't work;[12] *Bowfinger* did. He's great in the second one. Maybe it's not a top-five Eddie movie, but it's unequivocally one of his best performances. As Dan Silver pointed out on Grantland earlier this week, Eddie played two different characters so well that it felt like watching two different actors. He absolutely should have been nominated for an Oscar (and wasn't).[13] You can guess what happened next.

NUTTY PROFESSOR II (2000), *SHREK* (2001), *DR. DOOLITTLE 2* (2002). Kids, kids, kids! Eddie had a big family at this point—if you already did everything you ever wanted to do in Hollywood, and you were wealthier than your wildest dreams, would you be able to resist the urge to make big-budget movies for your kids? We should mention that the *Nutty Professor* sequel made $166 million worldwide; *Shrek* made $484.4 million (Eddie provided the voice of the donkey); and the *Doolittle* sequel made $176.1 million. If you rip Eddie for making kids' movies these past 15 years, make sure you point out that nobody enjoyed more success cranking out movies for that genre … a genre which, by the way, became infinitely more important in the DVD/Blu-ray/

12. I alway thought *Life* was his retroactive response to Spike Lee killing him publicly for not caring enough about African-Americans in his movies (it's basically an all-black cast).

13. Your Best Supporting Actors that year: Michael Clarke Duncan for The Green Mile, Haley Joel Osment for The Sixth Sense, Tom Cruise for Magnolia, Jude Law for The Talented Mr. Ripley and winner Michael Caine for The Cider House Rules. Michael Clarke Duncan and Haley Joel Osment? Really?

PPV/iTunes-"I need to throw something on to entertain my kids for 90 minutes" era. I would argue shifting this way was a good career move, not a bad one. But whatever.

ADVENTURES OF PLUTO NASH (2002), **I SPY** (2002), **DADDY DAY CARE** (2003), **THE HAUNTED MANSION** (2003), **SHREK 2** (2004). Rough stretch here with the exception of *Shrek 2*, even if *Haunted Mansion* and *Daddy Day Care* made a combined $346.7 million worldwide. Suddenly, we're approaching the quarter-century mark of the Eddie Experience.

STAGE 5: THE GRAVY YEARS

I turned 50 in April. I know this is a business where success is the exception not the rule. There's nothing you could say—even if you don't like me, you have to give it up. I've been around for 30 years. I think Stallone said it: you don't do 25 years in this business being stinky.

DREAMGIRLS (2006). Yet another Eddie comeback, yet another special Eddie performance ... yet another time when the Academy Awards robbed him. Eddie lost the "Best Supporting Actor" Oscar to Alan Arkin (*Little Miss Sunshine*), in what turned out to be his only Oscar nomination. He should have had three: *Dreamgirls*, *Bowfinger* and ... (wait for it) *Trading Places*. You tell me, what was a better supporting actor performance in 1983: Rip Torn in *Cross Creek*, Sam Shepard in *The Right Stuff*, John Lithgow in *Terms of Endearment*, Charles Durning in *To Be or Not to Be* ... or Eddie's iconic performance as Billy Ray Valentine?[14] That could have

14. Nicholson won for *Terms of Endearment*. And should have.

been one of those excruciating Chris Rock parts and Eddie singlehandedly saved it. He's fantastic in it. Too bad the Academy ignores "funny" performances unless there were mitigating circumstances ... you know, like someone dying in the movie. This is a whole other column.

NORBIT (2007), *SHREK THE THIRD* (2007), *MEET DAVE* (2008). Norbit made $159 million worldwide. Shrek made $484.4 million. Meet Dave sort of bombed, but not really ($50.7 million). Two for three, along with more paper and gravy. True fact: According toboxofficemojo.com, Eddie's movies have grossed over $6.5 billion worldwide before adjusting them for inflation. Will Smith's total: $5.735 billion. Denzel Washington's total: $2.788 billion. I'm just sayin'.

IMAGINE THAT (2009). Eddie in *Rolling Stone*: "Would the 27-year-old Eddie have wondered what I was doing in *Dr. Doolittle*? Or *Shrek*? No. Or in those *Shrek* movies? No. But you know, both the 27-year-old and the 48-year-old was like, "Why am in *Imagine That*?" That movie didn't have a chance at the box office—it's just me and a little girl and a blanket." They should put this quote on the Blu-ray cover.

SHREK FOREVER AFTER (2010). More paper, more gravy. Eddie to *Rolling Stone*: "After all these years, I've done well and I'm cool. I feel comfortable in my skin. I've saved some paper, everybody's healthy, my kids

Top Grossing Eddie Murphy Movies (Totals Adjusted for Inflation)	Shrek 2 $564,144,400	Shrek The Third $372,441,300	Doctor Doolittle $244,051,900
	Beverly Hills Cop $533,171,100	Beverly Hills Cop II $312,046,100	Shrek Forever After **$238,436,500**
	Shrek $375,487,600	Coming to America $247,574,000	The Nutty Professor $375,487,600

are beautiful and smart, doing different things, it's all good. I'm trying to maintain my shit like this and do a different project now and then." Can you really mock him for this? And yet ...

Tower Heist (2011). There's been a subtle Eddie renaissance these past few months: his decision to host the Oscars[15] next February; his candid *Rolling Stone* interview; a few late-night interviews; even a well-reviewed performance in Ben Stiller's new movie. Could Eddie enjoy one last run of mainstream relevancy? Could he rip off a few movie-stealing supporting roles, a little like how Nicholson kept things fresh post-50 with *Broadcast News*, *Batman*, and *A Few Good Men*? Would Eddie have the balls to return to 30 Rock and host *SNL* for the first time in 27 years? Does he realize that two generations of people don't remember when he truly mattered? Does any of this matter in the first place? Could you begrudge him for just being 50, rich and happy, for doing whatever he wants, for trying to "maintain his shit?"

15. Murphy has since dropped out of hosting the Oscars. He had agreed to do it when Brett Ratner was the director, but Ratner was forced to resign from the job after he used some gay slurs in November 2011.

Here was his best *Rolling Stone* quote (in my opinion, anyway): "I saw this documentary on Ronald Reagan and it was like, 'Whoa.' They say he came into the house, and he had the toy White House that he had taken out of the fish tank, and he goes, 'I don't know what I'm doing with this, but I know it had something to do with me.' He had even forgotten he was the president. No matter what you do, all that shit is getting turned into gobbledygook. In 200 years, it's all dust, and in 300 years, it ain't nothing, and in 1,000 years, it's like you weren't even fucking here. But if you were really lucky, if you really did something special, you can hang around a little longer."

It all depends on your definition of hanging around. He's right—all that shit is getting turned into gobbledygook someday.

But in the meantime, couldn't we remember that gobbledygook a little more accurately? Why don't we remember Eddie's peak from 1981 to 1988 a little more reverentially? How he exceeded any other non-musician's apex in my lifetime? How he meant more, did more, wielded the highest approval rating, earned a ridiculous amount of money, took the best chances, bridged classes and ethnicities ... I mean, what else could he have done?

Why don't we think about race when we think about Eddie? Why doesn't Eddie get mentioned with Poitier, Cosby and Pryor every time? Why doesn't it matter that every successful black comic or actor that came after him—Chris Rock, Dave Chappelle, any of the Wayans brothers, Will Smith, you name it—profusely credited Eddie for influencing him?

Why doesn't Eddie get more credit for flipping *Saturday Night Live* on its lily-white ass, reinvigorating itand becoming its only truly successful black cast member?

Why doesn't Eddie get more credit for, as he puts it, becoming "the first black actor to take charge in a white world onscreen?"

Why doesn't everyone ever point out that Eddie is the most successful comedian ever, by any calculation ... and really, it's not even close? That he's one of the best stand-ups ever? That, before Eddie, only white actors were considered sure things at the box office? That Eddie made more money making kids' movies than anyone ever? Doesn't this seem ... I don't know ... relevant?

I don't know why we stopped caring about Eddie, why we never give him the benefit of the doubt, why we never consider him a pioneer, why we were in such a hurry to marginalize him. I just know that we don't, and we don't, and we don't. And we did.

Originally published November 4, 2011.

SNOOKI'S WILT CHAMBERLAIN PERFORMANCE

An epic meltdown,
a reality television legend

by DAVID JACOBY

If there are any lessons to be learned from professional sports, it is that anything can be improved by creating a scoring system and holding a draft. From this lesson, the Grantland *Reality Television Fantasy League was born. A group of owners, including* Grantland *editors and a few friends of* Grantland, *completed a draft to build teams of the most debaucherous reality stars. Each week, David Jacoby takes stock and keeps score.*

You know that famous picture of Wilt Chamberlain holding up the "100" sign? If I were halfway decent at Photoshop, I would replace Wilt's face with the *Jersey Shore*'s Snooki's tan-, tear-, and mascara-covered one.

What happened to America's favorite spherically-shaped human this week made "Hamlet" look like a bad romantic comedy. Snooki's preparation for the arrival of her boyfriend Jionni was one of the happiest things we've ever seen. A woman so excited to see her love that she could not control herself. Spray-tan was applied, hundreds of outfits were auditioned, and the smush room was Febreezed. Jionni rang the bell and immediately Snooki embraced him, nuzzled his familiar (allegedly) PED-enhanced chest, and wept tears of joy. It was pure beauty. One of those moments that makes you believe that the meaning of life can be explained in one word: love. They ran upstairs, he kissed the cheeks of the ladies, awkwardly bro-hugged the fellas, and the couple retired to the smush room. All was well.

When they two emerged, it was time to return to the environment in which they first met: one filled with Italians, thumping house music, and enough alcohol to rid the world of all bacteria. Snooki wore her finest attire, a hot-pink leopard-print number that looked like a bandana being held together with jumper cables. Being a sexually conservative gent, Jionni remarked that he might prefer something a little more demure, but love was in the air and booze needed to be in the bellies, so they left for the club. All was well.

The presence of her lover transformed Snooki. She danced with a lust she had never felt before. She announced the she needed to dance where her soul was, above the crowd, on stage, to show the world her passion. Possessed by her love, she raised her dress and truly showed the world her passion. Jionni was not impressed. All was not well.

Ashamed, Jionni fled. Shocked, no longer possessed by desire, Snooki gave chase. Unable to find her *Guido*, she melted onto the streets of Florence into a weeping heap of rage and sorrow. Inconsolable, she retreated to her bed and continued to wail. Hours later, Jionni returned, announced that her behavior at the nightclub was unacceptable, grabbed his suitcase, and left. Under her hot-pink satin comforter, Snooki found no comfort. Hours earlier she held her true love, but now she held only her stuffed alligator. Reliving it makes me want to cry myself—I must be on my period.

Watching the ballad of the Snooki unfold was exhilarating, exhausting, and ultimately deeply depressing. Seeing her experience joy and nervous anticipation for the arrival of her Guido in bedazzled armor, and the melancholy of his midnight exit, was as close as a healthy human being will ever come to knowing what it is like to be manic depressive. Her box score[1] (pun intended) this week only begins to encapsulate the range of extreme emotions our heroine displayed last night:

1. For a complete list of the categories for which GRTFL players are awarded points, visit Grantland.com.

- Setting up a "prank" thats not really a prank (putting Brittany in Mike's bed)   10
- Crying (when Jionni arrives)   5
- Coitus   25
- Open-mouth kissing (at club with Jionni)   5
- Crying (after Jionni storms off)   5
- Intentional nudity (on the dance floor)   20
- Verbal fighting (with JWOWW)   5
- Falling over in public due to intoxication (chasing after Jionni)   10
- Verbal fighting (with Jionni)   5
- Crying (when talking to Jionni—she had stopped and then started back up)   5
- Unintentional nudity (when she gets into bed after Jionni breaks up with her)   5

Total	**100**

There is only one person who watched this episode and didn't want to jump into the television, wrap Snooki in their arms, and tell her everything was going to be OK—her GRTFL owner, Lane Brown.

This story is an excerpt from a longer Grantland Reality TV Fantasy League column originally published September 23, 2011. The complete text can be found on Grantland.com.

THE "TALENTED ONE" STARTS OVER

After a twenty-year hangover,
Noel Gallagher goes solo

by CHUCK KLOSTERMAN

Noel Gallagher's first official solo record won't be released in America until November, but there was already a party for it in August. It's described as a "listening party," so that's what I expect it to be: six or seven people sitting in an otherwise quiet room, listening to an album titled *Noel Gallagher's High Flying Birds*. For those who care about the music of Oasis, anticipation for this record is greater than for anything Oasis has done in the past 10 years. This is not only because Noel was the principal songwriter for the band, although that's certainly part of it; equally significant is the fact that the finest moments in Oasis' two-decade trajectory have generally occurred when Noel was singing: "Don't Look Back in Anger," the chorus on "Acquiesce," their live cover of Neil Young's "Hey Hey My My (Into the Black)," and a 1996 episode of *MTV Unplugged* (when Noel sang everything while his brother drank beer in the balcony). Oasis completists are interested in Liam Gallagher's new project, *Beady Eye*, the way Smiths fans were interested in *Electronic*, but Noel's material is what matters. The potential is real. Considering the circumstances of the Oasis split, it seems entirely possible that Noel might make a memorable album purely out of spite.

The so-called listening party is not what I anticipated. It's not six or seven people, but 60 or 70. It's held in the penthouse of the Mondrian luxury hotel and sponsored by (or is perhaps just uncommonly supportive of) UV vodka. The walls are white, the couches are white, the light is white. Everything is white (except the audience, which is maybe 4 percent Asian). There are at least two guys who look and talk like Adam Scott's character from *Step Brothers*. At 7:35 p.m., Mercury Records president David Massey picks up a microphone and explains how most people in the 1990s incorrectly assumed Oasis would "just flame out in a drug haze." This is an odd compliment, particularly since that's precisely what many casual fans believe must have happened. After his speech, we get to hear six tracks off *High Flying Birds*. No one even pretends to listen. The partygoers talk the whole time and stand in line for free vodka. I'm told that Noel is allegedly coming to this party later, but I don't stay long enough to find out. As I ride the elevator down from the 26th floor, I find myself hoping he never shows up at all, mostly because I suspect he'd really hate it.

T he next day, I'm scheduled to meet Gallagher at a similar hotel in a different sector of Manhattan. He is 43 minutes late for our 45-minute interview, so I sit and listen to a pair of publicists discussing a third hotel that's 2,462 miles away. It's the Friday before New York will be hit by Hurricane Irene, presenting the Gallagher camp with a strange problem: Noel is now flying to Los Angeles a day early, but he can't get into his room because the King of Tonga (George Tupou V) has supposedly booked an entire floor of the Sunset Tower Hotel. The King of Tonga rocks harder than anyone you know. I have a brief conversation with one of the publicists about a lawsuit Liam recently filed (and then reportedly dropped) against Noel: During a July 6 press conference, Noel claimed Liam had missed a 2009 festival date because of a hangover. Liam saw this as an attack on his professionalism and legally charged Noel with slander, which is a little like Kanye West charging Rickey Henderson with overconfidence. Noel publicly apologized and the problem seemed to evaporate, although Liam continues to insist otherwise.[1] It will likely drag on indefinitely. Ever since Oasis were propelled into existence, Noel and Liam have seemed like boyish versions of Andy Capp who despise each other equally—but this recent schism feels different. It's less fun, somehow. There will undoubtedly be a day in the distant future when Oasis reunites, because just about every group eventually does. But it won't be because these guys suddenly stopped disliking each other.

When I finally meet Gallagher (he'd been having a long lunch with his wife), he seems tired. He looks healthy but grouchy. My suspicion is that he's probably spent his morning talking to other people like me, most of whom have either asked him leading questions about Liam or tried to goad him into insulting other bands at random (as this is something he does not mind doing). He slouches on a couch while we navigate 10 minutes of small talk. We chat about the weather[2] and about why he finally married his girlfriend[3] after dating for 11 years. For no clear reason, he's wearing a garish class ring from a high school in Louisiana, purchased in a Japanese pawnshop 21 years ago. He briefly imagines the backstory of the ring: "I reckon the previous owner was a G.I. who was stationed in Tokyo and pawned this ring for prostitutes." I momentarily get the sense this is never going to become a real interview. But I start to

1. Liam's take on the affair, as reported by the BBC: "I didn't want this to happen. It's not nice suing your family, but like I said, he was telling porkies for the sake of his mates and journalists to get a wise crack on me." (Porkies fired!)

2. "In Britain, we don't get earthquakes or hurricanes," says Noel. "But my assumption is that the preconceived notion of what will happen is usually pretty far off the mark. It will probably be windy. I was here once when they were shutting

ask a few questions and Gallagher starts answering them. And everything he says is hilarious. I don't even know if this can be properly reflected in a profile, because it's not so much what he says as it is the way he says it; Gallagher just has a naturally comedic, endlessly profane delivery that seems unbound by the parameters of normal conversation. He doesn't even have to try. It just happens. I suppose this might all be premeditated, but that's not how it seems. Gallagher's dialogue is like his music: The straightforward virtuosity is a by-product of its apparent effortlessness.

"I've never understood musicians who don't enjoy doing promotional interviews," he says. "I just can't believe it. I always think, 'Your life must have been so brilliant before you were in a band.' Because my life was shit, and this is great. Even after all these years, at 44 years of age, whenever the label asks if I want to go to New York to do promos, I always say yes immediately. And the label is always like, 'Are you sure? It's going to require a lot of interviews?' And I'm like—I don't give a fuck. You're gonna fucking fly me first class to New York and put me in this amazing hotel? And my wife can go fucking shopping four hours a day? What is not to like about that? I fucking love doing press conferences. I don't want to suggest it's all a joke, but come on—the president holds fucking press conferences. Why am I here? Why not enjoy it? I've never felt like I had anything important to say. I can tell a few jokes and we can talk irreverently about fame and success and sport and bullshit and all the crazy people you meet. But I have nothing to say."

This is not accurate.

down the city when there was supposed to be a hurricane. I was like, 'This is what it's fucking like in London every fucking day.' What's wrong with these people?"

3. "The no. 1 reason is just because it's what you do. Reason 2 is that we really do love each other." The couple also has three children.

When you like a band, you want to hear about the good times. When you love a band, you want to hear about the bad times.

I want to hear about *Be Here Now*.

"At the time, I was taking a lot of fucking drugs, so I didn't give a fuck," Gallagher says. "We were taking all the cocaine we could possibly find. But it wasn't like a seedy situation. We were at work. We weren't passed out on the floor with a bottle of Jack Daniel's. We were partying while we were working. And when that record was finished, I took it back to my house and listened to it when there wasn't a party happening and I wasn't out of my mind on cocaine. And my reaction was: 'This is fucking long.' I didn't realize how long it was. It's a long fucking record. And then I looked at the artwork, and it had all the song titles with all the times for each track, and none of them seemed to be under six minutes. So then I was like, 'Fucking hell. What's going on there?' But you know, those were just the songs I wrote, and we recorded them to the best of our abilities. When we had recorded *(What's the Story) Morning Glory?*, nobody from the label bothered us, and we hatched the Golden Egg. So the label was like, 'Don't bother those guys. They're geniuses. Just let them do what they want.' The producer was really just the recording engineer. There was nobody around to say, 'These songs are too long.' It was a good wake-up call, to be honest. I really wonder what would have happened if *Be Here Now* had sold like *Morning Glory*. What would we have done the next time? Just imagine if that album had sold 30 million copies. I probably would have grown a mustache and started wearing a fucking cape."

Because of how the music industry has evolved (read: collapsed), there will never be a situation like 1997's *Be Here Now* again. There are no more situations in which a rock album that's impossible to hear in advance is collectively anticipated by the monoculture. But that's how it was before the release of *Be Here Now*. At the time, Oasis were in a weirdly unassailable position: They were of simultaneous interest to the critical community, the tabloid press, and the populace at large. They were the first post-grunge band to be massive in every context. But the 71-minute

Be Here Now failed, even though it supposedly sold 8 million copies in six months. Its earliest reviews were mostly positive, but the actual reception was disappointing (and the sales proved top-heavy). It's sometimes viewed as the record that killed Britpop. And people turned on Oasis when this happened. The bloated, bass-empty, blow-stretched songs validated critics who'd claimed their early work was overrated, and the absence of a ubiquitous single (such as 1995's "Wonderwall") eroded their position in the culture. From a public-opinion standpoint, they never truly recovered.

"At the end of the cycle of *Morning Glory*, I was hailed as the greatest songwriter since Lennon and McCartney," Gallagher recalls. "Now, I know that I'm not, and I knew I wasn't then. But the perception of everybody since that period has been, 'What the fuck happened to this guy? Wasn't he supposed to be the next fucking Beatles?' I never said that I was the greatest thing since Lennon and McCartney … well, actually, I'm lying. I probably did say that once or twice in interviews. But regardless, look at it this way: Let's say my career had gone backwards. Let say this new solo album had been my debut, and it was mylast two records that sold 20 million copies instead of the first two records. Had this been the case, all the other albums leading up to those last two would be considered a fucking journey. They would be perceived as albums that represent the road to greatness. But just because it started off great doesn't make those other albums any less of a journey. I'll use an American football analogy since we're in America: Let's say you're behind with two minutes to go and you come back to tie the game. It almost feels like you've won. Right? But let's say you've been ahead the whole game and you allow the opponent to tie things up in the final two minutes. Then it feels like you've lost. But the fact of the matter is it's still a fucking tie. The only difference is perception. And the fact of the matter is that Oasis sold 55 million records. If people think we were never good after the '90s, that's irrelevant."

The premise of Oasis' career happening in reverse is an interesting thought experiment and not altogether incorrect (had this inverted sequence actually transpired, it's easy to imagine the kind of person who'd argue that "Supersonic" sucks and that the real Oasis music can only be found on the likes of *Heathen Chemistry*). But it ignores a key element of artistic endeavor: motivation. The album that followed *Be Here Now* was the lowest artistic point in the group's career—and that was due to everything that preceded it.

"We should have never made *Standing on the Shoulder of Giants*," Gallagher says of the 2000 release, an album whose worst moments sometimes sound like an attempt at satirizing the Beatles. "I'd come to the end. At the time, I had no reason or desire to make music. I had no drive. We'd sold all these fucking records and there just seemed to be no point. Liam, to his credit, was the one who was like, 'We're going to make a record, we're going into the studio next month, and you better have some fucking songs written.' We should have gone to wherever it is the Rolling Stones disappear to, wherever the fuck that is. Rent a boat and sail around the Bahamas or whatever. But I went ahead and did it, even though I had no inspiration and couldn't find inspiration anywhere.[4] I just wrote songs for the sake of making an album. We needed a reason to go on a tour. But at the time, I wasn't thinking like that. We all thought the song 'Go Let It Out' was good. I was off [street] drugs, but to get off those I had to go on prescription drugs, which is fucking worse because they come from a doctor. It's just uppers and downers that replace the cocaine and booze. But after that, Gem [Archer][5] and Andy [Bell][6] joined the band, and we started to split up the songwriting duties because they wanted to write songs, too. I'd slowed down as a writer and didn't feel like I could keep writing 20 songs every two years."

4. Liam, however, was inspired by New York.

5. Formerly the guitarist of Heavy Stereo, now a member of Beady Eye. In an interview with Mojo, Gallagher mentioned that Archer is one member of Oasis he openly misses.

Gallagher makes a lot of reference to perception (both his own and other people's), so I try to reframe our conversation: I tell him that I want to run through various points of his life and have him try to recall how other people viewed him and how he viewed himself. He is totally willing to do this, but we never get past 1991.

"I was living in the center of Manchester, so I was always in clubs and at shows and kind of living on the periphery of the music business," he says. "The people at the center of the music scene would have seen me as an outsider. The people who were further outside than me, though, would have thought I was some kind of insider. But I just believed I was at where I would always be. It never occurred to me to be in a band or write songs, even though I played guitar. I'd always thought I might be in the music business, because I loved collecting records and reading about records and all of that. But just being in a road crew,[7] I thought, 'This is fucking great.' I was making $700 a week to plug in some other guy's guitar. I loved it. I never felt like I needed to be onstage. I liked being behind the fucking amplifiers. I had no ambitions. I got to travel the world—drugs, women. Nobody knew who I was after I left town. I didn't have to be anywhere or do anything. But then Liam said, 'You should join my band,[8] because you know how to write songs.' So I went down there on a few Sundays to jam, and it was the first time I'd ever heard other people play my songs. It was amazing to have that happen. And there was another pivotal moment about two years in,[9] before we'd done anything or anyone knew us: I wrote the song 'Columbia.' And the next song I wrote immediately after that was 'Up in the Sky.' And then right after that, I wrote 'Live Forever.' All of this happened in a row, very easily. And I just thought, 'These songs

6. Formerly the guitarist in Ride, now also in Beady Eye. One detail that's somewhat unexplained is the reason why the remaining members of Oasis have sided with Liam in this dispute, at least professionally. For elderly citizens who may recall the acrimonious breakup of Uncle Tupelo, this awkwardly positions Liam as Jeff Tweedy to Noel's Jay Farrar. Speaking to the Japan Times, Bell accused Noel of being more manipulative and media-conscious than he appears on the surface: "I know him, so I'm not disappointed [about what he said about Liam's hangover]. That's what he's like. I know how he spins the press. He's used the press for years. Interviews and press are secondary for us, that's his life."

7. At the time, Gallagher was the guitar tech for the Manchester alternative outfit Inspiral Carpets. You can see footage of this here.

8. This pre-Oasis band was called Rain.

9. The time line for this is a little confusing: In

are fucking great.' Especially 'Live Forever.' I remember thinking, 'I know enough about music to know that this is a good song.' So I took it to the band and we played it, and I instantly knew that I had written a bona fide classic song, even though nobody knew who the fuck we were. So that's when I started to take things quite seriously."

It's hard to tell exactly what "quite seriously" means in this context, since Gallagher is so adamant about not taking himself seriously under any circumstances whatsoever. Is his work on *High Flying Birds* more "serious" than his work with Oasis? That depends on what you thought of him before. It's very much in line with the music he's always made—the first single ("The Death of You and Me") has the most satisfying hook he's composed in many years, and the track "If I Had a Gun" would fit comfortably on any Oasis release after Definitely Maybe. All the lyrics are oblique and there are only two guitar solos on the entire album. Gallagher also has a companion LP coming out in 2012 that he made with the British electronic duo the Amorphous Androgynous, better known in some circles as the Future Sound of London; it still doesn't have a title, but it's an elongated '70s psychedelic record Gallagher compares to *Dark Side of the Moon*. How well these albums will perform is uncertain, mostly because gauging the success of modern records has become so difficult to calculate. But I suppose true success is never easy to quantify. It's not the same as fame, which Gallagher understands completely. He is not the type of artist who longs for success while hating the baggage of celebrity.[10] In fact, he feels the opposite. He sees success as a much more complicated predicament.

"Fame is something that is bestowed upon you because of success. Success is something you have to chase," he explains. "And once you've had success, you have to keep having it

other interviews, Gallagher has indicated that this specific songwriting stretch happened while working in a storehouse, which would seem to predate his actual involvement with Liam's group (although not necessarily).

10. In the 20 years I've interviewed celebrities, I think Gallagher might be the first one to ever directly say that the process of succeeding is more problematic

283

in order not to be a failure. In business, you can have one massive success that earns $50 million overnight, and that's it. You're successful. End of story. But in the music business, you have to keep on doing it. You have to constantly chase success. The fame you just get. I enjoy being famous, because I don't have to do anything. I can just turn up at nice restaurants and people are like, 'Oh, it's Noel fucking Gallagher. Brilliant. Sit down.' But success can ruin people, because you have to chase it, and that can drive you insane. You can get obsessed with the idea of a formula, and you start wondering, 'Why did I sell 20 fucking million albums in less than two years during the '90s, but now I can't sell 20 million albums over the span of 10 years after the turn of the century?' And it's not like I sit around thinking about that, but it's always there. And when you start really chasing success, you start to make mistakes, and that's when things spin out of fucking control."

As he says this, I suspect that he's talking about the real reason he can no longer work with his brother. Here again, the issue is not reality, but perception. The two brothers were able to maintain a working relationship for roughly 20 years, through periods of feast and phases of famine. Yet the perception during that whole time never changed: Noel was always the talented one and Liam was merely the charismatic singer. When they were younger, that perception was tolerable. But now that Liam is 39—and now that it's so clear that this perception will always be the defining image of what Oasis was—he simply could not accept the conditions of the contract.

"I think that's what it was," Gallagher says. "He'd never admit that, though. In the beginning, when I was writing all the songs and he was partying until the break of dawn, he

than the conditions that follow that success. Celebrities have been conditioned to insist that they want their work to be consumed and appreciated, but that they always dread the subsequent lack of anonymity and the vapidity of public recognition; in many ways, Gallagher's response seems like the first honest explanation as to why talented people so often seem depressed and uncomfortable. His perspective might also be colored by the fact that the Gallagher family was authentically poor growing up. I have a suspicion the guys in Kings of Leon might feel the same way.

didn't give a shit. D'you know what I mean? He was fine with it. But when he started to write songs … you know, this is really more of a question for Liam than it is for me, although you'd never get a straight answer from him. In my experience, you never see an older brother[11] jealous of a younger brother. Maybe he did get cast in the role of the performing fucking monkey by the press, and maybe I got cast as the man behind the curtain. Maybe he wanted to be the Wizard of Oz instead of the monkey. Maybe if I'd been a little more tolerant of his behavior things would be different. But at some point he had to take responsibility for the fucking words he was saying. I have a circle of friends, and he kept saying things that were upsetting to these people. And for years I ignored it, because I thought the band was more important. But at some point, I just decided I'd had enough of this. And when things got violent, I left. There is no point in being in a fucking violent rock band.[12] That's nonsense. We've always had a different view of the band: I thought the most important part were the songs, and he though the most important part was the chaos."

As one might expect, Noel also tries to downplay the degree of antipathy the two brothers share, since this type of breakup is more complicated than a typical, nonfamilial implosion. Certain issues between them might still stem from when they shared a bedroom as truculent teenagers. Sometimes, Noel seems amused by their fighting (I can tell he's still kind of proud that one of their 1995 arguments was recorded in the studio and released as a bootleg single in the U.K.). But sometimes he seems angry in a manner that's impossible to fake. There was a period when people assumed the animosity in Oasis might have been a marketing ploy, and perhaps—for a time—it was. But it's not anymore. Their dislike is at least as genuine as their music.

11. There is, of course, an even older Gallagher brother named Paul who maintains a good relationship with both Noel and Liam. I asked Noel how Paul views the situation in Oasis: "Oh, he's a crazy character. He's a DJ, so he's not really the voice of reason."

12. To be fair, it should be noted that—while recording *(What's the Story) Morning Glory?* in 1994—Noel allegedly hit Liam over the head with a cricket bat.

"We never hung out together outside of the band, ever," he says. "Now, of course, at some point I'm going to have to sit in a fucking room with Liam again. Hopefully time will heal some of these wounds. But if you're asking me if it's going to be this Christmas—not a fucking chance."

A s our interview draws to a close, I notice that Gallagher is sniffling and coughing, so I ask if he's getting sick. At first he says yes, but then he gets up for a cup of coffee and says, "To tell you the fucking truth, I'm kind of hungover." It turns out he did show up at the album release party the night before, just before it ended. It turns out he hated it a little less than I suspected.

"In England, we don't go for that kind of stuff," he says. "You just put the record out and people buy it or they don't. Over here, things are a little more corporate. You have to go to parties like that. I find it always helps to get drunk beforehand—not too drunk, but just a little. D'you know what I mean? You have to shake a lot of hands. I have no idea who those people were. My wife was like, 'How can you stand doing this?' But it wasn't that bad, except that now I'm hungover."

This, it seems, is why Noel is different than Liam (and always will be). Liam denies his hangovers and sues people for joking about them; Noel confesses his hangovers and will shake hands with anyone. And when you've been in a band that's been drunk for 20 years, that difference tells you everything you need to know.

Originally published September 6, 2011.

"THE BATTLE BETWEEN THE BIG MARKETS AND THE SMALL MARKETS."

(Bill Simmons and Billy Hunter, continued from 227)

SIMMONS: Last summer we had more dumb contracts handed out maybe any other summer, and this is when these owners knew a lockout was coming.

HUNTER: That's not the union's problem! I don't negotiate the contracts.

SIMMONS: I think it is part of your problem, though. But you—

HUNTER: In what way? Let me ask you; tell me what you would do. Give me your advice.

SIMMONS: Just hear me out. I think it's good for you for the fans to like you. I was in that position with Baron Davis and the Clippers where he was out of shape. He had signed a five-year contract, and he just didn't look like he really cared about being in shape and playing for that money. That's bad for you. That's bad for your union, and I don't think contracts should be longer than four years. I really don't.

HUNTER: Well, I don't agree with that,

SIMMONS: I know you don't. You're the Players' head. Of course you're not going to agree. [Laughter.]

HUNTER: But keep in mind: negotiated

salaries have gone down. That's why for the first time ever the NBA had to write a check to us, to the Players Union, because of the difference in the guaranteed BRI, versus where it actually came in. But I understand what you're saying. What you'd have to do is you negotiate provisions and clauses in the players' contracts that say if they don't come to the camp in shape or if they do this that and the other—

SIMMONS: You guys block all that stuff though. Latrell Sprewell got paid after he chocked his coach.

HUNTER: You think you can sell the NBA on the idea of arbitration? So that at any given moment a guy who wasn't performing and didn't deserve the contract, he would go to arbitration. But on the other hand if we thought the guy was being underpaid, then we could go to arbitration on that.

SIMMONS: Yeah, but that's logical. Nothing about this whole process is logical.

HUNTER: I'm with you! We're open to that kind of stuff, but the league is not open to it. They want it both ways: they want their cake and to eat it too.

I want the NBA to thrive and to be vital. I want the fans like you and others to be happy. Right now the hook is not what it is we propose, I think the hook is the battle in the room between the big markets and the small markets.

THANKSGIVING WITHOUT TURKEY

The surreal world of Las Vegas
during the holidays

by BILL BARNWELL

Vegas is simultaneously the most useful and depressing place in America on Thanksgiving. Useful, of course, because the city turns into a hundred different Thanksgiving dinners with no invitations needed. Virtually every elite restaurant on the Strip remains open and cooks a turkey dinner with all the trimmings that blows away the meal your aunt was going to slave over all day. Chances are that your aunt wasn't preparing pumpkin risotto, foie gras creme brulee, or toasted cinnamon ice cream. If turkey isn't your favorite, restaurants offered alternate options like bison tenderloin, Australian Kobe beef, and bourbon barrel-aged ham. And if you actually like turkey too much, the city's many buffets offered Thanksgiving dinner on a loop for ten hours straight. You are now hungry.

If you're like me, though, you end up spending Thanksgiving night in the sports book at the Stratosphere, watching the 49ers-Ravens game next to a guy with no shoes on shouting "Get his ass!" at Terrell Suggs and points in the general direction of Alex Smith. You recoil in terror as the same guy then clears his throat in some inhuman manner and the snot involuntarily flies out of his mouth onto the floor in front of him. And then you realize that you're basically spending Thanksgiving in a bus station waiting area with better TVs.

The bus station analogy was the one that kept crossing my mind as I sat through an admittedly exciting Ravens-49ers game. There was no-socks guy, who I've already introduced you to. There was muttering guy, constantly complaining that the presentation of the game focused too much on the Harbaugh brothers. "Let the games begin!", he forlornly shouted sometime during the third quarter. Later, in desperate pursuit of the over, he could take no more of the conservative Ravens offense. "Throw the ball for once, Flacco, you fucking jerk." Constant commentary guy gave instant reactions to anything that popped up on the television. "That's a good phone.", he exclaimed in response to an iPhone commercial. "An 80-inch television?" "Why would you want jewelry made of chocolate?" Valid questions all. Another fellow sat in the very corner of the book and drunkenly shouted at the walls in that terrifyingly random way, where you're left afraid in the aftermath of his yelps that he's going to turn around and insist that everyone in the room agree with him and make eye contact with you in the process. Virtually everybody in the half-filled book smoked, which was convenient, since there were ashtrays at each seat. Several were dressed in t-shirts and windbreakers from other casinos, the hallmark of a strong locals crowd. They brought in off-brand convenience store cups and poured vodka out of backpacks. If someone had only announced that the bus to Reno was leaving from Track 7, I would've sworn that 25 people would have gotten up to leave. And I might have gone with them.

It's a little unfair to give the Stratosphere book a review under these possibly atypical circumstances, but it wasn't a pleasant place to watch football. Even though the book is located directly on the casino floor, it was the smokiest book I've been in so far in Vegas. Since it was Thanksgiving night in a depressing casino, most of the people who were there clearly (and rightfully) wanted to be anywhere else. I asked the person working behind the betting counter how much drink tickets were and had two thrown at me with a response of "Don't worry about it." (Eventually, I found out that a bet of $50 on sports or $20 on races will get you a drink ticket.) No waitress ever came by for me to use the drink ticket, but the nearby bar was open and accepted the tickets. Without tickets, a 12-ounce beer was $5.

The 80 seats in the book (60 sports/20 race, but they're all the same) are like nice versions of your desk from junior high, since it has a leather seat and two cupholders, but they're small and each has a wooden armrest that doesn't move. Oh, and an ashtray. It's smoky, remember? The room's best feature is that it has 26 televisions, but even that's not ideal. The sports section has 12 smallish televisions and one very large square screen that the biggest game of the moment is splashed onto. Go look at your HDTV. Is it square? Right.

On Sundays, the Stratosphere offers a separate NFL-only experience in their showroom, similar to what the Hilton does in their theatre. This tends to be a much more comfortable experience. If you find yourself on the bleak North side of the Strip on a Sunday and need a place to watch football, head to the Strat's showroom and skip the sportsbook. If that's not an option, hop in a cab and head somewhere else. And if that's not an option, well, just make sure you're wearing shoes.

As for Thanksgiving dinner? After 27 years of turkey on Thanksgiving, I went to a steakhouse and got a steak, thank you very much. Trust me: You don't miss the turkey.

This story is an excerpt from a longer piece originally published November 30, 2011. The complete text can be found on Grantland.com.

IN DONALD
WE TRUST?

*The less-than-spectacular career of American phenom Donald
Young embodies the less-than-spectacular state of USA tennis*

by LOUISA THOMAS

Even if you're not a tennis fan, you've probably heard about Donald Young. He was the youngest winner of a junior grand slam, a former junior world no. 1. He was the phenom, the kid with the big Nike contract before he could drive, the Future of American Tennis, the men's answer to the Williams sisters, the lefty from the South Side of Chicago who had caught the eye of Agassi's coach, the Next Big Thing who, at the age of 10, impressed John McEnroe with his incredible hands. Young was also a cautionary tale—the brash kid who "had too much too early" and brought attention to himself in unwelcome and regrettable ways, most notably cussing out the United States Tennis Association on Twitter a few months ago. But on Sunday, Donald Young beat Juan Ignacio Chela in straight sets. Now the excited chatter, in a tournament that has been decidedly short of excitement, is that Young is living up to the hype.

But the hype around Young predicted that he'd one day be a championship-level player. This week marks the first time he's ever made it past the third round of a Grand Slam tournament. Jim Courier once said that, at 15 years old, Young was part of a rare pedigree of "obvious bets." Presumably, Courier was betting on more than Young's reaching the round of 16.

When the tennis establishment talks about the 22-year-old now, it suggests that top 20 would be a plausible and happy outcome. Far be it for me to sneeze at being the top 20 in the world at anything. But it's not the stuff of an Ashe or a Sampras. Donald Young was supposed to be one of them.

What he might be, though, is a star. Someone who makes you stop and watch. And, when you assess the landscape of tennis, that might just be enough for Donald Young, because tennis has a star problem.

Tennis thrives and falters according to its personalities, its stars. It's a beautiful game, sometimes astonishingly so, and it's possible just to appreciate the geometry and the physics, the terrific movement of the ball. But people root for people. If sports are substitutes for religious worship, tennis offers a lot in the way of idolatry.

Especially watching on television. It's true that in a lot of ways watching a match is a much better experience in person, that you can see the way the ball (and the players) move in a way that you just can't on TV. You can appreciate the power and the angles, hear the soles of shoes skidding on the courts. There is nothing like the energy of being inside Ashe during a night match at the U.S. Open or happening on a top player on a practice court

---

The Essential Donald Young	Vitals	Tennis History
	DOB: July 23, 1989	Began Playing Tennis: At age 3
	Hometown: Chicago, IL	Compared to John McEnroe by John
	Height: 6'	McEnroe himself: At age 10
	Weight: 160 lbs.	Signed with Nike: At age 15
	Shoe Size: 12 ½	Played first ATP match: At age 15
	Plays: Lefty	Time needed to lose that match: 50 Minutes
	Writes: Righty	Rank of highest ATP seed Young has beaten:
	ATP Career Record: 32-60	5 (Andy Murray)
	All-time high ranking as a	Rank of lowest ATP seed that has beaten
	pro: 39	Young: 1050 (Michael Shabaz)

or having Ivo Karlovic serve toward your head as you sit at knee level in the front row of Court 17. (I flinched every time.) But a camera can train on the face (not to mention legs and other assets). It can emphasize the emotional arc of a match. It can really make you care about who's playing—not only how they're playing but who they are.

The heroes of tennis are not always the most skilled players. Martina Hingis dominated during her time but was not a star. Lindsay Davenport was one of the best of her era and American to boot, but not a star. (Relatedly, was she wearing a muumuu while behind the anchor desk on Sunday night?) When you consider the stars of yesteryear—McEnroe, Borg, Connors, Evert, Ashe, Billie Jean King, Navratilova, Sampras, and so on—some were assholes and some were model citizens, but there was no denying their dynamism, the way they commanded both the court and the camera.

When people wonder where all the Americans are, what they're really asking is where the stars are. There are a number of solid American men and women, and that was true even before a run of upsets by several of them sparked talk of a "resurgence."

The thing is that the American players don't seem to want the spotlight. Andy Roddick still does, but more and more people are having trouble buying it eight years after he won his only major, not least because he can seem bitter and entitled. Mardy Fish is the top American, but he's very open about not wanting to be a star. When he supplanted Roddick as the United States' top-ranked player, he demurred, "You can put his

---

Key Matches of 2011

PTT Thailand Open: Runner-up, lost to Andy Murray (October 2)

BNP Paribas Open: Upset world #5 Andy Murray, his highest ranking opponent to date, in the first round (March 12)

US Open: Defeated world #24 Juan Ignacio Chela in straight sets in the second round (September 4)

Most Ill-advised Tweet of 2011:

"F*** USTA! Their [sic] full of s***! They have screwed me for the last time!"

Inevitable Damage-Control Tweet

"That tweet was out of character. ive never been like that before. but im tired of it. sry about the language, but not the thought behind it."

career on top of mine about six times. He's always going to be the top dog in my generation." Fish practically applauds his opponents when they hit winners. When he defeated Kevin Anderson at Louis Armstrong Stadium, the no. 2 court, he told the crowd he always requests playing there. In a way this is understandable. If you could have a nice career, make it into the top 10, and earn heaps of money doing what you love, why not just enjoy it? The spotlight can be harsh. Even if he won the Australian Open this winter, could you imagine Mardy Fish as anything but a nice, really successful guy? John Isner is a real threat, but he's still known as the guy who won that long match at Wimbledon, and there's just something alarmingly ... tall about him. It's like his personality disappears behind his size. James Blake is still slightly star-ish during the U.S. Open, capable of wowing a crowd with a spectacular shot (like this one!), but he's no longer a threat to make a deep run. Ryan Harrison still seems one temper tantrum away from being sent to his room. Alex Bogomolov has his own incredible backstory, but I'm always confusing him with Alexandr Dolgopolov, which is not a good sign.

Donald Young is different. The story of his promise—the tennis-loving parents, the atmospheric early rise and subsequent unmet expectations, the Twitter outburst, the reemergence at this year's Open, including two upsets of senior players—is told in hundreds of places elsewhere. (To get a glimpse of the darkest days, read Paul Wachter's 2007 profile in the *New York Times Magazine*.) It's a great, simple story. What is even more incredible is that people still want for him, so badly, to be someone they want to watch—one sure route to stardom, as Michael Vick proved last year, is the path of redemption.

Young was rewarded early, and then punished. Some of the backlash he'll admit he deserved. "I felt I didn't need to work as hard as other people," he said the other day. But for now at least, that's changed. Not everything has. He's still got a temper, he's still a little edgy. He still promises to open up the game like the Williams sisters did. He still wears his cap skewed. He is still losing at challenger tournaments. But now he's working for position, and if there's anything that's more appealing than a prodigy, it's a prodigy who makes the most of a second chance. He almost quit tennis, but he's still playing. He's still someone you want to watch.

To his immense credit, Young is being circumspect about his future, even if others are anointing him once more. To hear him tell it after beating Chela in the third round, he knows he's got a long way to go. He's just relieved not to be losing so much, to get to play another day. "It wasn't that I didn't love tennis," he said about his lowest moments, "I just hated losing."

His words made me think of another tennis comeback kid, Jennifer Capriati, who declared herself "sick of losing" after falling to no. 267. She went on to win three Grand Slam titles.

Losing wasn't the worst problem Capriati faced, and winning was no solution. By the age of 17, she'd had two stints in drug rehab and was hospitalized last year after an overdose. People with great stories don't always have great lives. What we want usually has more to do with what's best for us than what's best for them. Of course I want Young to be a star, and I think tennis fans—sports fans—are right to want that, too. He has the potential to draw new people to the game, to make the sport bigger. And he has the potential to be such a fantastic story. But I also think he'll be lucky if his story is half as good as Capriati's—or half as bad.

Originally published September 5, 2011.

REQUIEM FOR R.E.M.

From rumor to rumble
to national noise

by JON DOLAN

It's like the bald man said: bad day. At least for some of us. I know there are those among you who never got it or didn't care or were too young or too dumb to bother. I know there are many reasonable people collecting paychecks and raising children in this very America for whom "Everybody Hurts" or "Shiny Happy People" can exist only in the space where Wimpiness and Pussiness get together to do unspeakable things to each other on grandma's favorite quilted duvet.

But trust a bitter, old, forever-youngish, middle-aged man for a second: To a certain kind of person (white, relatively privileged, vaguely annoying) living through a certain kind of '80s (white, relatively privileged, vaguely annoying), R.E.M. was the gateway band—the gateway to the cooler bands, to bigger ideas, better politics, to culture itself, the way to slip out of something and into something else. Of course, today everything's free and wide-open and no one needs gateways to anything. This isn't the place for one more howitzer round of boo-hoos about how much better it was way back when we had to walk through miles of driven snow and knee-high cigarette butts just to buy an Embarrassment record, when the only way to get the word on new, hot bands was by consulting wizards who lived under bridges and spoke only in riddles through the hair draped over their far-away eyes. But put yourself in that Precambrian mindset just for a second. Or better yet, let 1986 Michael Stipe—The Wizard King himself—do it for you:

MTV: What do you think of the media?

Stipe (SITTING ON A PORCH IN ATHENS, GA.): "I don't own a TV set, I don't read the newspaper, I don't own a radio. Any information I get about world events I get from other people [pulls hands toward self in gathering gesture to signify people coming toward him, as if harvesting souls]."

As a newsgathering resource, this method had its limitations. But it was a nice way to make friends and influence people. The term future anthropologists will use for this process is "word of mouth." [Cue Robert Plant voice from the film *The Song Remains the Same*]: Does anyone remember word of mouth?

That's how the Former Biggest Band in America got built. R.E.M. began as a rumor ('80-'82). Then they were a rumble ('83-'86). Then they were the bright, new national noise ('87-'96). Then there was a decline ('97-'07). Then a soft rebirth ('08-'11). And now they've seen that great and golden exit sign everyone from Bush to Toto finds a way to ignore even though it's slamming them in the forehead, and they've taken the high road of early golf and 3 p.m. mint juleps. And probably reunions. Today, they're in Venerable Band Heaven, where the guys in Faster Pussycat are bringing them drinks and calling them "mister."

Peter Buck always enjoyed saying that when R.E.M. broke up he wanted to be able to look back and know he hadn't done anything to embarrass himself. A couple of British Airways flight attendants might have something to say about that. But you have to admit it: 31 years on the job and a career arc like one of those lush, green, softly sloping hills drawn in children's books. They built their fame on their own terms, and lost it that way, too, in a process that seems almost geologic in 2011.

Thirty-one years is a nice, weird, meaninglessly evocative number, and also a prime number; it's obscure and irreducible, just like a lot of their best songs—be it "Wolves, Lower" or "Ages of You" or "Harborcoat" or "Finest Worksong" or "Losing My Religion," or "New Test Leper" or "Imitation of Life" or "Überlin" or everything on Murmur or everything on Automatic for the People. But it's also appropriate. Had they split as recently as four years ago, "break up" would've seemed too strong a word. People were forgetting they were even around. But now, after 2008's Accelerate and this year's Collapse Into Now—records that revisit old dreams without trying to relive old glories—calling it quits proves once again their vaunted discretion and good taste.

Good taste is kind of an odd engine for worldwide pop appeal, but with a little goofiness thrown in there (see: "Stand"), that's how they did it. Sure, Stipe had his overweening enthusiasm for bold-faced names and Mike Mills had his unfortunate fling with Nudie suits and, hi, Peter Buck's mid-'80s black vests (actually, those have kind of aged OK). But no transgression could ever really shake their air of propriety. They always managed to convince you they wanted it less than they actually did—an almost un-findable stance today. Murmur, 1983's masterpiece, got to no. 36 on the Thriller-era Billboard charts, and they played RFK and Shea while opening for the Police, and yet Buck could always reasonably maintain well into their fame years that they were "the acceptable edge of the unacceptable stuff" rather than vice versa. As marketing, it was genius. People who loved contorting themselves in weird directions, looking for ways to prove (to no one in particular) how "appalled" they were by the "decadence" of the "Reagan '80s," found such studied sheepiness irresistible. Who else would land a top-10 album (1987's Document) then take pains to remind everyone how long they'd struggled to earn it by calling their big cash-in tour the WORK Tour: Yeah! Woo-Hoo! Work! Fuck Motley Crue and their fun tours! I'm gonna spend my $14.95 to go hear some blurry folk-rock jams about the dark side of U.S. policy in Latin America over at the Work Tour!

In retrospect, this seems like a much weirder thing to do with your '80s than dress like Jim McMahon and listen to Cinderella, or pronounce Duran with a "j." But it turned out to be the way a lot of people wanted to spend their '90s, when even in deeply annoying moments, like the famous Stipe VMA's strip-tease of 1991, they reigned as Nirvana's not-as-rocking weird uncles (Kurt Cobain famously had *Automatic for the People* on the stereo the day he killed himself). For a while it seemed like they'd just be giant rock stars forever, in that resilient integrity-swilling way Neil Young is, only bigger. But the brain aneurism that sidelined drummer Bill Berry in 1995 removed their musical motor and seriously waylaid their recording greatness. History may reclaim 2001's Reveal, but I bet Stipe himself can't even name more than three songs on 1998's Up. In a sense, R.E.M. were living only as legacy long before they made it official on Tuesday.

And that's fitting, too. Their songs obsessed over the distance between reality and memory, action and perception, reveling in disconnect and blur: "Fast songs that made you think slow," as critic Ann Powers observed. Musically, their trick bag was never that big: a blammo shake-it-up beat, some sleek, off-handed guitar sex, lyrics that balanced drift and foreboding, all coiled tight then finally unfurling into a chorus of the gods. They had their gimmick like anyone else. But they blew the shtick up in a thousand directions: whether it was making a concept album about Reconstruction that's really mainly about Michael Stipe's love life (1985's Fables of the Reconstruction), or building a parallel between the images of Christ and Marc Bolan on 1996's New Adventures in Hi-Fi, or putting KRS-One and Kate Pierson of the B-52's on the same record (1991's Out of Time), or making a bubblegum tune from a Douglas Sirk movie title (2001's "Imitation of Life") or working references to Lenny Bruce and Lester Bangs into an unlikely radio hit ("It's The End of the World As We Know It (And I Feel Fine)"). They were really quite something, as Former Biggest Bands in America go. And now they're gone. Oh well, it's like that radio hit said: birthday party cheesecake, jelly beans, BOOM! Thanks, fellas.

Originally published September 22, 2011.

JOHN A. WALSH
in conversation with
BILL SIMMONS

The film adaptation of Rum Diary by Hunter Thompson was released in October 2011. Bill Simmons and Grantland consulting editor John A. Walsh seized the occasion to devote an entire episode of the B.S. Report to tell stories about Thompson.

BILL SIMMONS: When you thought about bringing Hunter to Page 2—this is 2000—he had been pretty much out of the limelight for awhile. You were launching Page 2. You had some big name writers—it was the right idea. The Internet, at that point, wasn't being taken seriously as the kind of medium that had big, big talent on it. You went after Hunter, David Halberstam, Ralph Wylie. Did you honestly think, deep down, that he had anything left in the tank at that point?

JOHN A. WALSH: I really didn't know, and I hadn't spoken with him in a couple of years. I spoke with John Skipper who was and is my boss now, and I said, "what if we try and see what we can get out of Hunter?" He was all in. So I said, "Hunter, we'll pay you the top price that we're paying everybody else, the most we can. It won't be Rolling Stone price, it won't be Simon & Schuster. But I think it'll be good for you. You started your career as a sports writer. Wouldn't it be to nice to spend some time at the tail end doing some sports writing?" He loved that analogy—that he had started off in sports and now toward the end he could do something in sports.

SIMMONS: Was it weekly?

WALSH: We said it was weekly. It was weekly during the football season—almost. It was scattered until the basketball season was over. And then it disappeared. He was motivated by the emotion of the moment. If something bizarre happened in sports—if something really crazy happened—he would call up and say "I want to write about that." If he had a crazy idea, like the last column he wrote on shotgun golf (shooting golf balls in the air with Bill Murray. I thought it was one of his really better ones!), it was because he wanted to try and write. If you talked him through a piece, you'd get a couple good pieces. But if you weren't paying attention, he would file because he knew he would get paid for that week's column. It wasn't necessarily a great filing.

SIMMONS: That was still a good signing though, in retrospect, because—for what happened with Page 2 and how it was coming out—that was the lede. Hunter was going on the Internet. That felt like a big deal when it happened.

(Continued on 309.)

The NBA draft has been an annual event for commissioner David Stern to show off his steadfast leadership and good-natured relationship with the players and owners. That was until the 2011 lockout.

WHERE HAS EASY DAVE GONE?

*The story of David Stern is
not so linear anymore*

by BRIAN PHILLIPS

"You take me more seriously than sometimes I take myself," David Stern said during the lockout, and he's been saying the same thing, or at least acting it out, for twenty-five years. It's the key to his whole persona. Stern is the tyrant-as-entertainer, the mob boss who winks while he's calling in the hit. He's always kidding when he seems serious, but he's always deadly serious when he's kidding. Having decided that one of his tasks is to chaperone a skittish (white) public through an intimidating (black) sports league, he's cast himself simultaneously as the cop who keeps you safe and the clown who reminds you that really, it's only a movie.

For a long time, the two pillars of David Stern's commissionership were his air of absolute authority and the sense of easy whimsy with which he inhabited it. Other sports commissioners were functionaries or bureaucrats: Paul Tagliabue was a responsible steward more than a dynamic leader, Bud Selig was a slack-haired joke. But when Stern took the stage to his annual chorus of boos at the NBA draft, he radiated the amused self-confidence of someone who knows he's invincible. That's OK, it's only a game, his smile seemed to say, and everyone knows no one fucks with me. His perspective was always larger than yours, which meant he could afford to be patient with you—even if you hated him, you just couldn't see the whole picture. It also meant that if he decided to kneecap you,[1] you might never understand his reasons, but either way you weren't getting up.

In 1994, during an earlier round of collective bargaining, Stern famously called himself "Easy Dave." For all the achievements on which his legacy supposedly rests—instituting the salary cap, expanding the league's global reach, and so on—it's the creation of the Easy Dave persona that's really Stern's signature accomplishment. Easy Dave could be a buddy from Wednesday-night poker; he could also be a breezily nicknamed crime lord who's launched a fleet of corpses into the East River.[2] Compared to football and baseball, which embody unhumorous American virtues like family and militarism and Kevin Costner, the NBA has always been about show business, and Easy Dave was above all a master of show business, a wry emcee whose union-busting was part of the act. Where other commissioners pushed paper and signed contracts, Stern transformed himself into another item on the NBA's varied menu of entertainment, a sort of dry hybrid of Vince McMahon and Kenesaw Mountain Landis.

Like all born entertainers, Stern has always had an instinct for giving the public what it wants. In the past 15 years or so, the NBA has been haunted by a specter, one that began to coalesce around the advent of Allen Iverson before fully emerging in the wake of the Palace brawl. The specter is, to

1. Stern was arguably 5-0 in NBA lockouts—three with players and two with referees—before whatever the hell happened last week.

2. Quick story: Three weeks after Stern gave himself the Easy Dave moniker, Charles Grantham, who was then the executive director of the players' union, had the gall to use it during a press conference. "I consider him a friend," Stern smiled. Then after a beat: "I didn't say a close friend."

put it simply, the Red State Fan. To put it a little less simply, the specter is "the guy who boasts about preferring college basketball to the NBA without examining the reasons why," or "the suburban dad who wants to take his kids to a game but can't because Stephen Jackson might go on a rampage and kill them." There's a very distinct form of punitive desire that tends to well up in sports fans who see young men living lavishly on their nickel, and it's not always related to race.[3] As the lockout showed, though, it's practically impossible to separate race from the tangle of fan/player and player/management relations in the NBA. Stern, who is almost certainly not personally bothered by hip-hop, gave the Red State Fan what he wanted by handing down a lot of petty decrees that—whatever the intention—came off as an attempt to make the NBA more palatable to white fans. There was the dress code in 2005, the automatic suspensions for taking two steps forward during a fight, the infamous Iverson-tattoo airbrushing, last season's ejections for "excessive complaining," and on and on, all culminating with the mildly amazing 2010 rule that headbands shall not—must not!—be worn upside-down.

The Easy Dave persona took some of the sting out of this, since there was obviously nothing behind it but canny pandering. Step right up! Stern seemed to be shouting. Zach Randolph will not eat your family! What's more, the player-humiliation era happened to coincide with some of the most exciting and profitable NBA seasons in recent memory, so from a league-management standpoint, it might even look like a tactical success.

The problem is that you can't run a sports league on the premise that the players are the fans' natural enemies without undermining the compact that holds the sports league together in the first place. We're supposed to like watching these guys play. The moment Stern started pushing coded cultural messages about making NBA players look and act like the world's

3. One of the first things Fabio Capello did after taking over the English national soccer team in 2008 was to leak a bunch of details about all the rules he'd imposed on the players—they had to eat together every night, no cell phones, etc. This had nothing to do with developing the players and everything to do with humiliating them in front of a public who saw them as pampered underachievers. Capello quickly developed a popular reputation as a Godfather-like enforcer, "Don Fabio," which was not entirely unlike Stern's persona in the NBA.

last Bear Stearns interns, the league's wires got crossed in a very ugly way. It's hard to reduce all the overlapping messages of the NBA's self-presentation over the past few years to one line, but if you tried, it would look something like: "Carmelo Anthony is spectacular! Buy a ticket and we'll put him in his place."

David Stern didn't create American social realities, he only tried to exploit them. But because he did, two things happened. (1) Stern's persona curdled into something far more paternalistic and unlikable, "perspective" suddenly turning into condescension and "authority" turning into arrogance; (2) the conditions that made this lockout so much more damaging and acrimonious than anyone expected fell into place. The most widely reported scene from the negotiations—Dwyane Wade effectively telling Stern to get his finger out of his face—was the worst possible thing that could happen to the Easy Dave character. It revealed the limit of Stern's power. It killed any sense that he was still in sync with basketball as a mechanism for delivering entertainment. And it showed the extent to which he'd alienated the players by, essentially, siding with soft cultural bigotry against them.

And so, with the lockout finished, Stern finds himself in a strange place. He won the negotiations. But he looks like he lost. He's less relevant and more vulnerable than at any previous point in his reign. The Easy Dave of dry quips and unchallenged power has been replaced by a nastier and more bitter figure, one who no longer seems like a perfect fit for the NBA's mood. The old twinkle has been replaced by a bleary impatience. Among wide swathes of the audience, the attempt to caricature the players as greedy thugs fell totally flat during this lockout. For the first time, he's lost the crowd. They're not just booing him, they don't believe in him. Well, crowds can be won back, and he works for the owners, anyway. But it's hard to escape the sense that right now David Stern is a ringmaster who nearly burned down his own circus and can't understand why we don't want him to go on with the show.

Originally published November 29, 2011.

"EVERYTHING CHOCOLATE ON THE MENU."

(Bill Simmons and John A. Walsh, continued from 303)

SIMMONS: You read that Thompson was so revered by his friends and everyone loved having him in their lives. Then you read these stories and he just seems like a nut. What was it about him that made everybody revere him and overlook all of his faults?

WALSH: Because his faults were not as grandiose as the critics ... You could have a bad experience with him—and I've had a couple of very bad ones in my life—but mostly the experiences were memorable, they were funny, they were sweet, they were gentle.The critics who write these things didn't see that.

SIMMONS: Let's say somebody made a movie about him, and the movie consisted of twelve stories that his friends tell in their own voices about some night they had with Hunter. They are acted out by whoever. What would be your story that you'd contribute?

WALSH: I was in Washington DC, I was living with my brother. I was moving back east to work at the *Washington Post* after the West Coast. Hunter called, he was at the Hyatt on Capitol Hill. It was a Sunday and he wanted to watch football. He said "come on over, we'll watch football." So I go over and I sit down. We're ready to go. He says

"Let me call room service." The first order is, "I'd like everything chocolate on the menu."

WALSH: Everything chocolate on the menu?

WALSH: Yes. Then he said, "I'd like a bottle of wild turkey. I'd like a case of Heineken. I'd like six bloody marys. I'd like a dozen grapefruits." The order went on and on, and they actually rolled this stuff into his room! He was there to be a speaker at the NORML Convention, which was at that time a group trying to legalize marijuana. We sat and watched tv. He was given over to making wages. What he would do—and since I was out of work, I didn't have a lot of money—whenever we made a bet, we would scotch tape the bill to the screen. We would have at the top and the bottom of the screen a $20 bill and a $50 bill. Whatever the bet was for that quarter, the winner just took it.

People would come into the room—you didn't know who they were! There were lawyers, there were lobbyists. They would all sit wih him, and have an audience with him. He must have entertained a dozen to two dozen people. The chocolate was sitting there, the Heinekens were sitting there. Whatever you wanted! Hunter was entertaining. That was his idea of being the Perle Mesta of the underground.

WHAT THE JOKER WAS DOING NAKED

*Attempting to explain
the DC Comics reboot*

by ALEX PAPPADEMAS

The most enduring fantasy character in the world of superhero comics is the New Reader. The myth of the New Reader goes like this: Somewhere out there, there are supposedly these people who don't currently read comics, but don't have anything in particular against them, either. And (supposedly) these New Readers even go see movies based on comic books from time to time, and afterwards some of them charge across the (figurative) street into their local comic-bookery, full of bright-eyed, openhearted curiosity and eager to read a monthly periodical with Green Lanterns in it. And then, per myth, they're confronted, there at the new-release rack, with a paralyzingly broad selection of comic books so clotted with incomprehensible backstory, so custom-tailored to the arcane expectations of superhero-comics lifers, that they might as well be printed in Dothraki or C++ or Nadsat instead

Being a comics fan is like being a conservative, because you're always complaining about the mainstream media.

of English. Plus, the guy behind the counter is usually kind of a dick. So instead of buying anything, the New Readers slink out of the Android's Dungeon confused and deflated and maybe ashamed, and an angel loses its wings, and superhero comics slip a little further into cultural and commercial eclipse.

And the other part of the myth is the idea that this doesn't have to happen—that if superhero comics could just figure out how to speak to the people it doesn't currently speak to, if the medium could do away with or at least down-play the qualities that make it seem juvenile or stodgy[1] to outsiders, if comics could just put on a clean shirt and some jeans that fit and order a real drink and stop making tentacle-rape jokes in front of the New Readers, everybody on earth would suddenly get what's so great about them. This is first and foremost an argument you hear from comics creators and people on the business side, but it's one that gets echoed by fans and comics-blog types all the time. And it's weird that fans even care about this, but they do; no other niche pop-cultural fan-cohort is as concerned with how the thing they like is perceived by the world at large. As the great comics critic Chris Sims once joked, being a comics fan is like being a conservative, because you're always complaining about the mainstream media.

In September 2011, as DC Comics rolled out its "New 52" initiative—a line-wide continuity reboot in which the vast and frequently confusing metastory of DC's fictional universe would begin again, younger and fresher, in 52 new #1 issues released over the course of five Wednesdays in September—

1. I know it's weird to imagine a medium being both juvenile and stodgy, but the fact that both of those things are part of the problem sort of testifies to the depths of the problem.

people like DC co-publishers Dan DiDio and Jim Lee did a lot of interviews with the mainstream media, and the New Reader thing got a lot of play. "It's all about getting comics into the hands of new readers," Lee told Today.com. DiDio, in the *Washington Post*: "We told [the writers], 'Leave the past behind. Look to a new audience.'" DiDio, in the Village Voice: "This isn't about rehashing stories, but providing things that new readers can relate to." And on and on, in USA Today, on the front page of the "Arts" section of the *New York Times*, on ABC News and MSNBC and Wired and Ebony.com and MTV Geek, in so many places you'd think they'd killed Superman again—and that was just the first week. This was comics in a shirt with a collar, standing up straight—two industry heavies acting like representatives of a major-media-company subsidiary with a branded-entertainment experience[2] to promote.

This isn't the first time DC's hacked away at the Gordian knot of its own master narrative in order to render its books more accessible and not so, y'know, old-seeming. The 1985 miniseries *Crisis on Infinite Earths* introduced a villain called the Anti-Monitor who was bent for reasons I can't remember on wiping out all the parallel universes and alternate timelines that were supposedly making DC's books hard to follow. Written by Marv Wolfman and drawn by George Perez, who managed to give force and energy to some of the most incredibly overpopulated panels the form has ever seen, *Crisis* was a massive in-story solution to an essentially extra-narrative problem—the fact that DC's universe, unlike Marvel's, which was basically created all at once in the early '60s by Stan Lee, Jack Kirby, and a few other people, has always been way more ad hoc and random, an edifice built up around a bunch of characters who were never supposed to share a world. At the end of the book, after a lot of fighting and screaming and

2. DC recently announced that they've hired the market-research firm Nielsen NRG to gauge reader reaction to the New 52 (the news broke on a couple of comics blogs, and on the Twitter feed of Patton Oswalt, who basically live-Tweeted the experience of being hassled by Nielsen drones during his weekly comic-book run.) What's the weirder part of this, to you—the fact that DC's doing it, or the fact that comic-book companies aren't exit-polling comic-shop customers *all the time*? *What year is it?*

heroic dying, that world ceased to exist, kind of, and a new and more internally consistent DC Universe was born.

Crisis ended up being a nerd-culture turning point; it made it OK to futz with time-honored continuity if the futz itself was part of that continuity. (Think of how J.J. Abrams & Co. jumped through all manner of narrative wormholes to establish that their 2009 Star Trek movie wasn't a wholesale reboot, just a new story set in an alternate timeline created by Romulan Eric Bana; very post-*Crisis*, in that it was an ingenious workaround for a problem 90 percent of the audience didn't even realize was a problem.) And while it wasn't explicitly touted as an attempt to modernize the DC Universe, the notion that the cosmic odometer had been reset to zero gave DC's writers an in-story excuse to excise whatever they wanted from the official canon, including a lot of goofy stories and characters dreamed up in the '50s and '60s by earlier DC creators who assumed (correctly, for the most part) that they were writing for an audience of children who didn't care about realism. New titles launched post-*Crisis* included *Man of Steel*, about an '80s Superman who'd never had whimsical adventures as Superboy or owned a superdog named Krypto, and Frank Miller's paradigmatically gritty *Batman: Year One*.

Anyway—and I swear I actually left a bunch of stuff out of the previous paragraphs for clarity—the New 52 is DC's biggest Ctrl-Alt-Delete moment since Crisis, but it's happening in a completely different cultural landscape. In 1985, comics mostly competed with other comics; the four Batman #1s DC launched in September are competing for the attention of people who like Batman with the latest leaked footage from Christopher Nolan's next Batman movie on YouTube, with Batman games for Xbox and PlayStation, and the DC Universe Online MMORPG featuring Batman, and the Cartoon Network's *Batman: The Brave and the Bold*, and also all other comics, and girls, and the outdoors, where it is sometimes sunny. Obviously, there are Batman die-hards out there with the time and money to blow on all of the above, but the subtext is that DC no longer has the market cornered on the experience of Batman—and that comics in general no longer have the market cornered on the experience of superheroes, and that comics people should maybe be wondering if all these movies and video games and TV shows based on their work are actually making it easier for a generation of potential New Readers to leave comics alone. And yeah, most superhero movies are terrible—but a 14-year-old who digs superheroes these days is more likely than ever to have caught that bug in a way that bypasses print media entirely, and that evolution is only going one way.[3] The New Reader myth says that rising water lifts all Bat-boats and the omnipresence of the Caped Crusader as a transmedia figure will somehow trickle down to comics. But to believe that, you have to believe that screens can somehow lure people back to print. But ask anybody who used to work at a magazine how that's working out.[4]

A lot of smart people have written a lot of smart and/or funny things about what's wrong with the New 52 books. There's a fair amount of sex in these books, and a fair amount of violence, and it's been pointed out that it's the kind of sex and violence that sends a fairly unambiguous message about exactly what kind of New Reader these books seek to service. The stripper superheroine in *Voodoo* who's naked or almost-naked on 15 of the book's 20 pages, and the *Saw*-grade torture-porn in *Suicide Squad*. The slash-fictiony Batman/Catwoman rough-sex scene at the end of *Catwoman #1*, complete with a postcoital-Batman panel you'll want to unsee and dialogue you'll want to unread ("This isn't the first time. Usually it's because I want him. Tonight I think it's because I need him. Every time … he protests. Then … gives in. And he seems … angry. But that doesn't slow either of us down. Still … it doesn't take long … and most of the costumes stay on"). The portrayal, in *Red Hood and the Outsiders*, of Starfire from the *Teen Titans*—who's got a lot

3. DC made the New 52 books available for sale digitally the same day they hit stores, something they've never done before, but it's unclear if anybody's buying them that way, because the company—which hasn't been shy about touting the impressive physical sales of these books—has yet to release any digital-sales numbers. Take that how you want to.

4. It's like Justin Timberlake says (to the guy who's going to play Spider-Man next summer) in The Social Network: "Do you want to buy a Tower Records, Eduardo?"

of preexisting brand awareness among young girls thanks to the Cartoon Network's Teen Titans series—as a brainless fuckdoll who offers no-strings sex to one of her teammates before the first issue's half over.

I should point out here that (1) it's been a while since I've read any DC book regularly, except for Scalped, which is part of the company's exempt-from-the-relaunch Vertigo imprint, so I'm technically a New Reader, and (2) I actually bought and read all 52 of these books, and more than a few of them did not make me die inside.

I liked Animal Man #1, a kitchen-sink horror story written by Jeff Lemire and populated with spindly, extruded-looking humans by artist Travel Foreman. First page of that one is the cleverest piece of exposition in any of these books—a fake Believer magazine Q&A with Buddy "Animal Man" Baker that reproduces the Believer's house style right down to the display-type fonts. (In addition to being a superhero, Animal Man's an animal-rights activist and a part-time movie stuntman; he's totally the kind of superhero the Believer would interview.) I liked the way Men of War #1, a War on Terror update of Sgt. Rock, manages to set a war-comics story in a superhero universe—when the superheroes turn up, they're just red and blue projectiles moving so fast and causing so much collateral damage that they're more dangerous to the grunts on the ground than the insurgents they're supposed to be fighting. I liked the pure mainline insanity of Red Lanterns #1, which was basically 20 pages of aliens vomiting blood and soliloquizing about the hatred burning in their "napalm hearts" and played like Alan Moore on bathtub 'roids or a glossier, more purplish update of Vice cartoonist Johnny Ryan's demented Prison Pit . I liked Keith Giffen's art in OMAC #1—rubberized Jack Kirby homage, but colored like a packet of Smarties. And—I should point out that these are in descending order, by the way—I liked Aquaman #1, in which Geoff Johns confronted the main problem facing anybody trying to make Aquaman cool (namely, the fact that every hack stand-up comedian has a joke about

DC no longer has the market cornered on the experience of Batman.

how Aquaman's not cool because all he does is talk to fish) by having a central-casting emo-kid blogger interview Aquaman at a seafood restaurant and ask him what it feels like to be nobody's favorite superhero. Steer into the skid, baby!

So that's five titles out of 52, at least three of which I'll be sticking with, at least for a while. There are at least five more books from the initial run of #1s that didn't necessarily blow me away as comics-qua-comics but read the way really competent TV pilots play, which, in a comics marketplace increasingly dominated by comics that read like movie pitches written by really smart parrots, has to count for something. But the ones with the strippers and porno-Starfire and jumper-cable torture? Those were as bad as everybody says they are. And their badness had conviction. These books were really going for itwith the not-right. Personally, I'm still trying to process Detective Comics #1, the first new Batman title out of the gate. It starts with Batman thinking, "I'm trying to figure out what the Joker was doing naked"[5] while driving back to the Batcave from a crime scene. It ends with somebody cutting off the Joker's face with a knife—at the Joker's behest—and nailing it to the wall of his cell in Arkham Asylum.[6] "That felt ... fangasmic," the Joker says. (Welcome, New Readers! The Joker just fangasmed! Detective Comics! Rated T for Teen!)

Brand-wise, there's something superweird about DC deciding that the face they want to show the unconverted is a face that's bloody and clown-white and nailed to a nuthouse wall, no question. But ultimately that doesn't really matter. The fact that these books are still as rife with confusing continuity as they've ever been—Superman's a sneering, dungarees-wearing social-justice crusader in Action Comics, a scary alien from Krypton in Justice League, and

5. A line that becomes even unintentionally-funnier if you read it to yourself in Ron Burgundy's "The Human Torch was denied a bank loan" pre-show warm-up voice—although I guess that's true of any line.

6. Besides being pretty over-the-top horrifying for the first Batman comic published as part of what's ostensibly a new-reader outreach program, the face-peel is a straight lift from issue #5 of Garth Ennis' Preacher, except

an upstanding original-flavor benevolent-demigod Man of Steel in Swamp Thing and Supergirl—doesn't matter, either. Because the thing about the New 52 line is that very little of it actually feels like it's aimed at New Readers. There's a lot here for readers who already know they like superhero comics but need a cleavage shot or a disembowelment on every other page to reassure them that they're not wasting their time with children's literature. Lots of books scripted or penciled by dudes who made their bones in the tulip-frenzy-ish-speculator-market-driven gold-foil-stamped comics of the '90s, too—writers like Scott Lobdell and Fabian Nicieza, artists like Lee and Rob Liefeld, names that evoke as much '90s nostalgia in certain circles as a sweet live version of "Yellow Ledbetter" does in others.

And there's enough somber first-person I am a character and here is my motivation *derp derp derp* narration[7] to ensure that any novices who do run across one of these things will have no trouble grasping who Nightwing is and how he feels about being Nightwing, and enough window-dressingy references to YouTube and smartphones and blogs and WikiLeaking and "basement-dwellers who spend all day whining on the Net" to ensure that all these comics will someday be carbon-datable to third-quarter 2011, regardless of how many of them were actually created by dudes who've been deep in the game since '92. What's not here is verbal/visual storytelling that actually attempts to echo the brain-voice of readers whose approach to narrative consumption has been shaped by YouTube, smartphones, and blogs.[8] I'm not even sure what that would look like—a little bit like Crank, maybe, and a little bit like Joe Casey's info-noise-saturated teen-superhero comic The Intimates, which came out way back in 2005. Can you imagine if they'd tried, though, instead of just pushing

in that one the guy doing the peeling nails his victim's face back on upside-down, which sort of makes the whole thing impossible to take as seriously as Detective writer-artist Tony Daniel clearly wants us to take this Joker moment—and also it happened in Preacher, a book that had a "Suggested for Mature Readers" warning on the front cover and didn't have Batman in it.

7. Batman, in *Batman: The Dark Knight #1*: "Fear is a cannibal. A goblin. An unruly tyrant armed with a bludgeon of doubt. But you are the Batman. You are never afraid. Fear lives around every corner. So do you."

8. It's there, a little bit, in the whirlwind pacing of Lemire's *Frankenstein: Agent of S.H.A.D.E.*, and the way that book out-sources exposition

the rough trade further into hard-R territory? Comics that want to look and read like they're from the future, starring superheroes with decades of symbolic weight behind them?

Instead, these are just superhero comics, except for All-Star Western, and even that one's set in Gotham City. There's a ceiling on how many people are going to need this sort of thing in their lives. So call it a retrenchment move disguised as a reimagining. A company doubling down on the kind of stuff that has, historically, brought surly 16-year-olds and grown-ass men with the taste of surly 16-year-olds in the door. That's a stereotype, but that's what target audiences are—straw men with money. The tits and gore aren't there because anybody's confused about how to speak to their intended audience; they're there because DC knows exactly what it's doing, and when other media are eating your lunch you play to your base, and you print the books in a language called Badass. Movies can give you a Joker played by Heath Ledger and video games can give you a Joker you can punch in the nads, but no one in those industries would sign off on a Joker who's naked and asking to have his face flayed. Only comics can give you that, because only comics would.

Originally published October 6, 2011.

to the voice of a database called "S.H.A.D.E.net"—this sort of thing has been done before, but never to my knowledge in a book where you'll also see Frankenstein, now a black-ops monster-hunter, say "Father Time was under strict instructions not to interrupt my vacation on Mars unless it was of the utmost importance."

DISPUTED: HAGLER v. LEONARD

An oral history of the 1987 middleweight championship fight

by ERIC RASKIN

The 1980s were a golden age for the welterweight and middleweight divisions of boxing. The era was headlined by four all-time greats: "Sugar" Ray Leonard, "Marvelous" Marvin Hagler, Thomas Hearns, and Roberto Duran. Between 1980 and 1985, each of them fought all the others, except for Hagler and Leonard. When they finally clashed in 1987, it was the climax of that extraordinary series—not literally the last fight among the foursome, but the last one that mattered. Hagler, the middleweight champion making his 13th defense, and Leonard, the former welterweight champ who was coming off a three-year retirement, were fighting for bragging rights over all their rivals. Who could have guessed that they would still be fighting over those bragging rights more than two decades later?

OWEN FREEMAN

"Sugar" Ray Leonard: Someone comes up to me and says, "The Hagler fight. Great fight, man, great fight." I hear it every day of my life. And every now and then, I hear, "Ray, you know, you didn't win that fight, man."

"Marvelous" Marvin Hagler: I've been talking about this fight over and over for almost 25 years. It's like we just can't get away from it.

I. "MARVIN WAS A BOXER-BUSINESSMAN. RAY WAS A BUSINESSMAN-BOXER."

Stephen Wainwright (HAGLER'S ATTORNEY, 1977–1984): Every time Ray Leonard fought on television, the housewives turned it on. The advertisers understood that Ray was somebody the housewives enjoyed watching, so he became a big draw. He got endorsements because of his performance in the '76 Olympics, which is where he got his fame. Marvin had no Olympics. Marvin had no fame. He had to make it all himself.

Hagler: I wasn't that marketable as a fighter. I had to knock the other guy out.

Larry Merchant (HBO ANALYST): Ray Leonard faced the same challenge Muhammad Ali did early in his career. The hardcore boxing world was always suspicious of a good-looking guy who the women loved. They thought he wasn't serious. He wasn't taken seriously as a fighter until he lost to Roberto Duran in 1980. Before that, there were questions about whether he was just a telegenic fighter with a top-flight amateur career who wasn't tough enough to be an elite professional fighter. But the way he fought against Duran, being willing to mix it up and fight Duran's fight, resonated in the boxing world. And even though he lost a close decision, he actually finished stronger than Duran, which I don't think anyone had ever done before.

Bernard Hopkins (MIDDLEWEIGHT CHAMPION, 1995–2005; CURRENT WBC AND THE RING MAGAZINE LIGHT HEAVYWEIGHT CHAMPION): I always was a Hagler fan. I identified with him. Bald head, black guy, never really smiled. I don't want to compare color—obviously, Leonard was black, too. But Leonard had an Oscar De La Hoya type of presence when it comes to marketing. Leonard had the smile; he had the charisma. Hagler, no disrespect to anyone, but he had the D-block look, like he was out of Rahway State prison. It was a hard look. It was his look. That drew me to him, and later I identified with the hard way he came up through boxing.

Barry Tompkins (HBO BLOW-BY-BLOW COMMENTATOR): I called fights with Ray as my partner for many years, but I also called a few fights with Marvin. Ray and Marvin, I don't know how many people know this, but they always had a relationship. And it was not necessarily a hostile relationship. I think there was respect on both sides. I think both had this appreciation for one another's boxing ability.

Tompkins: It was a white-collar guy and a blue-collar guy. Ray was the white-collar guy; he just knew how to work a room. He was always that way. He had a demeanor that just said, "I'm somebody important." Marvin was an everyman—no pretention at all. I remember when he was champion, one year he and his wife took a Winnebago and went to campgrounds all over the country. I think they took a month, driving around from campground to campground, pressing the flesh with people, barbecuing hamburgers. I really wish more people would have seen that side of him.

Seth Abraham (PRESIDENT, HBO SPORTS): Marvin was more a traditionalist and a purist. The money was great, but he didn't fight for the money. For Marvin, the belts came first, the history came first, the legacy came first. He was a boxer-businessman. Ray was a businessman-boxer.

Wainwright: It was always tricky for Marvin, even as champion, to get both money and exposure. He ultimately decided that fighting on HBO was better than fighting on ABC. He sacrificed the exposure. But he needed the exposure.

II. "WHAT RAY WANTED IN THOSE DAYS, RAY GOT."

Leonard: When I first retired [at the press conference] in '82, that's when I started to feel something missing from my legacy. It was Hagler. Being retired, having suffered a partial detached retina, that's when I really thought about him. I saw my career coming to an end, and that realization made me want the fight to come to fruition more than ever.

Abraham: Boxing was what Ray loved to do. He loved the smell of the sport. He loved the dollars of the sport. And Ray was always looking for challenges. It was going to be hard for him to stay retired.

Leonard: I had fought Hearns and Duran already. Then, during those years, Hagler fought Duran, and Hearns fought Duran, and Hagler fought Hearns. Me versus Hagler was the only one that hadn't happened. I didn't lose sleep, but it stayed with me. Also, I was doing Hagler fights on HBO, and I interviewed Hagler at his home for one of the shows. I'm sitting there, asking Hagler how did he feel, what's next, what's your future, and everything. And I was like, Whoa, this is really strange.

Ollie Dunlap (LEONARD'S ASSISTANT): I recall in San Remo, Italy, when Hagler fought Fulgencio Obelmejias, there was a black Italian kid that was on the card, and he rode up in the elevator with Ray to get a picture. In his broken English, he was saying that, "You can beat Marvin. You have speed." Over the next few years, Ray would hear that from different people.

"Leonard had the smile; he had the charisma. Hagler, no disrespect to anyone, but he had the D-block look."
—Bernard Hopkins

Tompkins: I know exactly when Ray decided that he could beat Hagler. Ray and I were doing

324

the Hagler-Duran fight in 1983. Hagler won, but it went the distance and it wasn't easy. And you have to understand, Ray and Roberto had a relationship. They had great respect for each other. At the end of the fight, Duran came to where we were sitting at ringside and stuck his head between the ropes right after the decision had been announced, and he said to Ray, "You can beat this guy." About six months later, Ray and I were in Florida for a fight, and the day before, he called me. "You want to know how to beat Marvin Hagler?" he said. "You gotta fight three times each round. For 15 seconds at a time, just don't stop throwing punches, and then get out. You've gotta do it at the beginning of the round, once in the middle of the round, and you've gotta finish the round. And that way you steal the fight."

Dunlap: I remember there were a few celebrities at the Hagler-Mugabi fight in 1986. Michael J. Fox was right next to Ray. And at the end of the fight, Ray kind of motioned for me to come up. He had an aisle seat, and I was kneeling down, and he turned to me and said, "I can beat him."

Leonard: I was sitting there with Michael, and I'm watching Hagler get outboxed by a guy who is known as a slugger, John "The Beast" Mugabi. I said, "Michael, I can beat Hagler." He said, "Yeah, Ray, yeah." Everyone thought I was being a smart-ass. But I really saw a sign [in that fight]. I mean, I always felt I could outbox Hagler. If Mugabi can do that, I can do an even better job. That had the most bearing on my decision to go ahead with a Hagler fight. I felt he was at a point that he didn't have that same fire in his body or in his heart. He wasn't the same guy.

Dunlap: That evening, we were in Michael J. Fox's room at Caesars. Whoopi Goldberg, Ray Leonard, and myself. The suite was crowded, so we ended up sitting in the bathroom—somebody was sitting on the toilet, [a] couple people on the side of the bathtub. Ray said to me, "Call Mike [Trainer]." I looked at my watch and said, "You know, it's three hours' difference. It's the wee hours in D.C." He said, "Call Mike. Tell Mike I want to fight Hagler." And we all kind of laughed. Whoopi and Michael J. Fox, they're like, "Yeah, Ray. Sure." The next day this conversation comes up again. Ray is talking about, "Yeah, I can beat Marvin, because I can do this and he's doing that." And everybody's like, "Yeah, Ray. What's the population of your world?" You have to remember, Ray's social life after the surgery was kind of wild. You didn't take his comeback talk serious. He had some hard recreational bad habits. I never thought he would fight again, especially not against Marvin.

Wainwright: A boxer is only entitled to so many beatings, then he slows down. Marvin had never suffered a beating before. That's the first time I ever saw Marvin suffer a beating, the Mugabi fight.

Hagler: Anyone who says I was slowing down from the Hearns fight and the Mugabi fight—no, I wasn't. But maybe I wanted them to think I was? If I looked good out there, Leonard would never come. Everybody's looking [for] a possibility. [If] I'm vulnerable, they could win. For me, I could have retired after Mugabi. But there was one more guy that I wanted to fight.

Al Bernstein (ESPN BOXING ANALYST): I did the Hagler-Mugabi fight, and I didn't think Hagler was slowing down. I thought Mugabi fought a terrific fight, and I thought Hagler was winning that fight by more than the judges were giving him credit for. I don't think he was slowing down appreciably. But you know, Marvin Hagler and Kenny Norton were probably the two boxers who made the biggest mystery of their ages, so we'll never know how well into his 30s Hagler was. And he'd had a very long career. So he should have been, maybe, a little less than he was before.

Leonard: I've heard this theory that I ducked the fight until I saw Marvin slowing down. That's bullshit. As he gets older, I get older, too! And I'm out of the ring! When I hear these things, I laugh. I'm a smaller guy, and I've had one fight in five years and a detached retina. If I did wait until I saw him slowing down, don't I slow down, too?

Bruce Trampler (TOP RANK MATCHMAKER): After the Mugabi fight Marvin didn't want to fight anymore. He couldn't quite formulate a response to the writers after the Mugabi fight. They were saying, "Are you going to retire? You going to fight?" And he couldn't answer them. I think we all knew what the answer was. But he got goaded into [the fight] by Ray, who is kind of a needler, a witty guy. And what Ray wanted in those days, Ray got.

Nigel Collins (*THE RING* MAGAZINE EDITOR-IN-CHIEF): One key event was a supposedly innocent dinner between the two at Leonard's Bethesda, Md., restaurant. With Sugar Ray involved, you have to wonder exactly how innocent it really was. The way things turned out, he was probably setting a trap.

Leonard: The way Marvin thinks, if you're not a threat, Marvin's cool with you. So we sat there at Jameson's, my restaurant, had a few glasses of champagne, and he just started telling me things. He said, "I'm not motivated, I cut easy." He was telling me things that normally a fighter wouldn't [say], because I'm retired. He felt like I felt when I was retired. You don't have that same commitment in your heart, or that edge that we had from day one. I think you become civilized. You're not the fighter you used to be because now you're flying in private planes, you're staying in suites, girls tell you how cute you are. That's not conducive to being a great fighter. He had one foot out the door, I think, after the Mugabi fight. He had all the fame he wanted, he'd made a substantial amount of money. There's not as much reason to keep fighting.

Hagler: I might have retired if not for Leonard wanting to fight me. But I guess you want to prove to yourself that you're the best out there. I didn't want guys to say, "You know what? Hagler never gave me the opportunity to fight him. I would have beat him."

Merchant: The fight was coming together, and my recollection is that the narrative was, "Is Sugar Ray Leonard crazy?"

William Nack (*Sports Illustrated* boxing writer): A great boxing observer, Barney Nagler, always called it "the great delusion." When Ray decided finally to fight Hagler, people were wondering [if] he was a victim of the great delusion—he thinks he can do it again?

Wainwright: There were three things that ultimately were of importance to negotiations for the Leonard-Hagler fight: the number of rounds, the size of the ring, and the size of the gloves. The people negotiating for Marvin allowed Mike Trainer to dictate the terms because they were so confident that Marvin was going to walk right through Ray Leonard. So they gave up on the gloves, they gave up on the number of rounds, and they gave up on the size of the ring. Leonard got a huge ring with huge gloves and 12 rounds instead of 15.

Angelo Dundee (Leonard's head trainer): Whenever I had a fight with Ray Leonard, it was in the contract it had to be a 20-foot ring.

Tony Petronelli (Hagler's assistant trainer and Pat Petronelli's son): What you have to understand is we all thought Marvin was going to beat him. You could have given them the whole parking lot to fight in. I just thought Marvin was too much for him, you know?

Roger "Pit" Perron (Hagler's assistant trainer): Leonard had a lot of demands. Money wasn't one of them. Leonard already had a couple hundred million in the bank, but Marvin had about $20 million. And the concession was that it doesn't matter which kind of gloves they used, it doesn't matter if he went from an 18-foot ring to a 20-foot ring, it doesn't matter if he went from 15 rounds to 12 rounds. Marvin conceded all that in exchange for the pay-per-view revenue from the whole country. And that's why Marvin made $21 million and Leonard made $13 million.

> "When you have a fighter who hasn't lost in 10 years, losing doesn't cross your mind."
> —Lee Samuels

Lee Samuels (Top Rank publicist): Hagler hadn't lost in 10 years. When you have a fighter who hasn't lost in 10 years, losing doesn't cross your mind. Nobody at Top Rank expected him to lose.

III. "MY FACE WAS NOT USED TO GETTING HIT. IT WAS USED TO HAVING MAKEUP PUT ON IT."

Brown: Mike Trainer decided that after not fighting since 1984, Ray needed to have a couple fights before Hagler. So we did simulated fights. We brought in guys from around the country that were in the top 20, and Ray had four fights. He was 4–0 with two knockouts. The other guys had headgear on with small gloves, and Ray had no headgear with bigger gloves because he wanted to get used to getting hit. They were ten-round fights, and the guys got paid good money. No outsiders came in, the gym was closed down completely, nobody knew what was going on.

Leonard: The first few weeks in training camp were just monstrous. These young sparring partners were kicking my butt. My face was not used to getting hit. It was used to having makeup put on it. My cardiovascular was not great. I don't want to train this day. I don't want to train the next day. You know what? I want to go home. The first time I thought about packing it in, I went home and [my wife] Juanita said, "You wish you hadn't said yes to fight Hagler." I got very defensive. She said, "Ray, it's OK." And I looked at her, I said, "Yeah, you're right. I just had a bad day." Then I remembered: I want this.

Carlino: I went out to Palm Springs for Marvin's training camp, and I could tell he was slowing down a little bit. But you didn't want to say that to anybody.

Brown: One night I got a call from Mike. He told me to come to Ray's room, and they told me they wanted me to go spy on Hagler for a couple days. I disguised myself—my hair was black, so I dyed it gray. I put these horn-rimmed glasses on. And I went and sat in the back and watched him train for three days. I picked up a few things. He wanted to be in the center of the ring for all the sparring sessions; when a round would start and the guy would come out of the other corner, he'd be standing in the middle, waiting for him. And he got mad at his sparring partners, the Weaver triplets, because they weren't fighting him. They were boxing him. They were hitting him, moving, and he's like, "Come on, stop moving. Fight me, you little bitch!"

Samuels: The Weaver triplets had a lot of energy. That's why they were brought in, to get Marvin ready to deal with Leonard. And they did pose some problems. That's what they were supposed to do.

Carlino: I remember when J.D. Brown showed up. He was roaming around and I recognized him, but the Petronellis didn't know who he was. I didn't say anything to anyone because I didn't think it mattered. I figured there wasn't anything he could learn from watching public workouts.

Leonard: I said to J.D., "You show me that you were there by taking a picture with him to document it."

Brown: At the end of his training sessions, Hagler would sign autographs and take pictures. So I took a little camera up there, I put my arm around him, somebody took the picture, and I left. I came back and reported what I saw to Ray, and he put it to good use.

Nack: Ray was going to lose this fight until about six weeks before the fight. Even his handlers were demoralized. It was like he wasn't taking it seriously. He was getting in the ring with a murderer, in the boxing sense: a hard-hitting middleweight legend. And even though he might not be the same Hagler he was five years before, he still punched tremendously hard. And Ray was just saying, "It'll be OK, it'll be OK." Well, it wasn't going to be OK. Mike Trainer kept saying to him, "Ray, you've got to suck it up and train like you've never trained in your life." Some people don't know this, but Angie Dundee was never there for Ray's whole training camp. Angie usually came in two to three weeks before a fight. But Mike called him six weeks before and said,

"Angie, you've got to come now. Please come now, the kid needs help. He's taking things too easy." And Angie came in. Every day, they plotted strategy and tactics. Every day, they sat and talked about what he'd have to do to win. They put him in the ring with bangers, hard-hitting guys. Some of the rounds he fought in sparring were seven minutes! That's a long time to have your hands up in front of your face. But that's what Ray started doing.

> "You know what? People think that I'm going to lose this fight. But Hagler can't beat me."
> —"Sugar" Ray Leonard

Brown: I brought in Quincy Taylor to be a sparring partner. He was 3–0 at the time, a young hotshot. I thought he would be good because he fought from both sides, like Hagler. And he could punch.

Leonard: The fight was getting close, and I'd gotten so strong that I was breaking these sparring partners down. I was feeling so strong; I was going to fight Hagler toe-to-toe. I was sharp. And then, five days before the fight I was sparring Quincy Taylor, and I fell asleep for just a second and he hit me with a shot.

Brown: Quincy landed a punch that rocked his kinfolks. Ray was out on his feet. They were over near the corner where I was standing when Quincy hit him, and Quincy kind of realized he hurt him, and I said, "Go to the body! Go to the body!" Ray laid on the ropes like Ali and wiggled, but he was hurt. I think Janks Morton was the person who hollered, "Time!" There was still another minute to go, but if Janks let it go any further, the fight might have gotten canceled. Ray might have gotten knocked out if Quincy landed one more big shot. The van ride back to the hotel, nobody said anything. Everybody was kind of like, If Quincy Taylor did this to Ray Leonard, what would Marvin Hagler do? I remember—it was almost midnight that night—Ray called me on the phone from his room. He said, "You know what? People think that I'm going to lose this fight. But Hagler can't beat me."

Leonard: It changed my strategy. In the first months of training, my whole game plan was box, box, box. That's the logical thing to do against Hagler. But I kind of settled into being a middleweight. I was hitting guys to the body, hurting guys. I felt so strong. I became this beast who was going to beat Hagler up, open up the scar tissue over his eyes, cut him up. What a mistake that would have been. Thank god for Quincy Taylor. I should have paid him more. Best punch I ever took!

IV. "IT WAS LIKE BEING AT THE CENTER OF THE UNIVERSE. IT WAS LIKE THE NORMAL STUFF OF LIFE AND DEATH WERE TEMPORARILY UNIMPORTANT."

George Kimball (BOSTON HERALD BOXING WRITER)[1]: A poll in one Las Vegas newspaper found that 60 of 67 journalists covering the fight favored Hagler. One of them was Leonard's longtime HBO broadcast colleague Larry Merchant, who picked Hagler in nine.

Merchant: There was a personal element for me, because Ray had worked with me at HBO as an analyst. When we had our customary fighter meetings on the day before the fight, Ray asked what I thought, and I said, "Well, I have to pick Hagler." And I could see that he was disappointed—that he thought I had to be not just smarter, but more loyal. And, as he quotes me in his new book, when I left I said, "I'll be happy if you make me a liar."

Hopkins: I thought Hagler was going to walk right through him. Sugar Ray had been off for a while, and I believed [Hagler] was going to walk him down and wear him down and get him late.

1. Former *Boston Herald* columnist George Kimball died in July 2011. When the author requested an interview with him for this oral history, he declined due to health concerns but granted permission to use his book, *Four Kings*, which focuses on the careers of Hagler, Leonard, Hearns, and Duran. His quotes here are taken directly from that work.

Nack: The first piece I wrote was a lead-up to the fight. My editors at *SI* asked me to me to pick a winner. So I actually had a whole paragraph about why Ray was going to win. The fight in Las Vegas when Duran almost beat Hagler convinced me Leonard could win. There were moments in that fight that Duran made Hagler look foolish. And when I saw that fight, I thought, Jesus, Leonard could beat this guy.

Bernstein: There was great energy in that arena. There's something about outdoors at Caesars that was just special. It was in a parking lot when you get down to it, but it just felt special. And the build-up to this fight was unbelievable. It was the quintessential promotion of that time.

Tompkins: I've never been around an event that even approaches that, where there's all that buildup, and then there's the first sign of the fighters, and that sound from the crowd, you could really feel it. Here was the culmination—where the talk stops and the event really starts. It's the most remarkable feeling I've had in 40-some years of broadcasting.

V . "SLOW DOWN, YOU LITTLE BITCH. FIGHT ME LIKE A MAN."

Leonard: The bell rang. I saw Hagler in an orthodox stance. I wanted to say, "Hold on. Stop this fight. You're not doing the right thing!" It was that blatant. I was like, What are you doing? Then I thought, Well, shit, this is great! I had all this nervous energy, but when he did that, it settled me down. It occurred to me that he was a little bit more in awe of the moment than I was, and he was just as concerned as I was. That showed me a vulnerability that Marvin shows no one. When Hagler walks into that ring, he's a beast. But against me, he was more like a little lamb.

Hagler: A lot of people think I made a mistake by fighting him right-handed. But you know, the strategy was that I know he fought another southpaw—I can't remember his name, but [Leonard] looked good that fight. I knew that he knew how to fight southpaws, so you don't want to give him that look.

Brown: I wasn't surprised Hagler came out orthodox. When I spied on him, that's what he was doing. He was boxing guys on the right-hand side—that was his power side. You go back and look—when he fought Tommy Hearns, he knocked him out with a right. So when he came out like that, Ray was prepared because of what I saw in training camp.

Petronelli: That was Marvin's idea. My uncle Goody kept yelling at him, saying when he was fighting southpaw he was doing better. He was yelling, "Stay southpaw!" But Marvin got in his head that Leonard was expecting a southpaw.

Kenny Bayless (CHIEF INSPECTOR IN HAGLER'S CORNER): In the corner between rounds, the Petronellis were so calm. I felt they should have been in Marvin's face, yelling and screaming and saying, "What are you doing? You need to do this!" I thought that Marvin was giving up the early rounds. But they were calm. They were giving instructions. Everything was very professional. I just don't recollect them getting nervous or saying, "Hey, you're losing these early rounds, you need to pick the pace up" or anything like that.

Wainwright: Ray fought Ray's fight. Marvin didn't fight Marvin's fight. When Marvin fought Vito Antuofermo on November 30, 1979, for the title, they called that fight a draw. And the one thing that Antuofermo did in that fight was push Marvin. And as a result of that fight, people decided that the way to beat Marvin Hagler was to push him. But not Ray Leonard. Ray Leonard had seen all those fights and seen how effective Marvin was with anybody who wanted to go toe-to-toe with him, and said, "This is not for me—except the last 30 seconds of the round, then I'll do a little dance and throw a bunch of punches."

Leonard: At the start of the fourth round, I rushed right to the center of the ring. I did that in a lot of rounds. J.D. had come back from Palm Springs and said, "Ray, one thing about Hagler, he feels that the first person to the center of the ring wins the fight." So that's why I would do it. It's just the little things that I did to play with his head. Anything to prevent him from doing what he wanted. This was a small thing, but it was big for him. And later in the fourth round I landed that bolo punch to the body. It didn't hurt him, but it hurt his pride.

Merchant: All of a sudden the perception of the fight was completely different. Ray Leonard, the underdog, was winning. He was winning the drama of the fight as well as the fight itself. That builds a certain kind of emotional force and momentum, and maybe it influences some judges in close rounds.

Hagler: I still came on, fighting him on the inside, even trying to beat him with his own speed. Everybody was looking for me to knock him out, but you know what? I just wanted to beat him.

Leonard: He buckled me in the fifth round with an uppercut. That was the only blow that hurt me. But when I use the word "buckled," I mean I was knocked off balance, stunned, but I wasn't in trouble. It was nowhere near like how I felt after the Quincy Taylor shot.

Tompkins: Instead of taking a step back—it happened at close quarters—he got into Marvin and tried to body punch him. Something inside him said, "If I take a step back, I'll get knocked out." So instead, almost instinctively, he stepped forward and threw punches. He said Marvin never knew he hurt him.

Perron: There were a couple times where I jumped up and said, "I think we got him!" Marvin landed his best shot on Leonard's chin, and I saw Leonard was hurt. I was like, "Marvin, you got him hurt, finish him." But somehow Leonard wormed his way out of it. Marvin started winning a lot of the rounds from that point on, but Marvin never got to put the finishing touch on him. Marvin was a great finisher. He got all these knockouts not by being a one-punch knockout guy, but he'd wear you down when he got you hurt. It never happened in the Leonard fight. One of the low points of my life, I tell you.

Leonard: He shoved me when the bell rang to end the fifth. He was getting frustrated. I don't know what prompted that push, specifically. Maybe I looked at him a certain way, but it bothered him.

Hagler: People say his movement gave me problems. Movement? You mean running? The way the public looks at it, they say that was his strategy. I don't think that was strategy. I think he was fighting to survive. He tried to steal the last part of every round—that's amateur. Professional, you got to win the whole round, not 30 seconds.

Leonard: A couple days before the fight, I told Ollie Dunlap to tell me when there's 30 seconds left in each round, so I'd know to throw those combinations and impress the judges. It's not a bad thing! I wasn't really "stealing" rounds. I was keeping the round close, then winning the final 30 seconds. That was the plan.

Tompkins: If a judge is sitting there, thinking, This round could go either way, then at the end of the round somebody has a big flurry, that becomes the deciding factor.

Dave Moretti (official ringside judge): I gave Leonard, like, five out of the first six rounds, and when you do that, the guy's only gotta win two more rounds to pull it off. I just felt that he hit him at will the first four or five rounds. He was fast, he made Hagler miss, he did what he wanted to. He dominated the first half of the fight.

Hagler: He's running, [doing] that pitty-patty thing. He didn't hurt me. It's just me waiting for him to slow down or stop.

Leonard: He kept saying, "Slow down, you little bitch. Fight me like a man."

Steele: That was part of Leonard's plan. When you're talking trash, you ain't punching. I'd say, "Cut it out guys, let's fight," but he had Hagler's mind all messed up. If Hagler was talking, that meant it was going Leonard's way. Leonard needed that rest. Leonard needed him talking trash instead of punching.

> "We knew Leonard was going to run. But we thought somewhere along the line Marvin's gonna catch him."
>
> —Richard Steele

Hagler: I give so much credit to the guys like Roberto Duran and Tommy Hearns and Mugabi. Even guys before that, Mustafa Hamsho, even the second fight with Antuofermo, these guys came to take my title. This guy only came to survive.

Leonard: He wanted me to fight him the same way Hearns fought him. He says, "Ray wasn't fighting, he was running. I respect guys like Hearns and Duran." He beat those guys! Why would I stand there and fight him?

Perron: I couldn't believe what I was seeing. We knew Leonard was going to run. That's why he wanted a 20-foot ring. But we thought somewhere along the line Marvin's gonna catch him.

Steele: At the end of every round, I would say to myself, Well, I guess Marvin's gonna start the next round. We had conditioned ourselves that Marvin was going to just eat this guy up. But then it was too late.

Dunlap: Ray won the fight, in my opinion, in the ninth round. Marvin had him on the ropes, and Ray backed him off. And at that point, I felt like people were watching Ray rather than watching the fight. He backed up the beast. To me, that's when the fight turned. Marvin was getting back into the fight. He was making it close on the scorecards, and all of a sudden Ray took it away from him.

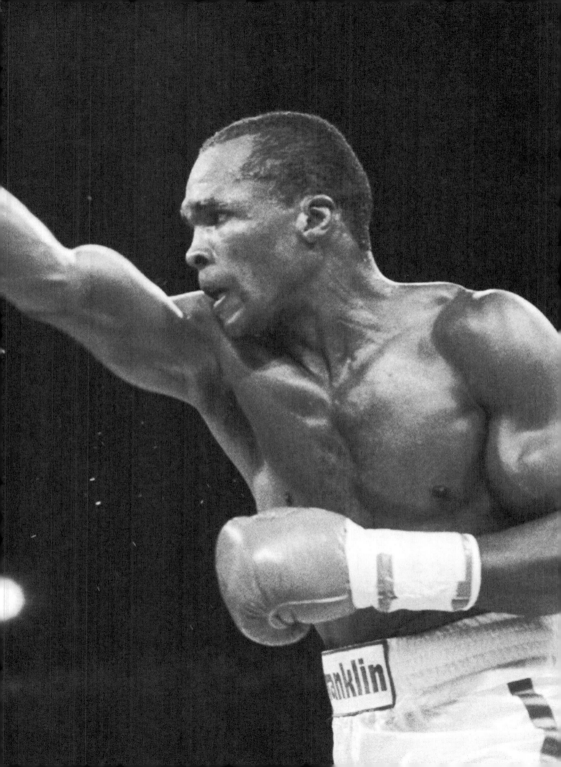

Hagler: They said maybe I lost the first three rounds. But it's not how many rounds that you win—it's how you finish the fight. This is a 12-round fight; you can lose three rounds and make up the difference by the end. I think I did that. In the last two rounds, I really had him going. I had him hurt in the 11th and the 12th.

Dundee: In the corner, between rounds, I'm yelling, "Six minutes left!" Then, "Three minutes for the title!"

Leonard: To be honest, I was exhausted. I was exhausted in the fifth round, sixth round. I was dead. I couldn't have won without Angelo. He said the right things, just what I needed to hear. That's the value of Angelo. He does the right thing at the right moment. Like with Ali, cutting the gloves against Henry Cooper.[1] Angelo's so cool under pressure. That's his magic.

Dundee: The guy who helped the most in that fight was the referee. Before the 12th round, he says, "Last round! 12th round!" I says, "Next champ!" Ray jumped up, put his arms up. You utilize every little thing you can get.

Nack: What I recall of that last round was Hagler getting desperate, trying to knock him out. He threw everything he had at him. He got him in a corner and was wailing away at him, and I thought to myself, Uh-oh, this is it. This is it for Leonard. He's had it. He's going to get hit on the button two or three times and he's going to go down and that'll be the end of it. It was like Hagler throwing punches at Hearns, that same kind of abandon, that same kind of ferocity—punches up, punches down, lefts, rights. Ray was covering up, and all of a sudden Ray threw a combination of punches that whipped Hagler's face left-right-left-right. And the crowd, 15,000 people, came roaring to their feet. All of the reporters came to our feet. It was unbelievable. It was like he'd come back from the dead. And then he spun away, and Hagler chased him, and by this time you could hear people chanting, "Sugar Ray! Su-gar Ray! Su-gar Ray!" People realized that they were witnessing something extraordinary in the history of the sport.

Steele: Leonard was through after 12 rounds. It took everything that Angelo had to push him through. If he'd had to go three more, he wouldn't have been there.

Leonard: If it had been scheduled for 15, I would have trained for 15. Marvin was tired, too!

VI. "WHEN WE HEARD, 'WE HAVE A SPLIT DECISION,' I SAID, 'UH-OH.'"

Hagler: I was bouncing around the ring, and I'm all happy and everything, because he knew it and I knew it—that I won the fight.

Leonard: He did things that were totally uncharacteristic of him. At the end of the fight, before the decision was announced, he was dancing! Hagler never does that crap. He knew ... he knew.

Hagler: As a matter of fact, he even told me himself. He said, "You beat me, babe." That was in the ring, right after the fight. He's now denying that he said that. Maybe he can't remember, but I remember because you whispered it in my ear. And between two people, you know. If you beat me, I would tell the world, "Hey, I lost the fight." There's nothing to be ashamed about. But you can't go around knowing that you did not win the fight and still say you did. After enough time, I guess you start believing it yourself.

Leonard: First of all, even if I felt he did win, I wouldn't tell him that. No fighter would say, "Oh man, he kicked my ass!" All the way back to Jack Johnson, a fighter never says, "I lost the fight; you won the fight." I didn't say that to him. I said, "Marvin, you're still a champion to me." And I kissed him on his cheek. He misinterpreted what I said, and now it's out there. Some people believe it, some people don't.

Leonard: I wasn't sure which way it was going to go. They say you gotta take the belt from the champion. I felt that I did enough. He was missing more than he was hitting me.

Nack: People were on the edge of their seats. And when it was announced it was a split decision, people in the audience booed. I think they figured that Leonard had won. I thought Leonard won clearly, but when I look at it on tape, it's closer than I thought. Anyway, what I remember is when the announcer said, "The winner … and the … " then he said "new," and the place went nuts, " … middleweight champion of the world, Sugar Ray Leonard!" Hagler was furious.

Moretti: I don't believe it was that hard to score. I had it 115–113 for Leonard. For some reason I was just locked in that night. After the fight I told Lou Filippo, who had it 115-113 for Hagler, "I can't find a problem with your score." Lou was the type who preferred harder punches. Well, they might have been harder, but they just weren't enough—in my opinion, anyway. Lou said he didn't have a problem with my score either. As for Jo Jo Guerra's card, I believe he had it 118–110 for Leonard—that's the way he seen it, and I respect him as a judge. I don't find fault in anybody's score. Where I was sitting, I didn't see that, obviously. But believe me, there's been fights where I looked at my score and then I watched it on TV, and then I wanted to change my score a little bit. It's a possibility that you don't see the same thing in these rounds where one punch or two punches make a difference. If the referee blocks you at a key moment, that can change your view of the round. This one, I've re-watched it several times, but never changed my score. I was locked in, and what I seen that night, that's pretty much what I see each time I watch it.

Wainwright: I did not score the fight round by round, but I absolutely feel Marvin deserved it. He was the one who took the fight to Leonard. Leonard never took the fight to Hagler. But Ray was too elusive. And that's what he planned on being—elusive for 2½ minutes, then performing in the last 30 seconds.

Merchant: I scored it a draw. I thought Hagler did enough to hold on to his title. But Leonard was able, as I said at the time, to steal the fight fair and square. As an underdog, he won the drama and looked like he was able to impose his boxing style on Hagler. If you go back in history, there were other examples of this, where the great fighter got the decision because he was the fighter that the public loved. I think this was a very close fight, but I also think Ray pulled off a historic con job to get the decision—and I think he earned that.

Tompkins: Marvin just seemed a step slow. He wasn't as busy. In my opinion, he let Ray steal the fight. I scored it for Ray, by a point or two. And believe me, I wasn't partial, because I liked both guys.

Bernstein: I thought that the right scorecard was Lou Filippo's, a two-point win for Hagler. While Ray surely won his share of rounds, I thought Hagler won more—simple as that. I would point to the CompuBox statistics as a very good reason why Hagler won that fight. He landed more jabs than Leonard. How is the boxer not going to land more jabs than the puncher? If Hagler outjabbed him, how did he lose the fight? I believe that the main reason Hagler ended up losing this is that people were amazed that Leonard was able to fight on equal terms with him. I've watched the fight eight or nine times, and I just don't see how Hagler didn't win by two points.

Trampler: This is going to sound like the all-time hedge, but I still have my scorecard somewhere, and I had it 6–6. Arum, to this day, he goes crazy: "Marvin won the fight." I never watched it again, to be honest, but there was nothing corrupt or sinister about it. It was just one of those fights.

Abraham: I had it 7–5 for Ray. He knew how to steal the last 15 seconds of every round. Ray admits he never hurt Marvin, but he ended eight of the twelve rounds with just beautiful, beautiful artistry.

Hopkins: I think Hagler won the fight. I think he did enough. He was the champion, so by Leonard basically throwing punches that [weren't] effective,

Ray wasn't handing Hagler his head. That shouldn't be enough to beat the champion. There's times in history where boxing is looking for the next guy. Not that Ray Leonard was a young guy, but he was younger than Hagler, and he was Ray Leonard. Leonard was the guy that was accepted in a way that Hagler wasn't. All of that plays a role with what the outcome's going to be.

Antuofermo: Leonard deserved to win. Plain English, he bullshitted Hagler. Running here, running there. Hagler should have gone right after him like he did everybody else, but Hagler didn't have it anymore. Leonard was able to hit him and jump in and out. Hagler couldn't get started. He didn't look mentally like he was into it. I think he just went through the motions.

Perron: Pat Petronelli had vicious words with Jo Jo Guerra after the fight: "You'll never judge another fight as long as you live!" You know what the irony of it all was? There were four judges there to judge the fight. Each camp has the option of challenging somebody off there, and Pat thought that [with] Harry Gibbs being from London and with Marvin beating Alan Minter for the middleweight title in London in 1980, he probably would have not favored Marvin too much. So Pat challenged Harry Gibbs off and put Jo Jo Guerra on. From what I hear, Gibbs went home after he was told he wasn't going to judge the fight. Somebody from the press called and asked if he saw the fight. He said, "Yeah." They asked him, "Did you score it?" He said, "Yeah." They said, "Well, how'd you have it?" "I had Hagler winning, 115–113."

> "Real boxing people, they know I won. And I just wait for the day—one day, Leonard's gonna tell the truth."
>
> —Marvin Hagler

Hagler: Real boxing people, they know I won. And I just wait for the day—one day, Leonard's gonna tell the truth. He's starting to tell a lot of truth about a lot of things,[2] so if he wants to tell the truth about this, I'm open.

Leonard: The second Hearns fight, when we got a draw, Hearns should have gotten the decision. I admit that. So don't you think if I thought Marvin beat me, I'd admit that, too? Look, I won the fight—whether I got the decision or not. I came from a five-year hiatus with one fight under my belt, fought the toughest guy in the world, [and] went the distance. I was a winner anyway, no matter what the decision was.

Hagler: I don't have anything personal about it. It wasn't Leonard's fault. It was left in the hands of the judges. I think what happened is that they wanted me out of the game. At that time, they wanted to split up all the titles. They don't like me having all the belts. We can't knock him out. We can't beat him. So we gotta steal it. That's exactly what they did. I know I won. In my heart, that's something you can't take away. You can take my belt, but you can't take the feelings, the pride.

Leonard: You know what? He's a proud man. He's an old-school guy, and he feels in his heart that he won the fight. If he's not ready to let it go, then I can understand that.

Originally published September 17, 2011.

2. In 1963, a 21-year-old Ali got knocked down by Cooper in the fourth round and was badly hurt, and Dundee bought him time by cutting a hole in his glove between rounds, forcing a delay while a new glove was put on. Ali stopped Cooper on cuts in the next round, and won the heavyweight championship from Sonny Liston in his next fight.

REUNION

A short story

by JAMIE ALLEN

The Friend Request from Allan Anson arrived on a weekday morning. Mike Oliver let out an involuntary "Holy shit" into the cool air of his office, the late-summer Florida sunlight bounding in and off things in obscene ways. It felt like someone had rung a bell in Oliver's chest at the sight of the alliterative name. Allan Anson. It was the same trill of the heart he had felt every time he had seen "Anson" blazed across the back of a red-and white jersey, over the number 9. In the sterile brightness of his office, the moment conjured images of a big kick, a ball hissing through summer's wet heat, and the stinging, dusty crack of his mitt.

"No chance," Oliver would say to the hitter after an Allan Anson fast-ball. "Might as well take a seat, my friend."

Oliver accepted the Friend Request and immediately went to Allan's page. Allan's Facebook account was new. He didn't have any photos; his profile picture was that cartoonish silhouette. The only action on his wall was the repetitive notices that he had become so-and-so's friend. Oliver was his 27th friend. So Allan Anson was new to Facebook, and Oliver felt a sense of importance at being on his list at all. He hadn't heard from Anson in, what, over 25 years? Oliver didn't recognize any of the other friends, so

Allan must've looked him up blindly through Facebook and not linked through a mutual friend.

How about that. Allan Anson. Where had he been all these years? Oliver felt aged and renewed at the same time— aged for saying "How about that" to himself, just like his old man would; renewed for being "friends" with Anson again. They had grown up together, had been best friends and teammates at Town 'n' Country Baseball in Tampa. Pinto to Pony League, inseparable battery mates every year, Allan pitching and Oliver catching, with last names that sounded like they belonged together. Oliver's dad, always the head coach, had every year picked Allan first, at his son's request. Allan played lefthanded shortstop when he wasn't pitching, and he hit like his league's version of Ted Williams. Oliver caught and hit homers and led his team. Oliver's mom kept score and recorded the boys' heroics in the Dugout Chatter.

Years spent like this, broken down by the league's two baseball seasons of Winter and Summer. Countless sweaty and clay-stained Saturdays of no-hitters and 18 strikeouts and doubles and grand slams. Wicked rivalries with teams named Dyser Plumbing and Prestige Cleaners and Tropicana Pools. Heartbreak and victory, strawberries on knees and elbows, sand in socks. Trophies with shiny-gold plastic men holding thin bats that broke too easily. Butts-Up and King of the Mountain competitions after games. Pool parties, All-Star tournaments, Atari and Intellivision and early MTV until 3 a.m.

When they were 13, they had taken a trip to Mexico City to play against several Latin American countries. They roomed together in a hotel that doubled as an oldperson's home, caught Montezuma's Revenge, and didn't play up to their potential. They finished fourth. Allan's mother didn't come along— she seldom even showed up to regular-season Saturday games—

and so the Olivers were in charge of him. The whole time— when he was sick, after he got well— Allan seemed happier, free. On that trip, on the second-to-last night at a party, Allan and Oliver had both experienced their first kiss to their team's Mexican batgirls, who were also best friends. Allan had fallen hard for his girl, even though he spent all of two hours with her and the language barrier prevented them from saying much more than "I like you" and "You are very beautiful" to each other. He wouldn't stop talking about her for weeks after they returned.

When they were 14, Oliver and Allan had snuck out of Oliver's house at 3 a.m. to dip tobacco and get drunk for the first time together. They choked on Copenhagen and guzzled Oliver's dad's bourbon out of a plastic liter Coke bottle in the field by the canal. Allan puked. When they stumbled home at 6 a.m., they ducked back in Oliver's bedroom window to find Oliver's father lying on the bed, head propped on pillows, watching an Abbott and Costello movie on the small television, waiting for them. He moved quickly toward them, grabbed them both by the ears, dragged them to the kitchen table and lectured them for an hour about their potential and how something stupid like this could keep them from playing baseball ever again. Allan had cried like a little girl whose horse had died. The sound of it woke Denise, Oliver's older sister, and Oliver could tell it humiliated Allan, who had a crush on her. Oliver's mom had made them eggs and bacon, which they were too sick to touch. Oliver's dad never mentioned any of it to Allan's mom, and only when Oliver was older did he understand why.

Later that year, an All-Star state championship closed out their Pony Baseball years. It was all over the Tampa Tribune Sports page. Allan struck out 14 and gave up one dink hit in the complete seven-inning game. Oliver went 3-4 with a homer. They were stars. The Leto High School coach, Simmons, clamored for both. Then, before the spring season could unfold, Allan was gone, across the country where his mother had moved with her boyfriend, to a town outside of San Diego, California.

O liver had written Allan a few times; this was before email, of course. The letters wentunanswered. Phones weren't used like they are now. People lost touch back then. You never heard from them again, and so you filled in your own stories.

Sure, Oliver was hurt that Allan didn't write back. But he also knew Anson like no one else. He was different. His brain functioned on an alternate current. He was lefthanded to the core, flighty but focused on whatever it was that he wanted to focus on. He might seem distracted, daydreaming about anything but baseball right in the middle of a game, blowing a Bubblicious bubble right in the middle of an at-bat. But then he'd turn on a pitch and jack it out of the park.

Or that odd sense of humor he possessed, communicated through competitive spirit: Facing the best hitter on the other team, Allan would shake off Oliver's signals simply for kicks, over and over and over, and soon Oliver would just put down a 1, over and over and over, until the ruffled hitter stepped out of the box. When he stepped back in, Oliver would throw down a 1 again, and Allan would nod with exaggerated satisfaction, as if Oliver had just put down an entirely new pitch, just invented. The hitter would be totally flustered now, not that it mattered. Allan's fastball would advance itself from hand to plate in half a blink, with alarming movement. The hitter had no chance.

Oliver and Allan would laugh about it later that night, and Allan would laugh longer, harder, until Oliver would be thinking just how odd it was to get such a kick out of something so ridiculous. Allan was different. And Oliver knew this. Expecting him to respond to letters was a little much, a little needy, a little girlish on his part. He moped for a few weeks.

One day, his dad walked into the living room where Oliver was lazing on the couch, thinking about Allan. His dad pinched his thigh hard and said, "Has your boyfriend written you back yet, Dearie?"

Oliver settled for remembering Allan fondly and wondering what in the hell happened to him. He grew up and moved on.

Then Facebook. In some ways it was a little much. Oliver was technologically capable; his job required it. He had the latest phone, and if he lost it he would have lost part of his brain with it. But Facebook. He had at first resisted it. It was for kids. Then it wasn't. Still, he had a good job and didn't want his personal life out there. And he wasn't the kind to seek attention, not the way people seemed to seek attention on Facebook anyway— with the clever status updates and the political rants and the pictures of themselves drunk in a bar.

But Oliver's wife, Tricia, had made a profile for him. Then she told him about it. He had no choice. He soon found himself enjoying it, reconnecting with high school and college mates. It was always the same: He'd get a Friend Request from a long-lost buddy or old flame, they'd chat for a few emails and take a look at each other's pictures. Mystery solved, they'd go back to their regular lives. How many high school and college reunions had Facebook ruined in this way? It was all a little too connected for Oliver; he didn't need to know what his old college friends were having for breakfast today. He logged in a few times a week.

But the one guy he wondered most about was Allan Anson. There is an unspoken connection between a star pitcher and his catcher, especially when they grow up together. It's a shared intellectual development that few other childhood friends experience. It comes from their collective attempts, their shared goal, to master a simple game. Pitching and catching. It's such an easy thing, and such a fine art. You're playing with something solid and natural, engaged in the environment, sure. But you're also lining up your mind with another's, talking without ever saying a word, trying to figure it out together. And of all the pitchers Oliver had caught, he had never felt a stronger connection than with Allan Anson. Hell, he connected more with Allan than he did with most of the girls he had dated.

Mike Oliver was 15 years' married with two children, ages 9 and 7. His youngest, a son, played Pony Baseball, Pinto League. Oliver served as the head coach. His oldest, a daughter, played travel soccer. His wife, Tricia, handled most of the driving for that.

After college and his baseball days were over, Oliver had moved back to Tampa, landed a job with Accenture, played softball as a ringer for his company team, met Tricia, gotten married. And in his spare time he had earned a Master's in information technology at University of South Florida. He was a senior manager now. He spent weekends with his family, fishing Tampa Bay and the Gulf with friends, or attending Rays or Bucs games. He spent his weekdays and evenings in air-conditioned offices in Tampa or whatever city the next convention or company gathering was held. His parents were still around, living in a condo across the bay in Clearwater, and Oliver had a three-bedroom house in one of the nicer neighborhoods of North Tampa, with a screened-in, kidneybean-shaped pool in the backyard. He drove a hybrid SUV. He voted for the candidate, not the party. He still had the same short clipper haircut that he had at 14, and the rest of him looked like an embellished version of that kid— friendly face with an un-offensive nose, playful blue eyes, dark hair, and a body that needed help to meet its full potential.

After the Friend Request, Oliver had emailed Allan with the simple, "Where is my old friend? Don't you dare shake me off." Then he had spent the rest of his workday checking and rechecking his and Allan's page. At lunch with a couple of co-workers, he told them about Allan. But could they really appreciate it? Another "glory days" story.

They nodded like they understood, told a few stories about people they had reconnected with through Facebook, and went back to their previous conversation about the Rays' middle relief. No one wants to hear stories about glory days, Oliver knew. The Bruce Springsteen song played in his head, and he couldn't get it out. He sang it to himself at work. He sang it when he got home, after telling Tricia about Allan's Friend Request. He sang it to his kids, who covered their ears and begged him to stop. He sang the song until Tricia told him to go to bed.

But he couldn't fall asleep. Oliver had read or heard somewhere that Allan had played well at his California high school and was drafted as a pitcher in, like, the 3rd round by the Reds. What happened after that? He heard a story from an old teammate, what, 10 years ago, that Allan had never made it to the Bigs. This was— and this said something for Allan— it was surprising that he never made it to the Bigs. That's how talented he was. You just knew the guy would get a shot. Oliver had been a solid catcher and clutch hitter on all levels, through college, but he had to work hard to stay that way. And solid and clutch gets you a college education, perhaps a low-round draft notice that a stupid 22-year-old might turn down out of a misfired sense of pride and post-college direction.

Allan, though— he was a volatile talent, something mixed and shaken in a capped-tight bottle. He was a great hitter, sure. But when he was pitching, kids would cry before they had to face him. And not just because of the angry-rattler fastball. He had the other two pitches at 12 years of age—an eye-crossing change-up, and a curve that broke like a fighter jet trying to duck an incoming missile. A handful of times, Oliver saw Allan's lefty curve break between a right-handed hitter's legs, and he knew that each time Allanhad done it on purpose to shake up the hitter. (It worked.)

And pitch selection! Oliver had allowed one guy, ever, to shake him off, and itwas Allan Anson. How many times had Allan disagreed with a pitch Oliver called ... and the pitch Allan had chosen had been so right that he had made the batter lose the grip on his bat (change-up) or collapse into the dirt (curveball) or just stand there like a victim of shock treatment (fastball). And this was when they were 13, 14 years old.

Everyone was certain Allan would make it. Even Oliver's dad. Even years later, when Oliver's dad had forgotten the names of most of the players he had coached, he made "Is Allan Anson on TV yet?" a regular starter to phone conversations with his son.

Allan had been destined for the Bigs, to throw no-hitters, make funny comments in the press conference after, fly mission trips to, what, Haiti, and marry (and divorce) a supermodel. He was that kind of guy.

Juan Dominguez, the guy who had told Oliver that Allan never made it to the Bigs, had also spit out the apparent reason: "Drugs." This was not an uncommon thing to be said about guys trying to make it to the Bigs. The ones that never had a chance in the first place, like fat Juan Dominguez, gossiped about the talented ones like girls in a sewing circle. "Drugs" was an easy slight, especially in Tampa, which had produced dozens of Big Leaguers, some of whom had very public struggles with addiction. While Oliver bristled at the suggestion—a reflex, defending his old friend—he had also thought it might be true. Allan's mother was— how else to put it— a lush. And Allan was a bona fide lefthander. He was different. As a kid, you love those people. When adulthood comes, it's those types that have the troubles. Where was he now? Still in California? On drugs? Married? Kids? He could be a good dad, Oliver thought, because he was probably still like a kid. Oliver could never see Allan growing up, and he didn't want him to be grown up. He was happy that he was alive, though. Part of him had wondered if Allan Anson had ended up dead somehow.

Two days later, Allan responded to Oliver's message. It read, "Mike, my old friend. Your family is beautiful! It's so good to see you doing well. I'm coming to town next week. I would love to meet up at the fields for a game of catch— and catching up. What do you say? Yours, Allan."

His Facebook page still didn't have a single photo on it, and his status remained blank. He now had 74 friends.

O liver and Allan Anson had only gotten in a few fights in all the years they knew each other, and the one thing Oliver learned from it was that you didn't want to get in a fight with Allan Anson. Even if you were lucky enough to get the better of him— right when you had him pinned and gasping for air, he went crazy. Literally crazy. He'd get out of the hold somehow, and he'd let out a girlish scream, his face deformed, his eyes blinded by rage. And you'd have to be the one to talk him down— from killing you or himself or some curious kid that came running up to see who was winning.

Aside from those moments, the only weird thing that had happened between Oliver and Allan occurred when they were about 8 or 9. Maybe 10. Allan had spent the night at Oliver's house; Ms. Anson was out again. They had played video games until late. They had watched a terrible movie on Showtime. It had promised nudity, but the only thing they saw was about three seconds of tits halfway through. The rest of the movie was dark and boring. They had gone to bed disappointed in that giggly but specifically frustrated way of boys who were denied a brief sighting of female pubic hair.

They had turned out the lights and settled into the same bed, Oliver on the outside, with his back to Allan. Normally, Allan faced the wall, but this night he was facing Oliver. They breathed into the dark, humid air of the room. Oliver's parents seldom ran the air-conditioning at night, even in summer. Oliver's face started to relax, its muscles falling asleep before the whole body.

"Do you wanna fuck?" Allan had asked.

"What?"

They must've been less than 10 years old, now that Oliver thought about it. Had to have been, because Oliver remembered that while he knew that the word "fuck" meant something dirty, he was still relatively unclear about exactly what it meant. And to "fuck" with Allan—asked like he wanted to play catch or something—made about as much sense as, what? Nothing. It made no sense.

"You never fucked anybody?" Allan asked. His tone was higher now. He seemed like someone else, like he had been taken over by a darker something, like that girl in "The Exorcist." Oliver wanted to turn around and face him, to see what was up. But he was frozen.

"What are you talking about?" he asked as casually as possible. He heard his own heart thumping against the bed sheet.

"Nothing, forget it."

As his best friend, as his battery mate, in the burning silence, Oliver felt an instinctual and chivalrous need to help Allan, to calm him just as he did in their fights, because though he did not know exactly what Allan had been asking, he knew they were in dangerous territory. He wanted to rescue him from it.

"Are you asleep? Are you sleep talking, Al?" He hoped this offered the out that Allan needed. Silence. Then, "Yeah. Go to sleep."

Silence. "I don't even know what you're talking about anyway."

"I can show you," Allan said. The dark boiled. It threatened a perfect friendship. Oliver needed to help his best friend. What followed had to have been one of the most awkward and unsuccessful

mating rituals ever. Oliver later recalled— at crucial, private times— that he had been soft the entire time. Allan hadn't. There was no real penetration but lots of heavy breathing on Allan's part. Was there a climax? Probably not, even though Oliver had no idea what to look for back then. They stopped what they were doing when they heard Oliver's dad get up to take a piss. They hardly looked at each other the next morning, and they never mentioned it again.

The sex talk Oliver's dad later gave him did not at all match up to what Allan had asked him to do, or what they had tried to do. So, the question had always been, from that moment until now: Where had Allan learned it? He had no older brothers and sisters. He had a drunk for a mom who brought home new boyfriends every other week. That was Allan's family. Where had he learned it? It was a question that had always bugged Oliver, but he had never asked.

O liver got out of a meeting later than he wanted and drove to Town 'n' Country. The Latin element had officially taken over the neighborhood years ago, and so a number of stores featured signs in Spanish. He took a brief detour by his old house off Elm. It was never the best neighborhood, lower middle-class, with 1960s and '70s houses that looked like they had been hammered flatter by the sun's rays. The trees, pines and palms, were much larger now, making everything look undone. He stopped in front of his old house, a whitewashed ranch with dark shingles and blue shutters. He wondered how four people could have ever fit in there. Five if you count Allan. The lawn was a patchy mix of half-dead St. Augustine and that bluish, powdery Florida dirt. The empty driveway was covered in oil and rust stains. Oliver hated looking at it all, so he drove away.

The road leading into the Town 'n' County baseball complex still had the bumps in it like rolling gulf waves. Oliver and Allan used to ride to the fields in the back of Oliver's dad's pick-up, and this road was their favorite part, the waves launching them in the air. They did that until some poor kid across town was killed when he got thrown out of his dad's pick-up into traffic.

The complex was larger now. It had paved parking lots and two new soccer fields. Oliver drove to the gate leading to the baseball fields and parked in front of it. Allan wasn't there yet. No one was. The two-story concession and storage building, circled by the fields, stood lonely and shuttered 100 yards behind the chain-link fence. The gate was unlocked. Not that it mattered; a locked gate never stopped them from climbing over.

Oliver's phone buzzed. It was a text from Tricia.

"Just be yourself," it read.

They had looked at Allan's Facebook page the night before. It still remained empty of any action except for friend updates. He had added a profile photo; it was a shot of him on a beach, and he was so far away that you could barely make out more than the fact that he was tall, thin, and wearing sunglasses on a beach. He now had 114 friends, including a few mutual friends with Oliver from their baseball days.

Oliver got out of his SUV and opened the back. He pulled out his old red Mizuno baseball bag. It smelled of salty leather and dried sweat. It held two catcher's mitts and two pairs of black cleats, a pair of shorts and a gray college t-shirt, a few balls, including one still in the box, and an old bag of stale David sunflower seeds. He had forgotten to bring socks. He would have to wear his black dress socks or nothing at all. Nothing at all was much better than black dress socks with cleats. He was concerned that he would look silly. He was nervous.

A tiny lime-green rental car came bumping down the road. It pulled into the lot and parked two spaces down. It was Allan. He turned off the car and got out.

The awkward moment of seeing a guy for the first time since he was a skinny kid: taking in every changed detail of the face, the hair, the voice and mannerisms, all in the space of a few seconds, all while engaging in the awkward handshake-hug, hellos, nice-to-see-yous, and the inevitable clumsy pause in conversation.

"God damn," Oliver finally said as they faced each other between their two cars, "look at you."

Allan's wraparound sunglasses were clipped over the neck of his white t-shirt. His eyes were light green; Oliver had forgotten that. He was a few inches taller than Oliver, and he was still thin. His hair was light brown with a few patches of gray, still long and feathered. His face was the same but longer and tanner and tired around the eyes. There was something else, a strange energy that Oliver couldn't quite name. He wore cut-off blue-jean shorts and white socks and blue cleats that were untied and looked too small for his feet.

"Look at you," Allan said back.

"Let's throw the rock, man," Oliver said.

Oliver gathered his bag and closed the SUV's back. Allan grabbed an old lefthanded glove from the passenger seat of his car, flattened by years of non-use, and a worn, brown ball.

"I have a new ball we can use," Oliver offered as they made their way through the gate along a shell path into the fields. They made small talk.

"I don't remember it being this hot here," Allan said. "I'm used to San Diego, I guess."

The sky was white, not from clouds but from sheer August blaze. It was animal instinct to avoid the metal of the chain link fences around the fields.

"It's hotter. Gets hotter every year."

Oliver didn't mind. It limbered his muscles and reminded him of things.

Augustwas when they used to end their All-Star tournaments, just before the start of school. The end of one thing, the start of another. You could smell this in the heat and dirt and grass.

"San Diego, huh?"

Without discussing it, they both walked toward the Pony field, the last one they played on together at these fields, before Allan moved away. They entered through a crooked gate. The mound and infield were flat and dry. The grass hadn't been mowed in at least a week, but it wasn't in bad shape for what it was. Old wooden signs hung from the backstop fence, including a faded and chipped white one with red and blue lettering that memorialized their final state championship.

"Sign's still up," Oliver said.

"You gonna catch in the suit?" Allan asked. His voice was deeper, but all the inflections were the same. Oliver wasn't wearing a suit, just a button-down and slacks. He looked at Allan to see if he was serious. He was.

"No, sorry, I got out of a meeting late. I have my stuff here in the bag. I'll just change in the dugout."

He walked into the cement-block dugout, practically had to duck entering it, and moved to the center of the wooden bench lining the wall. "No laughing at my pale oldman chest," he added.

"No funny business," Allan said, and Oliver wondered what he meant by it. Someone had pissed in the corner of the dugout, the dampness still apparent in the layer of dirt covering the floor. There was also the offensive but not uncommon smell— for some reason, Oliver had learned through the years, people like pissing in dugouts during the offseason. While he changed, Allan wandered along the third-base line, throwing the ball high into the air and waiting for it to come down. Sometimes he caught the ball behind his back.

"I saw that you're working at Accenture. Doing well, eh? Nice hybrid."

"Yeah, not bad," Oliver said. He had taken off his pants and was pulling on his shorts. "Just a company man these days. I sit in meetings and tell people what to do. Not unlike catching, actually."

"I hear that," Allan said, tossing the ball in the air again.

"What are you doing now, Allan?" Oliver asked. He had taken off his buttondown and replaced it with the gray college t-shirt.

When Allan didn't answer, he looked at him. A jet had flown over and Allan was watching it. Several seconds, 10 seconds passed with only the low, distant roar of the jet.

"Still blown away by the fact that those things can fly, by the way," he finally said. Oliver remembered Allan had always been obsessed with the passenger jets that flew over the field on their flight patterns to and from TIA. Sometimes he would stop in the middle of a game to watch one from the mound. Everyone on the field, including the umpire and the coaches, would see what he was looking at, shake their heads, wait. No one questioned the quirks of a star pitcher. The next pitch, whenever it finally came, was always powered by extra heat and precision, every time.

"Allan, where the hell have you been, man? What have you been doing with yourself? You never wrote me back, you bastard."

"I wrote you back. That's how we got here."

"No, I mean the letters I sent. When we were kids." It wasn't clear if Allan remembered this.

"Yeah, you know. I'm sorry, man. I'm bad at that kind of stuff."

Oliver took off his dress socks and stretched his cleats over his bare heels. He pulled a baseball cap out of the bag's side pocket, unfolded it and put it on backwards. He found an old protective cup in another pocket. He stood and stuffed it down the front of his pants until it was adjusted moderately well.

"You looked me up on Facebook though. You've got that going for you."

"Yeah, that's an interesting thing."

Oliver assumed he was talking about Facebook. He said, "My wife made me get on it. I have to admit, I kind of like it."

He walked out of the dugout with his mitt under his arm and a new ball in his hands. He rubbed the ball and spit on it and rubbed it more as they made their way down the foul line to the outfield. Allan dropped his old ball and his sunglasses in the grass, and he went to the outfield. Oliver stayed on the line. They took a few moments to pull their throwing arms behind and across their bodies, casually stretching.

"You ever learn to warm up before a game?" Oliver asked. Allan never properly warmed up. He just walked into the game and started playing.

"They made me," he said. Oliver assumed "they" were the Reds.

Oliver tossed the ball to Allan, and it began. They groaned with the first throws, but only for show. The pace of the throws picked up. They were both still athletes.

This was one reason Oliver had come here. He would never be able to explain it to his kids; not even Tricia could explain it. But here it was, this rhythm between them, the invisible line of communication that went deeper than throw, catch, throw, catch. It still existed.

"How's Denise?" Allan asked.

She lived in Orlando with her husband and three kids. Oliver hardly heard from her. She was a stay-at-home mom, the kind that used to be pretty but now went to church.

"She's fine. Married 17 years, three kids."

"She still hot?"

Oliver caught the ball. He took it out of his mitt and twirled it in his fingers for a moment.

"She's turned into a great mom, for sure," Oliver said, tossing it back. "I wouldn't say she's hot though."

Allan laughed. It was high, false. "Oh, man. You kill me, dude."

He hadn't looked Oliver in the eyes. That was it, the strange energy. He was always looking somewhere else. Had he always been like this? Oliver wanted to make him more comfortable. He figured more tossing would do the trick.

Oliver spun a slow curve that barely broke. Allan countered with a knuckle ball. Oliver followed with a split-finger. Every few times they tossed the ball, Allan took a step back, until he was about twice as far as when they had started. Oliver's upper lip and forehead and neck sweated. His throwing arm tingled somewhere between the bicep and tricep.

Allan still had his form, a weird little bump in his delivery as he drove toward the glove. His ball still moved, too, flying down and away or up and away when he let it go. But everything was slower, softer, less spastic. He was grounded by gravity now.

"How's your mom, Allan?" Oliver asked.

"Aw, well, let's see," he said. "She married that dickhead guy that moved us to California. He turned out to be a cocaine addict, and she left him about a year or two later, when I was a junior in high school. She married another guy, and something happened with them, I'm not sure what. Then she died."

"What? When?" Oliver had caught the ball from Allan and froze, the glove remaining in the exact spot where he had squeezed it shut, just below his chest.

"Years ago, man. Breast cancer. It's a real bitch."

"When you were playing pro ball?"

Allan had to think about it. "Yeah. I guess so."

"Allan, I'm really sorry to hear that," Oliver said. He meant it; he felt a sting in his eyes, and to clear it he threw the ball back.

"Yeah, she was always an odd one," Allan said. "Not the best mom, you know. My dad tried to get back in my life after that, but I told him to get lost." It might have been the first time Oliver had ever heard Allan mention his dad. He wondered if he lived in California.

"Hey, how's *your* mom?" he asked Oliver. "I loved that lady. And your dad?"

"They're doing great," Oliver said. He couldn't help but wonder if Allan even remembered their names. It was in the way he asked it— "that lady." "They said to tell you hello and to come by for lunch one day if you stick around. They're in Clearwater now."

"No shit. Wow. Hey, can we throw from the mound?"

"Sure."

They walked to the infield and took their places. The area behind home plate was a few inches deeper than the rest of the field. The clay was dusty.

Oliver moved it around with his foot, pressed it down with his weight. Allan was busy with the mound, which was closer than Major League distance and uneven with shallow holes where 14-year-old pitchers pushed off and landed.

"Don't hurt yourself on that thing. It's not exactly regulation."

Allan didn't respond. He was working intently on the area by the rubber. Too intently, like he was thinking about something else.

"Hey, you're also welcome to come by our house for dinner," Oliver said. "Meet my wife and my kids. I told them all about you. My son plays, you know."

Allan looked up. He said, with an exaggeration that nullified his words, "Aw, man, shit. That is really, really generous of you, man. I really mean that. I'm going to take you up on that. I really want to meet your kids. And your wife. You're really doing all right."

"Are you in town for long, Allan?" Oliver asked.

"Should be here a few days, at least."

"What are you doing here, anyway?" Oliver said. He was still standing, not yet ready to squat behind the plate and catch. "Allan, man, what have you been doing? Your freaking page is blank. Fill me in, dude."

He couldn't help but sound frustrated. They were friends, right? Friends were allowed to get frustrated with each other.

Allan looked over at the nearby Mustang fields. "Aw, man. I was married for a few years," Allan said. "I coached some in the minors. I was a substitute teacher." Then he said, "But it's interesting you ask."

He looked at Oliver, then away, then back again.

"Mike, things have been kind of hard for me lately. But I've been working with this company out in California," he said. "The owner has created this, this really unique athletic drink. He's put me in charge of marketing. I have a stake in the company. Sweat equity, you know? It could really turn things around for me. Anyway, that's why I'm here in Florida. I'm working all my sources. I immediately thought of you. I mean, I've always meant to get in touch and it seemed like a good time.'

You coach your kid, right?"

Oliver was either having trouble following him, or he couldn't believe where he was going.

"What? Yeah."

"The league would love this drink, man. It just glows in the bottle. I have some in my car. I'll show you. I brought a bunch of cases with me. I can give you a discount as a trial."

Oliver was careful to not make any sudden movements. His face burned. He wanted to call timeout. He wanted to pay a visit to the mound.

In all the years they were a battery, Allan's worst breakdown on the mound came in Mustang, 10 years old, random mid-season game. He just didn't have it that day, and the rival squad, Dyser Plumbing, had been lighting him up since the 1st. In the 4th, he went wild, beaning kids, throwing balls to the backstop, weeping between pitches. Total crybaby breakdown. And Oliver knew why. You didn't have to be a genius to see it had been a bad time at home for him; he had stayed at Oliver's house for days in a row even though they attended different schools.

Oliver had taken off his mask, called timeout and walked out to the mound. Allan's face was pink, and the tears mixed with the sweat. The kids from green-and-gold Dyser were shouting things from the dugout, laughing.

"Get your act together," Oliver had said quietly. "You're embarrassing yourself."

Allan had said, "Give me the fucking ball, you fucking prick. I fucking hate this game."

Oliver had held the ball in his mitt and looked over at his dad. He shook his head, and his dad came out to the mound. A pitcher was hardly ever taken out of a game back then, even if the score was out of hand, even if his arm was dead. He just took his lumps and learned from it. But Oliver's dad took Allan out of the game and sent him home with Oliver's mom.

"Is that the reason you called me here?" Oliver wanted to ask Allan now. "After everything, you want to sell me some copycat sports drink? Why didn't you just ask for help, you prick? Why didn't you just write me back?"

Instead, Oliver tossed the ball to Allan.

"Happy to take a look," he said.

"Aw, man. I appreciate it."

Oliver squatted. Allan's face changed at the sight of Oliver behind the plate. It became blank. He moved to one side of the rubber and waited for the signal. They were looking at each other now.

Oliver gestured with his bare hand and glove. "Serve it up, man. Let's see what you got."

Allan stepped back and then kicked up his right leg.

I never used to get tired," Allan said on the dugout bench after they had finished. They were both sweating through their shirts. Oliver felt the grit of sandy clay inside his cleats. He slowly pulled them off. "Never. I could throw for days. But now. Do you ever get that feeling in your shoulders and neck, somewhere inside there, there's a spot, and once that spot gets tired you might as well just lay down. You're done. I think that's what death must feel like."

Allan had his wraparound sunglasses on. The top of his left cleat and the ankle of his sock were stained with light orange clay from where he dragged his foot in his follow- through. Just like he used to. When he was a kid, he had to change his shoelaces every few games, Oliver remembered, because the dragging would tear the laces apart.

"What happened, Allan?" Oliver had asked in the dugout. It slipped out.

What had Oliver meant? He had meant, What happened. Allan Anson was not the same person; he was not even a shadow of the guy who had been his best friend. Forget pitching and making other kids cry and the Big Leagues. Allan Anson was not even the same person anymore.

CONTRIBUTORS

JONATHAN ABRAMS is a Grantland staff writer.

JAMIE ALLEN lives in Atlanta, GA. He has published work in *Eyeshot*, *Missouri Review*, *New South*, *Paste*, and McSweeney's Internet Tendency.

KATIE BAKER is a Grantland staff writer.

BILL BARNWELL is a Grantland staff writer

RAFE BARTHOLOMEW is a Grantland editor and author of *Pacific Rims: Beermen Ballin' in Flip-Flops and the Philippines' Unlikely Love Affair with Basketball.*

TOM BISSELL is a contributor to Grantland, and the author of *Chasing the Sea*, *God Lives in St. Petersburg*, *The Father of All Things*, and *Extra Lives*.

JOHN BRANDON is the acclaimed author of *Citrus County*. He writes about college football for Grantland.

CHRIS BROWN runs the website Smart Football.

REMBERT BROWNE is a Grantland staff writer.

KEN DRYDEN is a Hall of Fame NHL goaltender and six-time Stanley Cup champion. He is also the former president of the Toronto Maple Leafs and and a former member of the Parliament of Canada. He is the author of several books.

MALCOLM GLADWELL is a staff writer at the *New Yorker* and the author of *The Tipping Point*, *Blink*, *Outliers*, and most recently, *What the Dog Saw*. He is a consulting editor for Grantland.

ANDY GREENWALD is an author and screenwriter in New York. He covers pop culture for Grantland.

CHAD HARBACH is the author of the widely acclaimed *The Art of Fielding* and is the Executive Editor of *n+1*.

HUA HSU teaches at Vassar College. He is finishing his first book, *A Floating Chinaman*.

DAVID JACOBY is an ESPN Producer who somehow became a writer and editor for Grantland.

JAY CASPIAN KANG is a Grantland editor. His debut novel, *The Dead Do Not Improve*, will be released by Hogarth/Random House in the summer of 2012.

JONAH KERI is a Grantland staff writer and the author of *The Extra 2%: How Wall Street Strategies Took a Major League Baseball Team from Worst to First*.

CHUCK KLOSTERMAN is a contributing editor for Grantland and the author of six books. His novel *The Visible Man* was released in October.

MOLLY LAMBERT is a Grantland staff writer.

TESS LYNCH is a Los Angeles-based writer.

WESLEY MORRIS is a contributing writer to Grantland. He reviews movies for the *Boston Globe*

ALEX PAPPADEMAS is a writer for the *New York Times Magazine*.

CHARLES P. PIERCE is a staff writer for Grantland and the author of *Idiot America*. He writes regularly for *Esquire*, is the lead writer for Esquire.com's Politics blog, and is a frequent guest on NPR.

BRIAN PHILLIPS is a Grantland staff writer.

ERIC RASKIN is a former managing editor of *The Ring* magazine. He co-hosts the twice-monthly boxing podcast Ring Theory.

CHRIS RYAN is a Grantland editor.

MICHAEL SCHUR is the co-creator of *Parks and Recreation*.

BILL SIMMONS is the Editor in Chief of Grantland and the author of the recent *New York Times* No. 1 best-seller *The Book of Basketball*.

LOUISA THOMAS is the author of *Conscience: Two Soldiers, Two Pacifists, One Family—a Test of Will and Faith in World War*.

MICHAEL WEINREB is a Grantland staff writer and the author, most recently, of *Bigger Than the Game: Bo, Boz, the Punky QB and How the '80s Created the Modern Athlete*.